GEORGE W. CABLE

THE LIFE AND TIMES
OF A SOUTHERN HERETIC

GEORGE W. CABLE

THE LIFE AND TIMES
OF A SOUTHERN HERETIC

Louis D. Rubin, Jr.

PEGASUS NEW YORK

George W. Cable is part of a series, Pegasus American Authors, prepared under the General Editorship of Richard M. Ludwig, Princeton University.

813
Cable, G.W.

For Bob and Mildred Jacobs

1

Preface

When in the summer of 1967 the editor of this series invited me to take part, I proposed a critical biography of George W. Cable. What I wanted to do was to concentrate on Cable and his work in terms of their specific relationship to the Genteel Tradition in American literature and the long-range direction of Southern writing.

My use of Arlin Turner's biography of Cable has been extensive indeed—as a glance at my annotation will show. But my indebtedness to him goes far beyond my reliance upon his published writings. When I told him what I proposed to do, he immediately invited me to make full use of his research files, the fruit of a quarter century of devoted inquiry into Cable's life and career. I came back from his house bearing five thick volumes of Cable's correspondence, typescripts of most of Cable's magazine nonfiction, letters from his editors and others, microfilms of manuscripts from several libraries, transcripts of newspaper interviews, and articles about Cable, photostats of many of the "Drop Shot" columns, and so on.

I should like to acknowledge other debts. Mrs. Connie G. Griffith, director of the manuscripts division of the Howard-Tilton Memorial Library of Tulane University, opened to me the resources and facilities of that superb collection when I visited New Orleans, and subsequently furnished me with copies of the Cable–R. W. Gilder correspondence and several extant manuscript drafts of *John March, Southerner*. The manuscript division of the Library of the Louisiana State University in Baton Rouge allowed me to consult the Grace King Collection there. The libraries of the University of North Carolina at Chapel Hill and of Duke University provided much assistance. My colleague C. Hugh Holman discussed my findings with me throughout the writing of this book. C. Carroll Hollis was helpful on numerous occasions. Before and during the writing of this book I have profited much from working with my colleague Kimball King in the readying of his own book on George W. Cable and Thomas Nelson Page for publication. My neighbor Professor Guy A. Cardwell read and discussed the various drafts of *John March, Southerner* with me. Several of my graduate students, in particular Mrs. Susan Stone Provost, Miss Pamela Glenn Menke, and Mr. Donald R. Noble, helped me to understand some of the implications of my subject in the course of their engagement with their own research. The travel and research fund of the University of North Carolina at Chapel Hill awarded me a grant that materially aided me to further my researches. Finally, both C. Hugh Holman and Arlin Turner have been kind enough to read this book in manuscript and to offer suggestions for its revision.

Louis D. Rubin, Jr.
University of North Carolina at Chapel Hill
Chapel Hill, North Carolina
December 15, 1968

Contents

GEORGE W.
CABLE

THE LIFE AND TIMES
OF A SOUTHERN HERETIC

I
Mardi Gras

In the late winter months of the year 1872, the city of New Orleans, Louisiana, was once again preparing for the advent of the Mardi Gras. This characteristically Latin festival had for many years been celebrated during the week before Ash Wednesday, and since 1838 there had been a lavish parade each year. Even the four years of the recently concluded Civil War had failed to curtail the festivities entirely, and by the 1870's, though Louisiana was still under a Reconstruction government, carnival time had once again assumed considerable importance in the city's life.

It was rumored this year that the Mistick Krewe of Comus, whose parade was one of the oldest and most colorful of all Mardi Gras events, was preparing a spectacle for the 1873 Carnival that would have implications for the confused state of politics in Louisiana.[1] To ensure that the parade would be adequately described for readers of the New Orleans *Picayune,* the editor, E. C. Dill, asked a young local cotton exchange clerk and some-time journalist, George W. Cable, to report the event, just as he had done the previous year.[2]

The fame of the annual Mardi Gras doings in New Orleans had spread to all parts of the country, including New York City, so it was natural that another young journalist, Edward King, who had been commissioned to travel throughout the Southern states and report on the present and future prospects of the still-devastated former Confederacy for the readers of *Scribner's Monthly Magazine,*[3] should choose to begin his tour in New Orleans at Mardi Gras time. Accompanied by an illustrator, J. Wells Champney, he came down to New Orleans. While making inquiries about the forthcoming spectacle, he met young George Cable, who was seeking advance information about the plans of the Mistick Krewe of Comus.[4]

It was a fortunate meeting. For not only had King happened upon the man in New Orleans who could best aid him in searching out and appreciating the complexities and charms of post-Civil War New Orleans life, with its odd, exotic blending of Latin, American, and African customs and attitudes, but Cable had in turn made a friend who knew the ins and outs of the national literary and publishing scene. For some years now Cable had been writing about life in New Orleans, for a while as a columnist for the *Picayune,* at other times as a writer of feature stories for various New Orleans newspapers; less than two years earlier he had submitted to Charles Scribner and Company a volume of verse and prose sketches, which had been declined.[5] More recently he had been writing short stories, with the idea of making them into a book.

Just before King and Champney left New Orleans, Cable showed them several of his stories. Both were greatly impressed, and King took several of the stories along with him to show to editors in New York.[6] On July 22, 1873, he wrote: "The battle is won. 'Monsieur George' is accepted, and will be published in *Scribner.* . . ."[7] When the story, in its final form entitled "'Sieur George," appeared in the magazine in October, 1873, an important literary career was launched, and the Southern Local Color movement was under way. In the next several decades it would all but dominate the national literary scene.

Asked forty years later whether Edward King's magazine series on "The Great South" had played any considerable part in the rise of Southern local color writing, Cable said he thought it had not, and that "the two were merely coincidental."[8] Cable was probably correct; for the impulse that had prompted Scribner's to send King down to New Orleans to begin his Great South series also accounted in large part for the forthcoming vogue of local color in the national literature. Nevertheless, King's magazine articles, the first extended treatment of the South during Reconstruction to appear in the national magazine press, helped to prepare readers and editors for the literary use of Southern materials.[9]

Of more immediate importance for the South, King's series had political implications. The very first installment, about life in New Orleans and Louisiana, set the tone for the entire series. It was to the effect that the South had been sufficiently punished for its sins, and it was time to make amends. The picture that King drew of New Orleans for the readers of *Scribner's Monthly* was generally sympathetic. He portrayed Louisiana as a supine state, utterly defeated in war and broken in spirit. Upper-class society in New Orleans was depicted as discouraged and hopeless:

> Ah! these faces, these faces;—expressing deeper pain, profounder discontent than were caused by the iron fate of the few years of the war! One sees them everywhere; on the street, at the theatre, in the *salon,* in the cars; and pauses for a moment, struck with the expression of entire despair—of complete helplessness, which has possessed their features. Sometimes the owners of the faces are one-armed and otherwise crippled; sometimes they bear no wounds or marks of wounds, and are in the prime and fullness of life; but the look is there still. Now and then it is controlled by a noble will, the pain of which it tells having been trampled under the feet of a great energy; but it is always there. The struggle is over, peace had been declared, but a generation has been doomed.[10]

The onetime Confederacy, King emphasized, had accepted the verdict of the sword, and all thought of rebellion was completely dead. Now, fortunes gones, homes falling into decay, living under the yoke of a corrupt Reconstruction government kept in power by fraud and the presence of U. S. troops, the white South no longer deserved the nation's hatred, but its pity. King detailed the illegal means by which the Carpetbagger regime of Henry Clay Warmoth had maintained its control of the state government. "What has been the result of this usurpation?" he asked. "The State has been broken down by taxation and debt; the negro has been demoralized; the principal cities and towns are impoverished."[11]

Throughout his series of Great South articles, King implied that, given the opportunity, New Orleans and Louisiana were ready for swift economic progress. What was most needed was capital—to build railways, improve and modernize cotton warehousing and shipping facilities and the like; as well as some needed Federal aid in repairing levees and taking other flood control measures and in widening and deepening the Mississippi River channel to the sea. That and the return to orderly, responsible government through an end to Carpetbag domination would be enough, King suggested, to convert New Orleans, now a Paradise Lost, into Paradise Regained.[12]

It was not, however, politics and economics that King most emphasized in his articles about New Orleans. He chronicled the city's colorful past under French, Spanish, and American rule, and noted in detail how the old city still retained the marks of its heritage: "Step off from Canal Street, that avenue of compromises which separates the French and American quarters, and you will at once find yourself in a foreign atmosphere."[13] He gave much attention to the old buildings, gardens, churches, restaurants, as well as to the former slaves, the delightful patois spoken by everyone and, most exotic of all, the Creoles:

> Now and then, too, a knock at the porter's lodge will bring to your view a bustling Creole dame, fat and fifty, redolent of garlic and red wine, and robust in voice as in person. How cheerfully she retails her vices, as if they were blessings! *"An invalid husband —voyez-vous ca!* Auguste a Confederate, of course—and is yet; but the *pauvre garçon* is unable to work, and we are very poor!" All this merrily, and in high key, while the young negress—the house-maid—stands lazily listening to her mistress's French, nervously polishing with her huge lips the handle of the broom she holds in her broad, corded hands.[14]

Almost half of one installment was devoted to the Mardi Gras, which King depicted in considerable detail and Champney illustrated with his sketches. King related the history of the carnival, told of the Mistick Krewe of Comus parade, and noted that its 1873 theme had been "the 'Darwinian Development of the Species' from earliest beginnings to the gorrilla, and thence to man";[15] but he did not mention that each of the figures in the parade had been a satire on the Federal administration—General "Beast" Butler a hyena, President Grant a tobacco grub, and so on—nor did he say that the parade had ended in chaos and had to be disbanded before reaching its final destination.[16]

From almost every standpoint—the magazine's, the South's, the growing interest of the American reading public in the far-flung regions of the recently reunited republic—the Great South series which King began with his account of New Orleans and Louisiana was an immediate success. Politically, by depicting the Negro freedman's inability to govern the South, demonstrating that the Carpetbag governments were corrupt and remained in power only through force, and insisting that the white South had ceased to think of rebellion and was anxious to take its place in the Union again, the Great South series helped pave the way for the final abandonment of Reconstruction. Already weary of the cost and increasingly dubious of the wisdom of Reconstruction policies, the growingly apathetic Northern public was rapidly moving toward the belief that the white citizenry of the South should be allowed to govern the region. The Great South series, together with other accounts of the condition of the South in the early 1870's, helped to persuade the nation that the South could once again be trusted with self-government.[17] King made it quite clear that only with the return of the reins of government to the whites could the region progress economically and the investment potential thus afforded for Northern capital be properly developed. As the editor of *Scribner's Monthly* remarked at the conclusion of the series, the magazine could take considerable pride in the successful completion of "a task undertaken with the desire to enlighten our country concerning itself, and to spread before the nation the wonderful natural resources, the social condition, and the political complications of a region which needs but just, wise and generous legislation, with corresponding goodwill and industry, to make it a garden of happiness and prosperity."[18]

Everywhere there was widespread interest in and curiosity about the South. It was as if the people of the United States could for the first time in many decades give their enthusiastic attention to the differences and distinctions in the various regions of their republic. So long as the South had been a militant minority within the Union, possessing considerable political power and adamant in its refusal to conform to the majority view, any such acknowledgment of differences and distinctions had represented a potential threat to the will of the majority. Now that the threat had been effectively eliminated, so far as economic and political considerations were concerned, it was safe to recognize the differences.

The growing importance of the slavery controversy, which during the 1840's and 1850's had come to dominate the nation's political life, culminating in secession and war, had made it extremely difficult for either section to view the other objectively.

But now the passions and hatreds of the war years were receding and there was the abundant possibility of renewed discovery. That the inhabitants of the several American regions of the 1870's should be caring for each other, after their long sectional estrangement, was therefore hardly surprising. King and Champney had been instructed by the editors of *Scribner's Monthly* to "exhibit, by pen and pencil, a vast region almost as little known to the Northern States of the Union as it is to England." [19]

Thus when the opening installments of the Great South series began appearing in *Scribner's Monthly* in the summer of 1874, Northern readers eagerly devoured the accounts of New Orleans as "so richly varied, so charming, so unique" a city, one in which "the characteristics of an American city vanish; this might be Toulouse, Bordeaux, or Marseilles!" [20]

This interest was George W. Cable's opportunity. The renewed curiosity about the South that the Great South series exemplified was in part a hunger for just the sort of material that Cable himself found fascinating: caste, class, race, customs, and manners, the clash of the past with the present, the complex and colorful textural fabric of New Orleans society. He wrote his first stories, he told F. L. Pattee many years afterward, "because . . . it seemed a pity for the stuff to go to waste." [21]

Yet although this national appetite for stories about the South, and indeed for stories about the West and other distinct regions as well, was an advantage to Cable, it had its disadvantages too, and if at the time they seemed of little concern, in the long run they would be of considerable importance to his life and his art. For the growing popular taste in local color, as it developed throughout the United States and was interpreted in the editorial sanctums of the Northeast, was primarily for the quaint, the nostalgic, pleasing aspects of regional life—the exotic, the beautiful—and not for its ugly, unattractive aspects, which were equally real. The desire for sectional reconciliation was also a desire to put aside the unpleasant issue of the place of the Negro in American life. Unfortunately for George W. Cable, this turned out to be precisely what he did not wish to do.

When Edward King and J. Wells Champney first visited New Orleans in the early 1870's, Cable apparently had not dissented significantly in public from the racial attitudes of most of his fellow

Louisianians; but in the years that followed, his views on the Negro's place in Southern society were to become increasingly at variance with those of his neighbors, and his insistence upon arguing the unpleasant matter of the denial of civil rights to the Negro would run counter to the whole trend in public opinion both in the North and the South. Even more important so far as the ultimate shape and form of his literary art were concerned, instead of encouraging him to use the less pleasant aspects of Southern life in his fiction with ever greater artistic effectiveness, his editors in New York would do their very best to persuade him to leave out all such stuff from his fiction entirely, and to concentrate on quaintness and pleasantness. The result was tragic. In the words of Edmund Wilson, "The slow strangulation of Cable as an artist and a serious writer is surely one of the most gruesome episodes in American literary history." [22] In the 1880's, at the height of his art, Cable was frequently compared with Twain, James, and Turgenev, and not to his disadvantage; when he died in 1925, he was all but forgotten.

In the 1950's and 1960's, there has been a revival of interest in the fiction of George W. Cable. In part this is due to the belated recognition that in some of his fiction, as almost nowhere else in the literature of his time, is to be found an image of the South—or, for that matter, of American society—and the place of the Negro in it, that today seems of compelling truth and even urgency. Flawed though his work is, dated in some aspects, what he had to say and to show in his best fiction merits our attention, so that a continued examination of that fiction, and of the life and times of the man who wrote it, would seem worth-while.

II
Youth

Born October 12, 1844, in a rambling frame house on Annunciation Square in New Orleans,[1] George Washington Cable was the son of George Washington and Rebecca Boardman Cable. Cable's father was of German descent. One Jacob Kabell had come to America in 1710 with a group of colonists from the Rhine Valley, and had lived first in New York State, then in Pennsylvania, finally migrating down to Virginia, where about 1732 Sebastian Cable, apparently Jacob Kabell's son, was born in the settlement of Strasburg.[2] The Cables lived in Virginia for a hundred years or so. Sebastian Cable had a son, Jacob, whose son George was the grandfather of the novelist. This George Cable married Mary Scott in Winchester, Virginia, where in 1811 the novelist's father was born. Not long afterward, the Cables moved up to Pennsylvania, where they freed their slaves, and then migrated westward into Indiana, settling in Lawrenceburg, Dearborn County. It was here that George Washington Cable met Rebecca Boardman, whom he married in Ripley County in 1834.[3]

The Boardmans were New Englanders in origin. Amos and Sylvia Noble Boardman had moved from New York State into Indiana while it was still a territory, and their daughter Rebecca was born in Wilmington, Dearborn County, on November 20, 1813, the sixth of ten children. After Rebecca's marriage to George Cable, the family prospered; but when in 1837 the United States of America was caught in a financial panic, George Cable lost everything, and within the same year he moved his family down the Ohio and Mississippi rivers to New Orleans.[4]

Settled early in the eighteenth century by the French, New

Orleans by the 1830's was a thriving metropolis. Its strategic location near the mouth of the Mississippi River made it the port from which many of the export goods of the Mississippi River valley were shipped to Europe and the Northeast. The yield of the cities, towns, farms, and remote outposts of four great river systems—the Mississippi, the Red, the Missouri, and the Ohio— was floated down to New Orleans. Upstream and downstream between the river ports of the South and Midwest, fleets of flat-bottomed steam packets plied their trade. To New Orleans came the ships of seaboard America and Europe; by 1835, two years before George Cable and his family arrived, the city's exports had exceeded New York City's, and in 1840 the United States Census revealed that the city had a population exceeded only by that of three other American cities—New York, Baltimore, and Philadelphia.[5] The network of canals which was increasingly to tie the rapidly growing Northwest to New York and the industrial North-east was only beginning to cut seriously into the Southern port city's trade, while the railroad lines that would ultimately link the people of the cities and farms of the Midwest indissolubly with the North were as yet barely under way. River traffic was still dominant, and so complacent were New Orleans and its merchants with the trade that funneled through the city that little was done to improve transshipping facilities; cotton, tobacco, and other goods were left outside to rot in the hot, humid weather. There was no central market, no covered wharves, no auction rooms. Few city streets were paved, and those with cobblestones. Only in 1837 were the beginnings of a municipal lighting system in-stalled. Not until a half century later would there be public sewage disposal. The naturalist John James Audubon, visiting the city, wrote that the French Market was the "dirtiest place in all the cities of the United States."[6] Throughout the 1840's and 1850's, New Orleans steadily lost ground to New York and the Northeast as an export center; but since the loss was only relative, and the city's actual trade even continued to grow through the period, the complacent merchants of New Orleans went their way, tranquil and undisturbed.

New Orleans was a melange of races and nationalities. The Creoles, descendants of the early French and Spanish settlers, many of whom traced their ancestry back to French families of highest station, were the city's social aristocracy; disdainful of the *Américains* who had come swarming into the city in the years after New Orleans became an American city, they lived in the city's old French Quarter, frequented its opera and theaters, continued to talk French, and maintained their social exclusiveness in a community whose business and political life was increasingly dominated by the Anglo-Saxon Americans. As for the Americans, they came to the city from the South and the North both; brash, enterprising, energetic, they were predominantly Protestant, unlike the Roman Catholic Creoles and the thousands of Irish and Italians who also had come to live in the city. There were many Germans and Jews, too. Choctaw Indians came in to trade. Wildest of all elements in the population, perhaps, were the transients, the rivermen who came brawling and drinking their way down to New Orleans for a roaring time in the hundreds of saloons, gambling dens, and brothels that lined the area along the water-front. Lawless, roisterous, they were despised and feared by the city's resident population. The metropolitan police were hard put to maintain order among them.

Also, crucially, there were the Negroes, many recently come from the West Indies and still given to voodoo rituals and pagan ways. There were thousands of slaves within the city, and also a number of mulattoes, set apart legally as "f.m.c."—free men of color. The f.m.c. occupied a status somewhere between bondage and full citizenship; he could own slaves, pay taxes, but was nevertheless under severe legal and social disadvantages. Young mulatto girls, many of them octoroons or of even slighter Negro ancestry, were introduced at the famous quadroon balls to the young men of upper-class New Orleans society. These young aristocrats chose them for their mistresses, made precise financial arrangements with their guardians, and installed them in comfortable quarters, often continuing the relationship after marriage and maintaining two families.[7] Beautiful, customarily well-educated and socially accomplished, the quadroons and octoroons consti-tuted a highly exotic caste of their own in a colorful society quite unlike that of any other American city.

The climate of New Orleans was sultry, humid; spring came early, and winter late. Orange and fig trees bloomed in the gardens of the city. The spring floods often broke through the levee and inundated part of the city. Azalea and oleander flowered; so did yellow fever and cholera. Periodically epidemics would sweep the city, whereupon all who could, fled to higher and safer land. Stagnant water, poor sanitation, the arrival of ships from foreign lands whose sailors might bear disease, made the city a veritable charnel house at times.[8]

New Orleans was bilingual. English and French were habitually used; though the haughty Creoles clung to their language, the Americans were not so particular: Spanish from the Caribbean, African expressions retained by the slaves, the corrupt French of the humble Cajuns of the surrounding bayous and the delta, all blended into a patois virtually unintelligible to outsiders. Even today traces of this remain in the New Orleans speech patterns. In 1873, Edward King noted that when small children of indubitably American descent urged their comrades to make their kites fly higher, they said *"Poussez!"*[9] Negro vendors sold seafood, vegetables, and flowers on the streets, hawking their wares in several languages.

On his arrival in New Orleans in 1837, George Cable, Sr., a hearty, energetic man of commanding presence and unusual height,[10] straightway entered into the city's swirling commercial activity. Shortly after he had settled, his prospects momentarily waned and he was forced to send his wife and family back to Indiana. But soon he restored his fortune, and sent for them again. Engaged in the riverboat supply business, he became a partner in the firm of J. R. Borgstede and Co., and later purchased interests in various steamboats, so that by the time his fifth child, George, was born in 1844, he had attained considerable wealth and much esteem within the community. In 1845, scarlet fever took the lives of two of the Cable children; but a year later Rebecca Cable gave birth to another son, James. In 1847 George Cable, Sr., by now prominent in city affairs, was honored with the post of aide to Brigadier General E. L. Tracy, commander of the First Brigade of the First Division of the Louisiana Militia. The next year, 1848, dressed in full military regalia, George Cable paraded proudly with his troops on the Eighth of January as the city celebrated the anniversary of Andrew Jackson's victory over the British of 1815.[11]

For the young children of the Cable family the city which lay around them was a fascinating place. Their house on Annunciation Street was bordered by an unbroken row of orange trees; low, drooping fig trees grew beside the shady garden walks. Along the west side of Annunciation Square were large colonial villas, facing the Mississippi River. Nearby were the cotton presses, and young George Cable spent many hours watching the gangs of Negroes as they bore huge bales of cotton to be pressed into quarter size. The pressing machinery, with its clouds of steam and loud, gasping roar, and the Negroes singing lustily as they labored naked to the waist, would be part of his memories ever afterward.[12] Sometimes he would walk to the riverside to look at the sailing ships moored alongside. "I loved to study the spars, blocks and ropes of their beautiful and stately rigging," he remembered.[13] At other times, he might be taken as far as Canal Street, the thoroughfare that marked the division between the old French Quarter where the Creole families lived and the American sector of the city. Down by the levee were stacked huge quantities of freight, barrels, bales, and casks, their places marked by rows of little multicolored flags and other devices to guide the stevedores as they trudged back and forth loading the ships, while foremen called out instructions: "Go to de blue flag! Go to de red an' yellah! Go to de white cross! Go to de check flag! Go to de blue anchor! Go to de check an' green!" As five o'clock in the afternoon neared, hundreds of citizens would gather along the levee front to watch the steam packets depart. One after another, flags and pennants streaming and towering funnels blasting out clouds of black smoke, the ornate craft would swing away from the landing, turn bow upstream into the current, and with a parting salute from their guns move off, their huge paddle wheels churning the muddy water.

Sometimes young George might be taken marketing by his father before breakfast: "A bewildering chatter of all the world talking at once, mostly in German and French," he recalled; "a calling and hallooing, a pounding of cleavers, a smell of raw meat, of parsley and potatoes, of fish, onions, pineapples, garlics, oranges, shrimps, and crabs, of hot loaves, coffee, milk, sausages, and curds, a rattling of tins, a whetting of knives, a sawing of bones, a whistling of opera airs, a singing of the folksongs of Gascony and Italia, a flutter of fowls, prattling and guffawing of Negroes, mules braying, carts rumbling— . . . great fun!"[14] Or he might go fishing—not in the Mississippi, for its mighty current would allow no sinker to touch bottom for long, but sometimes in Lake Pontchartrain for panfish, croaker, sheepshead; and, more often by far, along the many nearby canals and drainage ditches for sunperch or other such less exalted species, and sometimes to catch crayfish.[15]

The late 1840's were the best years for the Cables. George Cable, Sr., was prospering, the family occupied comfortable quarters, there was the luxury of family slaves—as many as eight at one time, apparently.[16] Then came a severe financial reverse. Epidemics ravaged the city, a disastrous flood left much of New Orleans under four feet of water, cotton prices fell precipitously, at least one steamboat owned by Cable and Borgstede was probably burned, a schooner bearing a cargo in which Cable had invested failed to accomplish its objective, and by the end of 1849 Cable's property was being sold at auction and Rebecca and the children were back in Indiana. Though he was to send for the family again, the family fortunes were never to be retrieved. In 1859, now a customhouse employee, he died of chronic diarrhea, and was buried at Cypress Grove Cemetery.[17]

After the father's death, the family was left in straitened circumstances. The mother, Rebecca Boardman Cable, took charge. A resolute, determined woman, she was not given to self-pity. "Her supreme and constant characteristic was an heroic spirit," her son wrote of her many years later. "This feature belonged to the quietest hours and simplest tasks as much as to the greatest emergencies. She had at all times so emphatic a preference for the best way that often she almost seemed to choose the more difficult method because of its difficulty. She pursued all her tasks with a positive gaiety of temper. She had no such intolerance for anything else in life as she had for a spirit of indolence, whether it leaned toward ease or pleasure." [18] From her New England heritage she derived an austere morality and strong Presbyterian convictions. No doubt she viewed the Latin ways of the New Orleans Creole population with severe disapproval, frowning upon sin and complaisance in all forms. When many years later her son, by then a nationally renowned man of letters, struck up an acquaintance with the actor Joseph Jefferson and ventured at last to attend the theater in New York, she registered her disapproval emphatically. Doubtless it was from Rebecca Boardman Cable that George Washington Cable drew his own strong religious convictions, the rigidity of which would one day move his friend Mark Twain to exasperation and imprecation. Not until well into his middle years did Cable begin to relax his Calvinistic scruples.

Yet it is obvious that the young George Cable was strongly drawn, in spite of himself, to the lolling ways of the Creoles of New Orleans, with their love of ease and their delight in worldly pleasures, their sensual enjoyment of existence in a languorous, semitropical climate. From childhood on, he took great pleasure in the colorful life of the city, the balmy weather, the luxuriant vegetation, the exotic racial mixtures. Cable displayed throughout his life, as Jay B. Hubbell puts it, "a certain susceptibility to the voluptuous," [19] and his best fiction derived much of its excitement from the clash between his strong moral disapproval of the Creoles of New Orleans and his keen relish for their ways.

Upon his father's death, George Cable withdrew from school, where already he had displayed a talent for writing, and was given the same position his father had held at the customhouse. Only just over fourteen years old and unusually slight in stature, he began work as a marker at Private Bonded Store No. 7. In his spare time, he kept up his studies. His younger brother James stayed in school, and his older sister Mary Louise found work as a teacher.[20] Closely knit, strongly loyal to each other, led by their mother, the Cable family sought to make the best of their situation.

Meanwhile, political tensions were rising between the North and the South, until with the election of Abraham Lincoln as President in 1860, the Southern States began seceding from the Union one by one. Louisiana passed its secession ordinance in January, 1861, and with the firing upon Fort Sumter in Charleston Harbor that April, the Civil War was under way. New Orleans was swept up in a blaze of excitement. Creoles and Americans united in the common effort. Companies and regiments were formed; there was much parading and drilling. Then one by one the crack military units of the city—the Washington Artillery, the Crescent Rifles, the Orleans Battalion, the colorful Zouaves in their red breeches and fezzes—left for the front. General Pierre Gustave Toutant

Beauregard, a Creole of magnificent bearing, won an easy victory and immediate fame at Fort Sumter and shortly thereafter at First Manassas in northern Virginia.

Soon, however, a Federal fleet blockaded New Orleans and all the Gulf ports, and trade came to a standstill. The customhouse was turned into a sword-bayonet factory, and George Cable, out of a job, secured a position as cashier for a wholesale grocery concern.[21] The city's steam towboats were converted into gunboats and departed for points up and down the river. Except for the shipyards and foundries, all was silent. Gold and silver had disappeared from circulation; prices rose; there was widespread speculation. Now news of far-off battles in Virginia and Tennessee brought grief and woe. The body of the great Albert Sidney Johnston was brought home after Shiloh for burial in the city. The Home Guard drilled away, the middle-aged men who composed it going through their formations clad in a variety of uniforms.[22]

The Union Navy began its ascent of the river. On April 24, 1862, word came that the Federal fleet under the command of David Glasgow Farragut had passed Forts Jackson and St. Philip and was moving upon the city. Fire bells called the Home Guard out, schools were dismissed. Left alone in the store where he worked, George Cable locked the doors and joined the crowds at the levee. Cotton bales were emptied along the levee and burned, to keep them from falling into Federal hands. Ships were set afire to drift downstream. Across the huge bend of the river, Cable could see the mast tops of the Federal ships as they engaged the batteries at Camp Chalmette. Then, as Cable remembered it many years later, "they came slowly round Slaughterhouse Point into full view, silent, so grim, and terrible; black with men, heavy with deadly portent; the long banished Stars and Stripes flying against the frowning sky." He was to use the image often in his novels. While the crowds along the levee howled and screamed with rage, and rain began to deluge the city, two United States Navy officers came ashore, ignoring the threats and imprecations of the mob, walking calmly and steadily, to receive the surrender. Shortly thereafter a Union officer lowered the flag of Louisiana from the City Hall, and New Orleans became an occupied city.[23]

The Cables were loyal Confederates still. George continued to work as a grocer's clerk and cashier, but when General Order No. 62 of September 24 required all citizens over eighteen years of age to take the oath of allegiance to the United States under penalty of fine, confiscation of property, and imprisonment, Rebecca Boardman Cable refused to do so, declaring herself an enemy of the United States along with her daughters Mary Louise and Antoinette. The next spring Mary Louise and Antoinette left the city, and George, although now of conscription age, managed to accompany them. Dressed in short pants, he succeeded in getting through the lines, and with his sisters crossed over to Mississippi, proceeding to a plantation near Summit. Mrs. Cable followed them out some months afterward. On October 9, 1863, almost nineteen years old, just 5 feet 5 inches tall, and weighing about 100 pounds, Cable enlisted in Company J of the Fourth Mississippi Cavalry of the Confederate States Army.[24]

Cable's military experiences do not figure importantly in much of his fiction. Both his Civil War novels were products of the 1900's, a period when he was writing historical romances with little of his earlier interest in realistic description, and they contain little significant material from his own wartime years. Yet his army service was by no means uneventful. He was wounded twice, first when his squadron was involved in a running skirmish with a Union cavalry detachment near Port Gibson, Mississippi, and later in 1864 when his squadron charged a detachment of Illinois infantry ambushed in a lane and he received a shot in the armpit.[25] Years later Cable recalled how "I used to suffer with that bloody, ragged hole in my poor swelled back and stiff arm and not a little, too, from the vile smell of that sloughing wound that 'ran in the night' like David's. . . ."[26] Cable made a quick recovery from the arm wound, and was soon back in camp; shortly afterward he was assigned to quartermaster duty to relieve him of hard riding while his wound healed.[27]

For a full-fledged Confederate soldier, Cable was of very slight build. Once when his squadron stopped at a Louisiana plantation, the owner stared at him, and on being assured that the youth before him was indeed in the army, exclaimed, "Great Heavens! Abe Lincoln told the truth—We *are* robbing the cradle and the grave."[28] Quickly toughened to the saddle, however, Cable became wiry and bronzed, and participated in some of the most arduous campaigning of the war. During General William T. Sherman's month-long raid against Meridian, Mississippi, Cable rode 700 miles, 300 of them during one forced march.[29]

As the Confederate fighting forces disintegrated during the early months of 1865, and most available infantry was sent to the Carolinas to oppose Sherman, only General Nathan Bedford Forrest and his command were left in Mississippi and Alabama to contest the field with Union forces. Cable's unit joined Forrest in Gainesville, Alabama, and for the rest of the war he served as clerk for Captain T. Ellis and for Major J. P. Strange, Forrest's adjutant.[30] On one memorable occasion, Cable was called before Forrest, given pen, paper, and a legal form, and for four days wrote manumission papers for Forrest's Negro slaves. Forrest would call each Negro before him, give Cable his name, and Cable would make out the papers. "At the earliest moment when to a Negro in the South freedom was really anything but a mockery," Cable wrote later, "our modern Blucher was manumitting all his slaves. And he did not stop till he had finished." [31]

If Cable held any doubts of the South's ability to win its freedom, as surely he must have done during the last months of the war, they do not appear in most of the wartime letters that still survive. His letters to his mother and to his brother Jim, who was also in Confederate service by then, are cheerful, matter-of-fact, and often exhortatory. "So Jim, take care of yourself, be a good soldier, study army regulations, *read your bible, say your prayers without fear of comment,* write to us often, keep up your spirits, don't fall in love nor the enemy's hands," runs a typical adjuration.[32] Four days later, learning that Jim had been involved in an engagement in which his troop had been surprised and utterly routed, Cable wrote, referring to his own first experience in battle, "How lamentable our experience in this war! One brought out of a disgraceful skirmish with a slight flesh wound before the fight was done, the other hunted through the swamps, his horse and clothes captured and himself escaping by precipitate flight." Faced, like his brother, with the prospect of reassignment to infantry duty because his horse had been lost, Cable proposed that they transfer to foot-soldiering at once: "Oh pshaw! Don't suppose I *blame* you, for I know you could not do any better; but *let's get out of it!* I *know* that you will fight, and I am not afraid to trust myself, so as we will undoubtedly have to leave the cavalry let us hurry and make our arrangements. As for you going and me staying here, why that must not be thought of, it cannot be done."[33]

Cable fully realized the privilege he enjoyed in being assigned to clerical duty in the late days of the war. "It is raining quite briskly but thanks to a merciful Providence I am safe from the storm and am only aware of the rain outside by the pattering on the roof of our snow-white wall-tent," he wrote to his mother. "Poor soldiers! why should I be so much more comfortable than many who have breasted the storm of war from the beginning?"[34] Not until a letter to his mother written on April 16, 1865—eight days after Lee had surrendered to Grant at Appomattox and less than three weeks before Forrest's surrender—is a genuinely pessimistic note found in Cable's wartime correspondence. Urging her to see that his sister leave southern Mississippi, he wrote: "The way times are now, I think it is highly desirable and necessary that we should be as little scattered as possible. . . . These are the 'Times that try men's souls,' and my constant prayer is that when ours are tried they may go through the ordeal as gold thro' the refiner's fire."[35]

As a soldier Cable was apparently popular among his comrades, who valued his cheerfulness and encouragement. Years later, his onetime fellow Confederates recalled him kneeling to pray each night in camp or bivouac.[36] Throughout the war he read the Bible regularly, studied mathematics and Latin, and practiced drawing whenever he could. He carried books with him in the saddle, and particularly valued his assignment to clerical duty at headquarters because it "brought me much into contact with men of choice intelligence."[37] Undoubtedly one wartime memory which did find its way into his later fiction is found in Richard Thorndyke Smith's remark in *The Cavalier:* ". . . my unsoldierly motive for going to headquarters kept my misgivings alive. I was hungry for the gentilities of camp: to be where Shakespeare was part of the baggage, where Pope was quoted, where Coleridge and Byron and Poe were recited, Macaulay criticized, and 'Les Miserables'— Madame Le Vert's Mobile translation—lent round; and where men, when they did steal, stole portable volumes, not currycombs."

As Cable's war experience lengthened, he grew more mature; and while Confederate fortunes waned, he puzzled over the larger meaning of the events in which he was involved. In his essay "My Politics," written in 1888–89, he relates an incident in which he and some of his fellow soldiers were discussing headquarters gossip to the effect that various Georgia politicians were threatening their state's secession from the Confederacy. Cable rode along in silence without joining in the conversation until his companions, noting his failure to take part, began "bantering" him to speak:

> "This shows me," I replied, "that we are fighting to establish a scheme of government that will work our destruction as sure as we succeed. We shall go to pieces as soon as we are safe from outside enemies."
> "Then why do you fight for it?"
> "Because I am a citizen of this government, a soldier by its laws, sworn into service and ordered, not to think, but to fight." [38]

Yet, the essay goes on to say, at the time he saw no unrighteousness whatever in fighting to perpetuate slavery. When the war was over and he was paroled, he returned to New Orleans, still clad in his gray uniform, resigned to defeat, but without the slightest feeling of loyalty to the triumphant United States of America.

III

New Orleans Days

George Washington Cable came back to New Orleans in late May of 1865, with $155 in worthless Confederate currency in his pocket and no clothes to his name except the uniform he was wearing. An occupied city for three years, New Orleans now painfully began the struggle to win its way back to prosperity. Investment capital was largely lacking, commercial facilities were in disrepair, railroad communications were all but nonexistent, and a Federal garrison patrolled the city. Cable found work with the tobacco house of F. Van Benthuysen, but remuneration was pitifully small and he faced the need to support not only himself but also his mother and sisters, who were still living in Mississippi. On one occasion when he was sent on an errand to United States Army headquarters, his Confederate uniform aroused the ire of Union General Nathaniel P. Banks, who asked him, "Don't you know that there is a law that forbids you to wear that uniform?" Cable remembered that he "drew himself up to my fullest height and replied: 'Yes, sir; I know that, sir. But I know of an older law which I am bound to regard, which forbids a man to appear without any clothes at all, sir.'" Banks thereupon wrote an order to Cable's employer directing him to purchase appropriate clothing for his clerk.[1]

In the summer he found a job at Kosciusko, Mississippi, clerking in a store, which paid him a salary of $50 a month and included a job for his brother Jim as well. Meanwhile he sought to find a place back at home that would pay living wages, eventually locating a position as clerk to a family friend who was a cotton and commission merchant in New Orleans—Lloyd R. Coleman. He was looking forward, he wrote to his mother, to a time when

"we will have a little home of our own in New Orleans La Belle
& *one hearth, one circle, one interest, one motive, one faith, one love*—shall
bind us all together." [2] For a time, too, he was in love with
Coleman's daughter Bettie, telling a friend (in a letter dated
January, 1866) that he was to be married the following year.[3]
To his mother he wrote, "I am slowly learning, in my present
position, some of the hitherto incomprehensible parts of the great
machinery called Trade. I begin to see what I thought was not
to be found—the beauties of the *science* of Trade. The cotton
business is very pleasant—but I cannot help striking higher, and
trying for an honorable profession. May the world regret me when
I die!" [4] In early July, Cable left Coleman's employ to serve as
rodman on a surveying party on the Atchafalaya River. For
several weeks the surveyors worked along the river, and Cable
enjoyed the hard physical labor in the open air; but then malarial
fever struck the party. Cable was prostrate for weeks, and would
not for two years be able to resume steady work.[5] His months
of recuperation were spent studying the natural history of the
region.[6] Eventually he joined a commission merchant as accountant, and subsequently worked for two cotton firms and as secretary
of the New Orleans Oil Works Company. His lingering illness
incapacitated him at times, but his intelligence and reliability
earned his employers' respect.[7]

In February, 1869, Cable became engaged to marry Louise
Stewart Bartlett. Born in New Orleans, she was the daughter of
William Allen and Louise Burling Stewart Bartlett, both of whom
were of New England descent. Bartlett, who traced his ancestry
back to the Pilgrim fathers, had come to New Orleans from
Connecticut as a young man. Cable and Louise Bartlett were
married on December 7, 1869, by Dr. Benjamin M. Palmer at
the Bartlett home on Magazine Street. They had grown up within
a few blocks of each other, but not until adult years had they
met. Louise was of slight build, with dark hair and delicately cut
features. As deeply devoted to church work as her husband, she
shared his seriousness of purpose and encouraged him in all his
work.[8] Unlike Cable, who for all his slight frame was basically
of robust health, she was not strong, and throughout her marriage
she was frequently ill. Their first child, Louise, was born in November, 1870.

Meanwhile Cable had begun to write. The New Orleans newspapers commonly published unsolicited material, often in the form of poetry. Cable soon became a contributor. Together with several friends he formed a literary club with the idea of furnishing a weekly column to the *Picayune,* then edited by his friend C. Harrison Parker, to be entitled "Drop Shot." When, after the first column had appeared on February 27, 1870, the other members of the club failed to furnish any further copy, Cable undertook to write the weekly feature himself. For eighteen months he continued, for one month even writing it on a daily basis. As Arlin Turner points out, the "Drop Shot" column served as Cable's literary apprenticeship: "it afforded him ample satisfaction and it showed him where his ability lay. We see evidence of his rapidly widening acquaintanceship among books, and we see him groping after some bases for judging authors and their writings. We have here a detailed log of the development of his mind as he became more aware of the local scene and local characters and as he began to speak out more plainly and more persistently for the righting of wrongs in the world around him." [9] A good deal of the "Drop Shot" material was poetry and, as Turner notes, Cable discovered thereby that he was no poet. [10] However, he included in the column some of the love poems he had written to Louise Bartlett before their marriage, as well as frequent effusions on various topics, and some light verse as well.

Turner has estimated that in the total "Drop Shot" columns Cable referred to some fifty different authors—whether he read them all, or only borrowed apt quotations from various sources, is another matter. He wrote often on literature, giving advice to writers, commenting on craft and on style, describing and sometimes criticizing books and authors. The topics which most interested Cable, however, were apparently the local New Orleans scene and various contemporary matters. He wrote on such varied subjects as yellow fever, school newspapers, lotteries, the Mardi Gras, the lack of a literary society in the city, the customhouse, kites flying over the main streets, fishing, the climate, the city's fancy balls, walking canes, politics, women's rights, differences between North and South, the death of Robert E. Lee, the lack of good local writers, baseball, book blurbs, advertising, inventions, fairs, the streetcars of the city, children in the newspaper room, editors—whatever struck his fancy. It was excellent training for a man who would soon be writing fiction notable for its social texture. On one occasion, he remarked that for the poet in search of a subject, Louisiana's two centuries of history were "a rich and profitable mine. Here lie the gems, like those new diamonds in Africa, right on top of the ground. The mines are virgin." Only one man, Cable said, "has culled among these nuggets. The historian of Louisiana . . . in following the annals of colonization, has uncovered the mines of romance"—an obvious reference to the historian Charles Gayarré. "But the half, I am sure, has not been told," he continued, ending with a poem.[11] It would not be long before Cable followed his own advice, to the growing jealousy of Gayarré.

Some of the "Drop Shot" articles dealt with local history and descriptions of old forts, ruins, and the like. Cable also wrote a great deal about flowers, trees, and birds, sometimes producing rather self-conscious effusions on the natural scene, in particular the Gulf of Mexico as seen from coastal island resorts. Whereas at first, as Turner points out, he was little more than a local citizen commenting at random on local matters, his columns grew more and more literary as his tenure on the *Picayune* progressed. There was also increasing concern with questions of social justice, though there is little evidence that Cable was mistaken when he later declared that in those years he held no views on Southern problems at variance with those of his neighbors.[12]

One of Cable's best "Drop Shot" pieces was that for June 28, 1870, entitled "Going! Going!", in which he describes the scene as various townsfolk depart for summer vacation. He notes the general confusion as the outward-bound travelers board trains and boats:

How lively the depot! All sorts of people in all sorts of humors, but no one exactly serene. Here a little boy has caught his fish-hook in an old gentleman's hat; there that little girl's kitten has got away; that drayman has smashed a bird cage. Here comes a family of ten, and everyone has a basket; an old man, rich and genteel, has been giving way for everyone at the gangway—that's him in snowy side whiskers and white canvas shoes—and just steps to get aboard when up rushes a swarm of French children, as irrestrainable as a herd of buffalo, and he falls back. Now they're on the train—adieu, papa! adieu—smack—ma—smack—femme—smack! smack! The canvas shoes go into another car.

>There are two Irish gents saying good-by. "Good-by Jawny! If ye's can't stand it over there come back and tell us how ye's like it." There's a Northern group with their "ah's" and their "ha's" and their "psha's", poking their canes into everybody's baggage; and yonder's a Mexican family with half a dozen unbearable pets; phew!
>
>There's a masculine crowd out on a 3 days cruise, a single freedman with them, with some 17 fishing baskets on his person, trying to receive instructions from 17 jocose swells at once. . . .

The piece continues for several hundred words more, describing scenes aboard ship, and ending with a description of a determined pleasure seeker who assiduously attempts all the proper forms of recreation without enjoying any of them: "he is a martyr to pleasure-seeking by rule, and has sought it in vain the wide world over." [13] Though the column is not of itself remarkable, it will be recognized that within it Cable in one way or the other touches on many of the ingredients that would make his later fiction so distinctive: the crowded scene, reminiscent of Dickens perhaps but infused with the life that Cable would bring to such things; the mixture and contrast of races, especially the Creole element; the Negro freedman, his status here noted only for purposes of humor; differences between North and South, and between rich and poor; even, however slightly, a taste of that French-English dialect that would become his stock in trade.

So adept at journalism did Cable become that in early 1871 he was offered and accepted a full-time post as reporter on the *Picayune.* Some of the news writing was to his liking. For his report on the Mistick Krewe of Comus parade for the Mardi Gras that year—the theme of which was Spenser's *Faerie Queene*—he produced an extended account that opened with a poem of his own, discussed the *Faerie Queene* itself, and furnished an elaborate description of the pageant and its reception. When Horace Greeley, editor of the New York *Tribune* and by this time considered a friend of the South because of his support of amnesty for ex-Confederates, visited New Orleans in May, 1871, Cable accompanied him on his tour of the city and reported sympathetically on it in news stories and in the "Drop Shot." [14]

Soon, however, an incident happened which Cable found not at all to his pleasure. Assigned to cover a Teachers' Institute called by the Republican-appointed superintendent of schools, he reported in resentful terms that since all teachers were compelled to attend, Negroes and whites were thus forced to sit down next to each other in the same room. The other New Orleans newspapers joined in the hue and cry, whereupon Cable, in his own words, "suddenly weakened, slackened, ceased." "I did not see that I was wrong," he continued. "I only saw that there were two sides to the question and much doubted which side was least right. Naturally the proprietor of the *Picayune* was greatly vexed at me for losing the lead in this exhilarating chase." [15] The refusal to continue the attack on the Republicans for having thus forced teachers into an integrated meeting was of serious consequence to Cable, as he pointed out later:

> I was living from hand to mouth those days. My household consisted of a widowed mother, a young wife entirely without fortune but unused to a poor man's life, and our infant daughter. I did not feel like losing my place, but I submit the fact to the thousands who have since then accused me of pitching my public utterances to suit the public ear that I neglected to do it then. I did not lose the place at that time, nor at last for political reasons; but then and there I permanently lost grace with my employer.[16]

The incident whereby Cable actually lost his job on the *Picayune* involved his refusal to violate his religious scruples by going to a theater to report on a play, although, as Cable said later, this of itself would not have been cause for dismissal if his general performance as a news reporter had been more competent: "I had neither the faculty for getting more news, nor the relish for blurting out news for news' sake after it was got. . . . I wanted to be always writing, and they wanted me to be always reporting." [17] In any event, during the summer of 1871 it was suggested to Cable that his resignation would be accepted, whereupon he went back to bookkeeping, vowing never to have anything to do with a newspaper again.[18]

So Cable began work for William C. Black and Company, cotton factors. Black had once been Cable's employer before the war, and would remain his employer and friend until he died in 1879. Soon Cable—despite his vow—was writing for the *Picayune* again, the ownership having meanwhile changed hands. He began the "Drop Shot" once more, and also took on for the *Picayune* the task of attacking the notorious Louisiana Lottery Company, producing two editorials which charged the Lottery's management with bribery and called on other New Orleans newspapers, ministers, and townsfolk to join in the crusade. The Lottery Company, which was strongly entrenched, fought back with a libel suit and other legal measures, whereupon the *Picayune,* unable to withstand such powerful opposition, changed editors again and the assault on the Lottery abruptly ceased. Not for another twenty years would the Lottery be successfully opposed. Meanwhile Cable continued to write book reviews, an occasional feature, and some poetry for the *Picayune* and other papers.[19]

On October 17, 1871, not long after returning to clerical work, Cable addressed a letter to Charles Scribner and Co. in New York: "I have a small manuscript ready for publication and desire to arrange for its early issue," he began. It would come to about 120 pages of type, he said, mostly prose but with about 40 pages of occasional verse. "The work takes the form of a story, with scenes laid in and about New Orleans, involving descriptions of scenes and seasons especially characteristic of the place, and portraying three or four personal characters representative of classes peculiar to this community. The verses are component parts of the story, but do not comprise any portion of the narrative." Cable was apparently not certain of the finances of book publishing; he asked Scribner's what the cost of printing 2,000 or 3,000 copies would be in cloth or "flexible cloth" covers, how much of the total he would be required to advance, and "your lowest terms if undertaken entirely upon my own risk and charge." Scribner's asked to see his manuscript, and off it went.[20] Accompanying it was another letter, offering to subsidize 2,000 copies, explaining that the material came from his "Drop Shot" column with a narrative added, and declaring that two New Orleans friends had already offered to speak for 300 copies between them.[21] Not until late in December did Cable hear from Scribner's, and then without explanation, that his book was not accepted; he asked for further comment and apparently received it, although the manuscript itself has not been preserved. In reply, he expressed his thanks for "your advice which is, no doubt, the best," declaring that "after a while, when more at leisure, I am going to try to send you something that *will be published.*"[22]

In the early months of 1872 Cable began his series for the

Picayune on "The Churches and Charities of New Orleans." And no doubt it was during his historical research for the series, which carried him back to the earliest years of the city, that he came upon the city's old *Code Noir,* the inhumanity of which, he declared later, inspired him to write the story entitled "Bibi" which so impressed Edward King and J. Wells Champney the following year.[23] The original version of "Bibi" does not survive, but apparently the version later set into the novel *The Grandissimmes* differs only slightly. King took the story, which tells of an African prince being brought into early eighteenth-century Louisiana as a slave, and dispatched it to the assistant editor of *Scribner's Monthly,* Richard Watson Gilder, who kept it for some weeks and then rejected it.[24] "Bibi" went the rounds of the magazines thereafter but did not find a place, no doubt for the reason given by the assistant editor of the *Atlantic Monthly,* George Parsons Lathrop, who returned it "on account of the unmitigatedly distressful effect of the story."[25] It is appropriate that Cable's first mature story should have been declined for just such reasons, for, as we shall see, this first encounter with the Genteel Tradition of post-Civil War American magazine literature was to be all too typical of his later experience.

King had also taken another Cable story along with him when he left New Orleans, however, and he urged Cable to revise it: "Give Sieur George a reef on the head, and furbish up the first part; then let us hear about him, and if you would like me to forward it, I will."[26] Meanwhile, as he traveled about the South finding material for the Great South series, King kept Cable's spirits up with continued praise. "Fear not, O Cable, for your fortune is sure if you continue to make Bibis," he wrote from Mobile, Alabama.[27] From San Antonio: "'Bibi' rode me as a nightmare the other midnight."[28] And again from Houston, "Seriously, I think Bibi has a chance. But I am only a worm crawling before the Scribnerian throne."[29]

Then, from St. Louis, Missouri, on July 22, King sent the good news that *Scribner's Monthly* had accepted "Monsieur George" to appear in the magazine as "'Sieur George—A New Orleans Story." He had himself read the story to the editor, he wrote: "it trembled in the balance a day, and then Oh Ye gods! was accepted! I fancy I can see you waltzing around the office of the venerable cotton brokers, shouting the war-cry of future conquest! Courage!" [30]

Following " 'Sieur George," *Scribner's Monthly* accepted "Belles Demoiselles Plantation" and " 'Tite Poulette," and then "Jean-ah Poquelin," "Madame Déliceuse," and "Café des Exilés." One of Cable's best stories, "Posson Jone'," was rejected by *Scribner's Monthly* and subsequently taken by *Appletons' Journal.* Thus by the autumn of 1875, Cable had had seven stories accepted for publication. For each, however, he received an average remuneration of about $70, and three additional stories had been rejected by everyone. He was thus in the position of being a published author, of some reputation, but almost as far as ever from supporting himself and his family from the proceeds of his writings. Small wonder, then, that after November, 1875, he sent no more stories to New York for three years.

IV

Local Color: *Old Creole Days*

Since George W. Cable's first and apparently lasting reputation was as a Southern exemplar of local color, it is appropriate to consider what the genre was all about and what it actually meant for Cable's art and career.

The local color movement that for several decades after the Civil War was so prominent a feature of the American literary scene is generally said to have begun with the publication of Bret Harte's "The Luck of Roaring Camp" in the *Overland Monthly* for August, 1868. But, as Claude M. Simpson points out, it had actually been under way for considerably longer than that.[1] The first American local colorists might be said to be those "humorists" of the Old Frontier who, at a time when the historical romance was the dominant American fictional form, were devoting themselves to the delineation of the quaint and comic types who inhabited the more backward rural areas to the United States. Beginning with A. B. Longstreet's *Georgia Scenes* in 1835, there had been a series of Southern writers who had concentrated on giving an "authentic" presentation of everyday American life in its rural Southern forms. The immediate purpose was primarily that of comedy; the typical humorist of the Old Southwest (by which is meant the region between the Savannah and Mississippi rivers) was a Whig gentleman who sought to portray the crude, often barbaric customs and attitudes of uncouth backwoods folk. Frequently, however, the Whiggish superiority of the storyteller gave way to fascination and even to sneaking admiration—particularly in the writings of such non-Whigs as Johnson Jones Hooper and George Washington Harris—and along with the humorous exaggeration and relish for the bizarre went a genuine interest in the faithful recording of rural life. There was an interest, too, in the peculiarities of regional dialect; most of the material was borrowed from taletelling, and the transcribers labored to represent the way their characters talked with strict accuracy.[2] What they produced was not ordinarily considered literature by the official culture of the day, though in the *Southern Literary Messenger* for March, 1836, Edgar Allan Poe had praised Longstreet's *Georgia Scenes* as the work of a man with a "discriminative and penetrating understanding of *character* in general, and of Southern character in particular," and had hailed the book as "a sure omen of better days for the literature of the South." The fact that the frontier humor was viewed, both by antebellum readers and by the authors themselves, as subliterature, served to protect it from being tailored to the literary ideal of the day and allowed its unabashed use of raw, everyday subject matter to go unchallenged.

What the writers of local color did, in the years following the Civil War, was in effect to draw on the techniques of the old frontier humor, divested of its crudities, in order to achieve a specificity of regional textural detail that had largely been missing from American literature until then. American fiction was at a low ebb. Its chief artistic luminary, Nathaniel Hawthorne, had died in 1864. The man who today is recognized as its other great pre-Civil War master, Herman Melville, was already all but forgotten. The vogue of the old historical romance as practiced by Cooper, Simms, and Cooke was exhausted. The sentimental novel, written in large part for and by women, was in its heyday; the heartrending tales of Mrs. E. D. E. N. Southworth and Augusta Jane Evans sold in hundreds of thousands, and Hawthorne's earlier lament that "America is now wholly given over to a damned mob of scribbling women" remained appropriate. Yet there had come, notably through the success of Harriet Beecher Stowe's *Uncle Tom's Cabin*—which save for its scenes of high melodrama relied on quite realistic detail and description to tell its story—a desire for a greater fidelity to the facts of ordinary experience than either the old-fashioned romance or the sentimental novel could provide. It was toward this goal that American fiction had begun, however hesitantly, to grope. The call had gone out for "the Great American Novel," a book which would draw together the myriad details of American experience into a single great tale which would, as John W. De Forest wrote in the *Nation* in 1868, paint "American life so broadly, truly, and sympathetically that every American of feeling and culture is forced to acknowledge the picture as a likeness of something which he knows. . . ."[3] No claimants appeared for this honor, and it would shortly become apparent that instead of any single such national work, the various regions of the United States would provide for themselves in fiction quite successfully.

As noted earlier, the post-Civil War American Union was showing a renewed curiosity about its various regions. Freed from the danger of political separation, the country's geographical and social differences could be acknowledged. The cultural hegemony of New England, the distinguished visages of whose Good Gray Poets still graced genteel parlors and studies throughout the North and Midwest, was coming to an end, even as the war had clearly shown that New York, and not Boston, was now the financial center of the nation. Though the idealism that had evolved out of the earlier Transcendental ferment of New England would continue to dominate American cultural life for many decades to come, there was in general both a lowering of tone and a broadening of geographical and social horizons. Not for some years yet would the realism that William Dean Howells came to champion make important inroads on the inner nature of American fiction, but there was a notable demand both for more varied subject matter and more realistic use of everyday experience.

It was a time, too, when Americans began to acknowledge that their society was becoming increasingly an affair of cities. The Civil War had accentuated the trend toward industrialism, and the masses of immigrants from Europe brought in during the war to swell the Union armies were followed by hundreds of thousands of additional immigrants, most of whom took up residence in the large Eastern Seaboard cities. The network of railroads now drew the West into closer economic relationship with the East, and the rural areas with the cities. With industrialism clearly in control of the American political system, farm prices dropped, railroad combines exerted a growingly restrictive control over the marketing of farm products, and rural poverty was widespread, in turn stimulating the move into the cities from the country.

The tranquil agricultural society of the republic in the days before the war thus became increasingly a lost paradise, and stories of outlying regions where life was still apparently easy and bucolic, without the complexities of postwar urban society, possessed a powerful appeal for the American imagination. Mark Twain, writing his tales of boyhood along the Mississippi while living in a brownstone mansion in Hartford, Connecticut, symbolized the yearning of an urban America for a lost rural innocence.

In the years following the Civil War there was a tremendous demand for magazine fiction. *Harper's, Scribner's,* the *Century, Lippincott's, Appletons',* the *Atlantic Monthly,* were found on parlor and study tables everywhere. The discovery of a mass magazine market was tied in with the rising curiosity of Americans about their regions, and the fiction of local color, with its emphasis on setting and its concomitant tendency toward weakness in character and plot, was admirably suited to magazine publishing. Few of the local color writers proved successful novelists; their fiction tended to be episodic and to stretch out too thinly in book form. But at magazine length the lush scenic effects of local color were highly acceptable, and faults of story line and characterization minimized.

The typical local color story, as written by Thomas Nelson Page, Joel Chandler Harris, Mary Noailles Murfree, and, in his less original moments, Cable himself, was a hybrid literary form. It provided close detail of setting and, within limits, a realistic descriptive texture, but these were grafted onto an essentially romantic plot structure, commonly a love story. The characters, though given the particularities of regional life, tended to be types, with little depth or complexity to them, designed to exhibit the quaint eccentricities of provincial life. The typical local color story was a form of pastoral romance, with an emphasis on setting; if in their quaintness and simplicity the characters constituted something of a rebuke to the complexities and urgencies of post-Civil War urban America, the rebuke was gently administered, and comforting to the nation's widespread wish to believe that the simple American virtues of prewar days still existed. In any event, the appetite of the American magazine reading public for picturesque provincial tales seemed unquenchable, and the mass magazines competed for circulation with story after story of local color fiction.

Because it was shaped for a mass market and designed for family consumption, magazine fiction accepted the ideals and the inhibitions of the dominant Genteel Tradition. Sex was to be treated obliquely, and depiction of physical passion was taboo. Ideality was the pervading mode; religion was sacrosanct. Overt unpleasantness of setting or characterization was frowned upon; the rigors of life on the farm in a time of failing farm prices and widespread rural poverty, the exigencies of a meager existence in the defeated cities of the South, were not permitted to infringe upon the romantic plot structure and quaint descriptions of an idealized provincial life. Controversial topics and attitudes were to be avoided; when Southern writers such as Page ventured to exhibit traces of lingering Confederate prejudices, such passages were carefully excised. The world was essentially good, and magazine fiction must perforce reflect the goodness.

Thus, if in the history of American literature the local color movement represents a stage in the development of a realistic fiction, it is primarily because its technique, involving the detailed description of provincial life, served to introduce a more diversified subject matter and to place a premium upon accurate, if very much selected, observation. When, as sometimes happened in Cable's fiction, the attempt to render the details of regional experience drew the artist's eye toward the inclusion of unpleasant and even ugly elements, the magazine editors who guarded the sensibilities of their readers were quick to protest.

The story entitled "Posson Jone,'" perhaps the best of Cable's early stories—all of which appeared in magazines before being published in book form under the title *Old Creole Days* in 1879—is an example of the problems that a writer like Cable faced in his dealings with the magazine editors of the Genteel Tradition. This story, which involves a drunken preacher who is willing to gamble away his church's money, was rejected by *Scribner's Monthly,* and then in succession by the New York *Times,* the *Galaxy,* and *Harper's.* When Henry Mills Alden, editor of *Harper's,* returned it, he commented that "the disagreeable aspects of human nature are made prominent, and the story leaves an unpleasant impression on the

mind of the reader," adding later that the stories in *Harper's* "must
be of a pleasant character and, as a rule, must be love tales."
Ironically, "Posson Jone'" when published proved to be the most
widely commended of all of Cable's stories, and was praised by
Charles Dudley Warner for showing that actual life, even low life,
could be heightened to gain an idealistic effect.[4] Cable's editor
at *Scribner's Monthly,* Richard Watson Gilder, later regretted his
failure to recognize the story's merit.[5]

The public taste for local color provided, therefore, both a signal
opportunity and a potentially severe liability for George W. Cable
in his drive to become a successful writer. There can be no question
of Cable's good fortune in having been born and raised in New
Orleans; the lavish color, the romantic history, the exotic mixture
of races and civilizations, provided him with a setting that was
ideally suited to the growing American interest in provincial life,
and his own descriptive talents were precisely those best calculated
to take advantage of the situation. Highly conscious of racial
differences, strongly interested in society and the relationships
between people, alert to the sensuous possibilities of life in a richly
complex Southern city with a strong Latin heritage, he was
admirably equipped to answer the demand for fiction that emphasized a rich textural surface. The sound, shape, feel, and smell
of everyday life was his metier; he was a master of the composition
of place, writing at precisely the time when that quality was in
great demand. As for Cable's other qualities—a strongly developed
social conscience, a talent for probing boldly into the moral and
social subterfuges of the life around him, an unwillingness to
accept half-truths and convenient rationalizations—these were less
well adapted to the demands of his editors and the public. But
at first, as he wrote the stories that would make up *Old Creole Days,*
these liabilities did not seem crucial.

As William Malone Baskervill remarked, it is significant that
Cable's first published story began with the words "In the heart
of New Orleans. . . ."[6] The story, "'Sieur George," contains in
miniature almost everything out of which Cable was to make his
art, and it is dominated by a particular tone and his major theme,
the Creoles of New Orleans. The tale of an *Américain* gentleman
who spends the better part of his life and all of his fortune
gambling unsuccessfully with tickets on the Cuban lottery, "'Sieur

George" has about it an air of pervading languor, the futility and decadence, with a hint of the voluptuous, of a Latin race living in slothful ease in a Southern city under warm skies. The protagonist, known first as "Monsieur" and later, as his fortunes decline, merely as " 'Sieur George," dwells for fifty years in two rented rooms in a brick house in the French Quarter. His origins are unknown. Like the Creole landlord Kookoo whose attempts to find out the secret in his tenant's hair trunk constitute the framework of the story, we view 'Sieur George from without, a somewhat imposing but not quite heroic figure, who makes his living in obscure ways, drinks a great deal, and tells nobody about himself or his past. From the very first there is the sense of ruin, embodied in the description of the building, which itself stands for what we shall finally perceive is the moral ruin of 'Sieur George:

> With its gray stucco peeling off in broad patches, it has a solemn look of gentility in rags, and stands, or, as it were, hangs, about the corner of two ancient streets, like a faded fop who pretends to be looking for employment.

The street sides of the building are rented out for small and unprosperous shops, and within the courtyard children play amid clotheslines of wet laundry, while rotten staircases "that seem vainly trying to clamber out of the rubbish" line the sides. Once the neighborhood had been prosperous and fashionable—it was then that 'Sieur George first came to rent rooms—but it has long since declined, along with the physical appearance of the building. The whole atmosphere seems decadent—the apothecary shop is "dingy," the neighborhood is "given up to fifth-rate shops," a "decaying cornice hangs over, dropping bits of mortar on passers below," while the landlord, "an ancient Creole of doubtful purity of blood," has "grown old and wrinkled and brown, a sort of periodically animate mummy. . . ." Old 'Sieur George, stumbling home drunk, fits perfectly into the surroundings.

When 'Sieur George first moved in, he brought a small hair trunk; and when Kookoo took hold of this trunk to help in arranging the apartment, 'Sieur George had threatened to hit him, thus arousing the landlord's deepest curiosity as to its contents. After 'Sieur George had gone off to fight in the Mexican War—for he surprised them all one day by stepping out of the old house in full regimentals—Kookoo had hoped at last to find out what was in the trunk, but 'Sieur George's apartment was at once occupied by a Creole lady and servant who in their aloofness offered him no opportunity to look within. After the war, 'Sieur George fails to return for some time. When eventually he does so, it is with a scar from a saber wound on his forehead, and a friend in tow, a "tall, lank, iron-gray man." For a while it seems to everyone that 'Sieur George is preparing to marry the woman inhabiting his apartment, but apparently it was the tall friend who won the lady's hand. After the wedding, 'Sieur George returns to dwell in the apartment again. Turned momentarily garrulous, he tells Kookoo and others how the tall man, a "drunkard" for whom he had little regard, had attached himself to him during the war, and he makes it clear that he disapproves of the marriage. Then his forebodings are justified; the wife dies, 'Sieur George brings home her infant child, and soon afterward the father is found drowned. 'Sieur George raises the child by himself; he has reformed, no longer comes home drunk. Eventually the child turns sixteen, reaches womanhood. One evening there ensues a final dramatic scene, which the eavesdropping Kookoo witnesses. 'Sieur George tells the girl that she can no longer live with him: "You cannot stay with me safely or decently, much as I wish it. The Lord only knows how I'm to bear it, or where you're to go; but He's your Lord, child, and He'll make a place for you. I was your grandfather's death; I frittered your poor, dead mother's fortune away: let that be the last damage I do."

The girl weeps pathetically, sobbing that she cannot bear to leave the old man. Whereupon—and here Cable's instinctive artistry thoroughly redeems the story from the sentimental romance it has seemed to be turning into—'Sieur George "was encouraged by the orphan's pitiful tones to contemplate the most senseless act he ever attempted to commit." He tells the girl that she is not really blood kin to him, and that there is one way whereby she can with propriety continue to live with him:

> She looked up at the old man with a glance of painful inquiry.
> "If you could be—my wife, dearie?"
> She uttered a low, distressful cry, and, gliding swiftly into her room, for the first time in her young life turned the key between them.
> And the old man sat and wept.

This startling dénouement, with its sense of degradation, its suggestion of near depravity, its furtive understatement, destroys whatever admiration has been building for 'Sieur George in the reader's mind. His moral degradation is clear. When the girl departs to take up life in a convent, and 'Sieur George slumbers away in a drunken stupor, we learn the secret of his troubles; Kookoo steals into the apartment, manages to look into the mysterious trunk, and finds it filled with a mass of worthless tickets on the Havana lottery. We last glimpse 'Sieur George sleeping out in the high grass along the edge of the prairie, and still seeking in vain to talk to the girl in order to borrow ten dollars for yet another try at the lottery.

" 'Sieur George," we are told, so puzzled Richard Watson Gilder and his fellow editors at *Scribner's Monthly* that before it was accepted for publication Cable was asked to insert several clarifying sentences and to write a final paragraph. One can understand why; what is told is stated indirectly, and a great deal of the appeal and strength of the story comes from its delicate gliding over matters that if presented directly would doubtless never have won Gilder's approval. The sense of decadence, of moral ruin, is so artfully embodied in the physical dilapidation and decay that it is difficult to point to any actual, direct statement of the story's chief appeal, its depiction of sensual indulgence and moral squalor. The statement that Kookoo is "of doubtful purity of blood," the remark that the young Creoles of the neighborhood think that the mulatto maid, "a tall, straight woman," is "confound' good lookin'," and above all the eloquent understatement of the passage in which 'Sieur George's niece recoils at his proposal—"She uttered a low, distressful cry, and, gliding swiftly into her room, for the first time in her young life turned the key between them"—are almost the only specific sexual references in a story with nonetheless profoundly sensual overtones. The extent of Gilder's comprehension of the story's true nature may be gauged from his statement to Cable that he must "work as religiously as if you already had Bret Harte's reputation—and perhaps you may have one as lasting." [7]

Bret Harte, with his sentimental prostitutes, tender-hearted gold miners, and the like, was hardly of the same rank as Cable; the unsentimental, almost savage depiction of human degradation in

" 'Sieur George," with its acceptance of decadence, strikes a note that Harte never attained. The statement of Gilder's assistant, Robert Underwood Johnson, that "it was a fresh and gentle southwest wind that blew into the office in 1873" when the story arrived at *Scribner's Monthly* seems almost comically inappropriate.[8]

It is probable that the exotic, faraway aura of the old New Orleans setting, with its introduction of picturesque Creoles into American fiction, so fascinated Gilder, Johnson, and their colleagues at *Scribner's Monthly* that the underlying harshness of the material failed to register. Certainly if the story had been set in a more conventional place, and 'Sieur George's degradation had been depicted amid less colorful surroundings, the story would never have been published in *Scribner's Monthly*. In any event, " 'Sieur George" is a remarkable psychological study, and in its time and place seems all the more startling; critics who complain of its absence of plot and its insipidity as social criticism miss the point. Its plot is completely appropriate to what the story has to say, and the story moves beyond mere social criticism to offer a compelling picture of human degradation. The artistry is a great deal more like that of James Joyce in *Dubliners* than that of even the best of Cable's contemporaries. If only, one laments, Cable had enjoyed editorial tutelage equipped to recognize what he had to offer, and critics able to perceive the nature of his artistic gift. But this was never to be.

Though Cable made his degenerating protagonist in " 'Sieur George" one of the *Américains,* his depiction of the Creoles, primarily through the landlord Kookoo, was hardly flattering. His remark that "your second-rate Creole is a great seeker for little offices," his description of Kookoo as "an ancient Creole of doubtful purity of blood," his insistence upon the pretensions of the little landlord, as in his statement that Kookoo "felt a Creole's anger, too, that a tenant should be the holder of wealth while his landlord suffered poverty," above all his depiction of the Creole as venial, acquisitive, and "intensely a coward," were not calculated to endear the author to Creole New Orleans.

"Belles Demoiselles Plantation," the second story to appear, fastens upon miscegenation. Like all the tales of *Old Creole Days,* the story takes place in the early years of the nineteenth century.

Cable begins by describing two lines of the distinguished Creole family of De Charleu: the legitimate branch which "rose straight up, up, up, generation after generation, tall, branchless, slender, palm-like"; and the sinister branch, product of a union of the original De Charleu and a Choctaw wife, its name corrupted by Spanish contact to De Carlos, now "diminished to a mere strand by injudicious alliances, and deaths in the gutters of old New Orleans," of which the single surviving representative is one Injin Charlie. The latter, "sunk in the bliss of deep ignorance, shrewd, deaf, and, by repute at least, unmerciful," owns a block of dilapidated buildings left to the Indian side of the family by his great grandfather, while the legitimate De Charleus, consisting of Old Colonel Jean Albert Henri Joseph De Charleu-Marot and his seven beautiful daughters, inhabit lovely Belles Demoiselles Plantation at a point below New Orleans on the Mississippi. Between Injin Charlie and the Colonel there is nevertheless occasional communication; they always converse in broken English, and however distant their social relationships may be, the family tie is acknowledged, for, as Cable remarks, "One thing I never knew a Creole to do. He will not utterly go back on the ties of blood, no matter what sort of knots those ties may be."

The story revolves about the Colonel's attempt to persuade his half-breed relative to sell him his town property—for the Colonel's seven beautiful daughters have been badgering him to move from Belles Demoiselles into New Orleans and its gay social life. Injin Charlie steadfastly refuses; what would people say? he demands: "dey will say, 'Old Charlie he been all doze time tell a blame *lie!* He ain't no kin to his old grace-gran-muzzer, not a blame bit! He don't got nary drop of De Charleu blood to save his blame low-down old Injin soul! . . .' " He proposes to trade his property for Belles Demoiselles, but the Colonel will have none of this— until he realizes one day that the Point on which the plantation house is located is eroding so rapidly that the house must soon be washed away. He then determines to make the trade, and Injin Charlie assents. But at the last minute the ties of blood are too strong to permit the Colonel to defraud his half-breed cousin; he takes him out to inspect Belles Demoiselles, then declares: "My God!—old man, I tell you—you better not make the trade!" "Because of what?" Injin Charlie asks "in plain anger," whereupon, as the two of them watch, "Belles Demoiselles, the realm of maiden beauty, the home of merriment, the house of dancing, all in the tremor and glow of pleasure, suddenly sunk, with one short, wild wail of terror—sunk, sunk, down, down, into the merciless, unfathomable flood of the Mississippi." The stricken Colonel, his seven beautiful daughters drowned in the river, lives on for a year longer, nursed by old Injin Charlie, until at last he dies, dreaming of his daughters in the garden: " '—I shall be with them at sunrise'; and so it was."

Despite the sensational melodrama of the conclusion, "Belles Demoiselles Plantation" is an effective tale, not least for its depiction of Injin Charlie. This dissolute, half-deaf old man, living in semi-squalor and idleness with an aged and crippled Negress, is a much more convincing figure than the proud Colonel; in his lazy corruption and sybaritism, he represents very much the same image of decay and unregenerate hedonism that characterizes the milieu of " 'Sieur George." For all his squalor, there is something at once exotic and attractive in his disdain for the hard work of moneymaking, his preference for sitting placidly in the sun on his bench in the garden, under a China tree. And despite the fact that throughout his fiction Cable's conscious sympathies are usually with the energetic, bustling *Américains* rather than with the indolent, pleasure-loving Creoles whether of higher or lower caste, one senses here, as often in Cable's fiction, a kind of admiration for and even envy of the lazy, sensual way in which the Creoles accommodate themselves to their circumstance. It is not that Cable portrays the Creoles as nonmaterialistic, but simply that their natural indolence keeps them from working too hard for anything. The portraits of both Injin Charlie and the Colonel, however, and particularly the emphasis on the mixed blood lines, were hardly flattering to the Creoles.

Lax Creole morality plays an even more striking part in the story entitled " 'Tite Poulette," this time in direct contrast to Nordic, or more precisely, Dutch attitudes. This story, the first, save for the rejected "Bibi," in which Cable dealt directly with the Negro situation, involves an octoroon woman, Zalli, called Madame John, and her lovely daughter, "white like a waterlily! White—like a magnolia!" who live across the street from Kristian Koppig, a rosy-faced, beardless young Dutchman. Zalli had been the mistress of a Creole, Monsieur John, who had loved her and had left her not only a daughter known as 'Tite Poulette, but also ample funds when he died. The money has long since been lost in a bank failure, however, and to earn her living Zalli, her identity masked, dances at one of the famed quadroon balls, which at this stage in New Orleans history have become quite degenerate. The Creole manager of the ball, having once spied 'Tite Poulette in company with her mother, seeks to force his attentions on the beautiful young woman. When he refuses to go away from their door, Kristian Koppig slaps him across the face.

Later, upon learning that Madame John must dance at the ball out of financial necessity, however much she loathes the task, Koppig goes to urge her not to do so, but discovers he is too late. So he goes to the ball himself to ask her to leave, and there is set upon and stabbed repeatedly by the manager and his friends. Madame John has him taken to her apartment, where she and 'Tite Poulette nurse him to health. The young Dutchman declares his love for 'Tite Poulette and proposes marriage, but the distraught maiden cannot accept—"it is against the law" for one of part-Negro blood to marry a white man. Whereupon Madame John reveals that 'Tite Poulette is not her child and Monsieur John's, but the child of a Spanish couple that Monsieur John had befriended—both of them having died of the fever: "I have robbed God long enough! Here are the sworn papers—here! Take her; she is as white as snow—so! Take her, kiss her; Mary be praised! I never had a child—she is the Spaniard's daughter!"

The happy ending, though Cable attempted to prepare for it by earlier hints, is very much a *deus ex machina* contrivance and, as Cable knew well, did not constitute a realistic solution to what he felt was the injustice of racial discrimination; in a later story, *Madame Delphine,* he would confront the matter more directly. Still, in presenting so forcefully the plight of the quadroons, Cable was criticizing racial discrimination both as it had existed back in antebellum days and, by inference, in the New Orleans of his own times, which still legally forbade persons of mixed blood to marry whites. And in presenting the Creoles as the perpetrators of the quadroon system, he was again placing them in an unfavorable light. When Kristian Koppig writes home to his mother in Holland about "this wicked city," it is the ways of the Creoles that he condemns. Again, it should be noted that Cable finds the theme of miscegenation, however morally unjust, very much the stuff of romance.

The famed "Posson Jone'," which appeared first in *Appletons'* because the editors of *Scribner's Monthly* and several other magazines found it too coarse, also contrasts Creole and Anglo-Saxon morality, this time for purposes of comedy. One Jules St.-Ange, an indolent young Creole down on his luck, leaps at the opportunity to bilk a tall American preacher from West Florida of his roll of banknotes belonging to Smyrny Church. He succeeds in getting the *Américain* drunk, but when the huge West Floridian preaches to a jeering multitude come to see a battle between a tiger and a buffalo, then lifts up the tiger and single-handedly places him upon the back of the buffalo in order to demonstrate that "the tiger and the buffler *shell* lay down together!", the little Creole is so overcome by admiration that he extricates the preacher from jail. Posson Jone' is filled with remorse, for he has lost the money entrusted to him by his parishioners. Jules, who has won a large sum of money playing cards, seeks to give the money to the parson to make up the loss; Posson Jone' refuses, but when he boards the schooner to go home, it turns out that his Negro slave has safeguarded his money all along. So moved is Jules St.-Ange by the whole thing that he resolves to pay his debts and become an honest man.

Here Cable, in spite of his satire of the naïve country American preacher, presents the Anglo-Saxon as morally superior to the Creole. In several fine dialogues, their attitude toward religion is humorously contrasted; Jules's religion is a mere form, in no way binding upon his conduct, while Parson Jones is theologically narrow and naïve, but, as Jules says, "the so fighting an' moz rilligious man as I never saw!" If Jules can separate an *Américain* from his money, he "might find cause to say some 'Hail Marys!' " Jules believes in providence because when his father had caused a barrel of sugar to be sprinkled with holy water, the purchaser had made a mistake of 100 pounds in his father's favor. Both the Creole and the Protestant preacher are equally convinced of the complete inferiority of Negroes, and the portrait of neither could be said to be flattering, but it is the parson who inspires the Creole to act in untypical Creole fashion and pay his debts. Jules extracts from the *Américain* a promise: "Posson Jone'! make me hany'ow *dis* promise: you never, never, *never* will come back to New Orleans." "Ah, Jools," says the parson, "the Lord willin', I'll never leave home again!"

This is the story which apparently proved to the satisfaction of Charles Dudley Warner that fiction could continue to be idealistic while achieving a much greater realism of setting and detail than had hitherto been tolerated by idealistic critics. Whether Warner could justifiably reach this conclusion seems, to modern eyes at least, debatable. What is most remarkable about this story, I think, is the aesthetic distance Cable maintains from both the rural Southern minister and the little Creole.

In retrospect it seems especially unfortunate that of all the stories of his early years, it was "Posson Jone'" that Cable had the greatest difficulty in placing for publication, for the discouragement surely had the effect of helping to convince him that this kind of broad, detached humor, which took no sides and made sport of the naïveté of Southern Protestantism, was an unprofitable literary business. The much greater acceptability of his more romantic, idealistic tales must have indicated to him that this, and not broad comedy, was the direction in which he should move in his future writings.

In the story entitled "Madame Déliceuse," there is no direct confrontation of Creole and Anglo-Saxon. Very much a romance all the way, it centers on the efforts of a young Creole woman, Madame Déliceuse, to reconcile her friend General Hercule Mossy de Villivicencio, a pompous and martial old veteran of the War of 1812–15, with his son, Dr. Mossy, physician and (unknown to his Creole neighbors) distinguished scientist, whom she loves. The General resents the fact that his son shows no interest in military matters and heroic attitudes, and for some years they have not spoken, but Madame Déliceuse cleverly arranges their reconciliation, and all ends happily with the espousal of Mossy and Madame Déliceuse. The story, however, contains considerable humor about the Creoles' vanity and showiness. There are digs at the Creoles' lack of awareness of what goes on in the world beyond New Orleans; they have no idea that Dr. Mossy is a distinguished man of science, and consider him only a mild little physician. Furthermore, the doctor at first refuses to fight a duel to defend his father's honor, and Cable makes it clear that his attitude toward dueling not only makes him morally superior to the Creoles but, even though he is himself a Creole, very much untypical of the race. As for Madame Déliceuse, though she is an admirable woman, she is so in Creole fashion, with "her principles, however, not constructed in the austere Anglo-Saxon style, exactly (what need, with the lattice of the Confessional not a stone's-throw off?)" She is virtuous and generous, but very much acquainted with the ways of the world, and by no means averse to using deceit if the ultimate goal be good. The story is slight, touches on no important themes, and makes its appeal entirely through the quaint characters and the exotic atmosphere of early nineteenth-century New Orleans. At the close, as the happy group—father, son, and bride-to-be— walk out onto the rue Royale, "The sky was blue, the air was soft and balmy, and on the sweet south breeze, to which the old General bared his grateful brow, floated a ravishing odor of—'What is it?'" asks the old General. Madame Déliceuse and Dr. Mossy blush: It was the odor of orange-blossoms.

"Jean-ah Poquelin," by contrast, is perhaps the most somber of all the stories of *Old Creole Days*. Old Jean-ah Poquelin, an indigo planter once, later a smuggler and slave trader, is a recluse. He lives in an old plantation house on a canal early in the nineteenth century, not long after American rule over Louisiana has been established. Once he had been popular and highly respected, but after returning from a slaving trip, he went into seclusion. There had been a brother whom he had revered, but who had disappeared from sight after the final trip. There are rumors of a ghost out on the Poquelin place, and some suspicion that the brother is being kept there. Meanwhile, New Orleans is expanding beyond the old city, and streets are laid out past the Poquelin place; old Jean-ah has sought to get the American authorities to forbid the draining and filling in of the swamp near his house, but in vain. A development company wishes to purchase the house, but the old Creole will not negotiate. When the secretary of the development firm, "Little White," is sent out to investigate, he sees something that sends him back determined to do what he can to ward off further encroachment on the old man. Finally a horde of Creoles, at the instigation of the Americans, goes out to the Poquelin place one night to shivaree its owner;

Little White succeeds in diverting them elsewhere for a time, and when finally they do move on to their objective, it is only to find that old Poquelin has died. Not until then does the secret of the Poquelin place reveal itself; from the half-ruined old mansion come a deaf-mute servant with the coffin of Jean-ah Poquelin, followed by a figure as white as snow—Jacques Poquelin, the long-hidden brother, now a leper. The crowd watches as the Negro mute and the brother go off with the coffin into the swamp, toward the leper colony there.

In this story the old Creole's nobility and loyalty to his brother stand out in sharp contrast both to the Americans who are bent on developing new areas of the city, and to the unfeeling, exuberant Creole townsfolk who go out to shivaree the old man. Only Little White, the secretary of the development firm, is able to appreciate the dignity and courage of the old Creole. With its stark outlines, its sense of tragedy, its playing off of the commercialism of the Americans and the callousness of the Creole mob against the lonely dignity of Jean-ah Poquelin, faithful to his terrible burden, the story is one of Cable's best. Cable gives a tragic dignity to the Creole past manfully confronting its sins (it was in Africa, on a slaving expedition, that Jacques Poquelin had contracted his dread disease), in doomed resistance to the irresistible forces of progress and commercial development. Yet the story could hardly be read with pride by Cable's Creole neighbors; the fact that old Jean-ah Poquelin had been a smuggler and slave trader, and the depiction of the brother as a leper, scarcely constituted a complimentary portrayal of Creole society.

The remaining story in *Old Creole Days*, "Café des Exilés," deals not with the old French-Spanish Creoles of pre-American Louisiana, but with a group of Spanish exiles from Cuba during the 1840's, who meet at the Café des Exilés to plot an expedition to Cuba and to plan ways of smuggling weapons out of New Orleans. Philip Butcher cites the story as an example of Cable's racism; the hero, he notes, is an Irish adventurer: "Always the male partner belongs to a race commonly regarded by Americans at the time as superior to the race of the woman. A beautiful Creole girl may win the love of an Anglo-Saxon, or an octoroon may capture a male Creole, but the coin is never reversed."[9] This is not strictly accurate: the tall man who wins the hand of the sister of 'Sieur George is apparently a Creole, while 'Sieur George and presumably his sisters are Americans; and in Cable's second novel, *Dr. Sevier,* Irish Kate Riley marries Italian Rafael Ristofalo. It is true, however, that Cable, himself a Protestant of German and New England stock, tends to make his villains dark-complexioned and his heroes light-hued, and he often seems to equate darkness, especially of the Creole sort, with lax morals—though not always, as witness Mossy and 'Sieur George.

Save for some grumblings in *L'Abeille,* the French-language newspaper of the Creoles, Cable's stories were received with praise by his fellow townsfolk. The virulent attacks on Cable by the Southern press commenced only in the mid-1880's, when he began speaking out openly against racial discrimination. Butcher suggests that because Cable's fellow Southerners of non-Creole origin felt that his portrait of the Creoles was accurate, they were not disturbed by the fact that it was unsympathetic and uncomplimentary; it was only when Cable began to write about events and issues closer to his own day, in which they were also involved, that Southerners began to dislike what Cable wrote.[10] This is undoubtedly true. For Cable and his fellow Southerners, the Creoles were something of a foreign race. Yet it will not do, as I have noted, to define Cable's attitude toward the Creoles merely as one of disapproval. The quality of the stories that make up *Old Creole Days* arises in large part out of the dynamic tension between their author's strong fascination with so much of Creole life and his disapproval, as a progressive-minded Protestant of Calvinistic descent, of their tribal ways. His secret admiration for and envy of old Injin Charlie's lazy acquiescence to things, as he sits in his garden under a blue sky in the sunlight, has already been remarked. His admiration for Madame Déliceuse and her Latin ideas of rectitude is also obvious; a richly sensuous woman, she appeals to Cable's senses, if not to his straitlaced concept of ethics.

Creole beauty fascinated Cable; his Creole heroines, whether of mixed or entirely white blood, are among his most alluring creatures. He admires the utter femininity and helplessness of Zalli and 'Tite Poulette; he finds the element of mixed blood allied with pure whiteness of complexion quite enthralling. What appeals to him as artist, and so distinguishes his New Orleans stories, is the physical texture of Creole life. For all his religious belief, as a writer he is secular in a way that almost no other American novelist of his century is.

The stories of *Old Creole Days* present a densely packed social panorama of class and caste. Cable's art is very much of the everyday, the ordinary; it is not the sometimes highly romanticized plots—Belles Demoiselles Plantation being swept away by the river, the beautiful Creole maiden nursing Kristian Koppig back to health, and so forth—that constitute the chief appeal. Rather it is the social scene, the rich variety of social life, with the coming and going of people, the confrontation of Creole and Anglo-American attitudes and customs, the impact of racial admixture. The art of the stories in *Old Creole Days* is founded upon realistic social observation.

When one views these stories in terms of Cable's later work, one sees both similarities and dissimilarities. That fine texture of experience that marks the best of *The Grandissimes* and his other work is already very much in evidence. In embryo, most of Cable's themes are present: the clash of Creole and Anglo-American ways, problems of race and caste, the delight in dialect (Cable would never surpass, though he would often equal, the language of Jules St.-Ange in "Posson Jone'"), the attractions of the *dolce far' niente* under Gulf skies, the decadence of the Creole establishment, the city falling into neglect and disrepair, above all the sensuous, carnal quality of human experience in a Southern city of mixed races and languorous ways. Present, too, is Cable's taste for plots based all too strongly on romantic sentimentality: in "Belles Demoiselles Plantation" he sacrifices plausibility to melodrama, and in "'Tite Poulette" and "Café des Exilés" (but not "Madame Déliceuse") his lovers, insofar as they are lovers, behave woodenly in the conventionally sentimental tradition of the genteel romance. Significantly, the best of the stories, "'Sieur George" and "Posson Jone'," are those in which the plot is least complex.

What is largely missing from these stories, however, is any important attempt at social *criticism*. Except for the implied relevance of the plight of the quadroons in "'Tite Poulette" to the plight of the Negro in post-Civil War New Orleans, there is relatively little evidence of the author's desire to protest social inequities. The attack on racism that is so prominent even in his next book, *The Grandissimes,* is hardly evident here at all. Only in occasional remarks—Jules St.-Ange and Posson Jone' on the subject of Negroes and heaven, the abrupt sale of 'Sieur George's sister's slave after her marriage—does Cable touch on racism, except in " 'Tite Poulette." To be sure, there is considerable *implied* criticism. The fact that 'Sieur George's ruin comes because of his mania for the lottery is not without its relevance to the existence of the infamous Louisiana State Lottery of Cable's own day. "Jean-ah Poquelin" comments obliquely but meaningfully on commercialism at the expense of human compassion. "Madame Déliceuse" has things to say both about dueling and about intellectual insularity. And certainly Cable goes to considerable lengths to criticize the democratic failings of the Creoles of Louisiana. But the point is precisely that most of this is suggested obliquely; it grows out of the fiction, and is in most instances a part of the characterization and the story line. The stories generally succeed on their own merit as fiction.

Obviously an attempt at a full-fledged novel was in order for Cable now. The talent for social portrayal was there, the ability to create a mass of convincing characters, to unfold a rich tapestry of everyday life into which an elaborate story might be woven, with adequate potential for deepening complexity and meaning. There need never be, for Cable, the thinness of textural specificity that sometimes brought Hawthorne so close to bare allegorical narrative. Nor need he, as Melville did, feel obliged to look to the South Seas for the stuff of romance. It was there all about him: almost two hundred years of Louisiana history and life, under five flags, two contrasting modes of civilization, with myriad gradations of caste, class, and race. Here were poverty and wealth, old loyalties and old hatreds, several varieties of lost cause, a provincial but thoroughly urban metropolis dependent for its livelihood upon a vast agricultural region around it; here were the Old World and the New, with their competing institutions and loyalties, a Latin, Catholic Church and an Anglo-American, Protestant Establishment. So much, then, was available to Cable if he were capable of using it.

But if, as I have suggested, it is not so much in the plots of the Cable stories as in the complexity of social texture, the variety of characters and themes and attitudes, that their chief appeal lies, then this might well have forecast problems in the longer form of the novel. In the stories of *Old Creole Days* in which plot is most prominent, Cable shows a tendency to rely on romantic sentimentality, to construct love stories in the conventional tradition, and to keep his protagonists within the confines of the demands of the genteel romance, so that they tend to be wooden and two-dimensional. If Cable was to develop as a novelist, he would have to find a plot, which is to say, a meaning, for his material that would permit a deeper exploration of the social texture of his chosen milieu than was required in a short story. But could he do this? Or was the ambivalence of his attitude toward the Creoles—moral disapproval, but secret sympathy and even envy—so complex and so contradictory that the unity of development required in writing a novel might be beyond his capabilities?

"You bother me," Richard Watson Gilder had written to Cable after reading "Madame Déliceuse": "Your conception of character is strong—artistic—your style is bright and witty—your plots are generally good—your field is all your own—and I consider your stories a great acquisition to the monthly—but you lack in the capacity to edit yourself. This is the only thing that makes me fear for your literary future." [11] Gilder was by no means an infallible critic; his role in Cable's eventual development is open to considerable question, and it is doubtful that the kind of self-editing he wanted Cable to be capable of was what should have been done. All the same, he may well have sensed, however indistinctly and vaguely, what might prove to be a severe limitation indeed to Cable's artistry: not an inability to edit his material as such, but literally an inability to edit *himself*—to recognize what it was that he was really trying to do, and to shape his material to that end.

V

A Published Author

In July of 1875, George W. Cable left New Orleans on his first trip to New York and the Northeast. He had by then published four stories in *Scribner's Monthly,* another had been accepted, and his work had already begun to acquire something of a reputation. His trip to New York, therefore, was in his role as a promising young author, and doubtless his editors at *Scribner's Monthly* were as eager to meet him as he was to meet them. Traveling by ship, he stopped off at Havana, Cuba, where he gained some of the background information for the story "Café des Exilés" which he was to write later in the year, as well as material for another story, "Don Joaquin," which came out anonymously in *Harper's* the following January, and which he did not include in *Old Creole Days.*[1] As the steamer *Juniata* drew near the Northeastern coast, he penned a brief note to his mother and sister, describing the ships in Delaware Bay and, obviously in high spirits, reported that "I am enjoying myself immensely."[2] He was making his first visit to the center of American publishing activity; like many a young man from the provinces both before and afterward, he doubtless looked upon the occasion with great excitement and anticipation.

If so, his hopes were not disappointed. He was warmly welcomed. Cable was *Scribner's Monthly*'s first real discovery. Though the magazine, first as *Scribner's Monthly* and after 1881 as the *Century,* was important in introducing the work of numerous other writers to the American reading public, all of them had published elsewhere first. Cable was entirely their own find.[3] In New York Cable met his magazine publishers for the first time, in particular Roswell Smith, the *Scribner's Monthly* business manager, and

Richard Watson Gilder, then associate editor but already by that time a major force in the magazine's policies. Born in 1844, the same year as Cable, Gilder had come into magazine editing by way of newspaper work, and by the mid-1870's was becoming a prominent figure in the New York literary world. In the decades that followed he grew to be the most notable and influential of all the magazine editors, and won widespread fame as a poet as well. In William Allen White's words, he was "the literary arbiter of the times. His magazine, the *Century,* represented in the mid-eighties and nineties the heights to which American literary culture had risen." Together with Henry Mills Alden of *Harper's* and Edward Burlingame of the new *Scribner's Magazine* which was formed five years after the *Century* had 'broken off entirely from Scribner's, he was part of a triumvirate of genteel idealism, "a blessed trinity that beamed over the America of that day, kindly lights of literature and learning, beacons that shone benignly unto the perfect day." [4] Gilder was a strong defender of ideality, alert to the slightest criticism of the moral tone of his magazine, sensitive to the point of prudishness, and determined to protect the American home from all contact with squalor, prurience, and irreverence. Though his defenders [5] claim that for his own day he was considerably more broad-minded and less prudish than his contemporaries, and though in public life he stood for political and social reform, there seems little reason to question Larzer Ziff's statement that Gilder "most clearly epitomized the suppressing tone of the literary establishment" of his day. [6] Gilder admired his authors, but he showed no hesitation whatever in editing them in what he considered the interests of good taste—which he was sure was identical with his own. Not only Cable, but Mark Twain, Henry James, William Dean Howells, Edwin Arlington Robinson, and others were confronted by numerous excisions and emendations from his editorial pen. (Gilder won for himself a lasting place in American literary history by excising from the magazine version of *Huckleberry Finn* the Duke's famous remark upon placing the words "Ladies and children not admitted" under the poster advertising "The Royal Nonesuch": "There, if that line don't fetch them, I don't know Arkansaw!" [7])

There is no doubt that Gilder thought highly of Cable's abilities. "I feel moved to say that 'we' hope you know that you have the

makings of one of the best story-writers of the day," he had written
him after accepting "'Sieur George." [8] And, even more strongly,
"You are a genius, and that is a rare article," in 1874. "Being
a genius you might feel the right of being grouty and cussed which
you are not." [9] All the same, he was in no way reluctant to
substitute his own taste for Cable's whenever he failed to understand or did not approve of what Cable had written. Repeatedly
he asked Cable to excise what he considered crudities and offenses
against good taste. "Write something intensely interesting—but
without the terrible suggestion you so often make use of," he once
told him. [10] Whenever he found Cable's style perplexing, he called
for insertion of sentences and paragraphs to make matters more
obvious. And he did so with an authoritativeness that the ambitious young Louisiana writer found most formidable. Now that he
finally met Gilder, he was amazed at his editor's youthfulness:
"The words of editorial counsel in his headlong handwriting were
so sage, so lucid, and so plainly impromptu, that they seemed
certainly to spring from the depths of a long-clarified experience,
and the inspiring surprise with which I first looked upon the
boyishness of his form, step, and smile, and saw a man of my
own years, is now a specially tender memory." [11]

Cable met others at the *Scribner's Monthly* offices, in several
instances people with whom he would form lifelong friendships.
There was Robert Underwood Johnson, Gilder's assistant, who
would later serve as editor of *The Grandissimes*. Like Gilder, Johnson was also very much in the idealistic mode of the day; a poet
of minor reputation, he later became ambassador to Italy following
Thomas Nelson Page, and until his death in 1937 remained a relic
of the once dominant Genteel Tradition. There was Roswell Smith,
the *Scribner's Monthly* business manager, with whom Cable struck
up an abiding friendship. There was the younger Charles Scribner,
who would publish Cable's novels for the next fifty years. [12]

The New York trip thus provided Cable with an intriguing
introduction to the literary life of the metropolis. He was shown
about town by the author Frank L. Stockton, invited to visit the
Philadelphia estate of the publisher William H. Appleton, and
otherwise made much of. "Don't I write like a college boy?" he
wrote to his wife in relating his adventures. "And why shouldn't
I? It's vacation, you know." [13] The contrast between the literary

life he saw in New York and the honor he was given by it, and his long hours of labor in the cotton exchange back in New Orleans, where he was just another impecunious clerk and scribbler, must have registered itself forcibly upon his mind.

The fact remained, however, that fascinating though his new role as author might be, in actual income from his stories he had little to show for his work. Obviously it would be necessary for him to produce not merely magazine stories, but books, if ever he was to achieve financial independence with his pen. Then as always, however, publishing houses were reluctant to bring out volumes of short stories, and Cable found that even his growing reputation did not suffice to ensure publication of his tales in book form. He offered to make up a list of 500 subscribers if Scribner's would bring out a book of his stories, but to no avail. Harper's likewise refused to publish the stories, and after D. Appleton and Co. informed him that they might be willing to do so only if some narrative thread could be developed to unify the volume, Cable, on Gilder's advice, let the matter rest for a while.[14]

He returned to his labors at William C. Black and Co., working as an accountant for the firm's cotton business. Cable was proud of his efficiency at his job, and fond of his senior employer, a Virginian who was highly esteemed in New Orleans public life. Black sympathized with Cable's literary efforts, and when the pressure of work permitted, he allowed Cable to hire an assistant in order to gain more time for writing. When Black became chairman of the finance committee of the New Orleans Cotton Exchange, Cable was also made secretary of the committee and treasurer's clerk of the exchange, which within a few years of its founding in 1871 had become the world's largest spot-cotton market.[15]

Cable was still far from comfortably fixed financially, however. To his children, vacationing with his wife at the beach in September, 1875, he wrote, "when I hear that you are enjoying the pleasures of the seaside, I am so delighted that I open my sleeve slyly and laugh right into it till it is as full of laugh as a bathhouse. I have a hole in the elbow for this very purpose. A man named *Pauvreté* (Poverty), a Frenchman, made it for me for nothing."[16] Unable to rent a home large enough to provide a study for himself as well as a bedroom for his mother, he longed to be able to afford to purchase a home. Apparently, too, there was some tension among the women in the family. "Again I would beg of you to be patient with Louise," he wrote to his mother on September 9. "It is the verdict of physicians that many women in her situation are barely morally responsible. Please try to brighten and cheer her; she needs some enlivening influence always at her side. Don't be so critical as is your (I might say our) wont. If you could see what I have to put up with now, here, in order to have my dear ones where they are—but let that pass." [17] Possibly Louise was pregnant again; between 1870 and 1877 she bore five children, and her health was frequently poor.[18] Some years later, thinking of his marriage, Cable wrote in a journal that "it has been nineteen years of half health for her. Years ago she had been sixteen times seriously ill since her marriage. I quit counting at that. It didn't benefit anybody." [19]

It was during these years that Cable began to draw further and further apart from the political beliefs of his fellow New Orleans townsfolk, especially in their attitude toward the Negro. It had been the feeling of outrage he had felt in the early 1870's upon reading the city's old Black Code of antebellum days that had prompted him to write "Bibi," which Edward King had vainly attempted to market for him before " 'Sieur George" had been accepted. Cable had studied American history and joined in a debating club with friends, and his logical mind was coming to question Southern attitudes toward the newly created freedmen. Until 1876, Louisiana had remained under Reconstruction rule; there had been considerable violence in New Orleans, including a bloody riot in 1874 when the former Confederate General James Longstreet led a force of metropolitan police against a mob of New Orleans white men and numerous persons were killed or injured. Cable had supported the white South's demands for a return to self-government, yet he felt privately that the refusal of Southern whites to participate in the Reconstruction government was a cruel abnegation of responsibility. As he later pointed out in his unpublished essay "My Politics," he had ample opportunity—working across the desk from his friend William C. Black and talking frequently with him and other leading New Orleans citizens—to hear the best arguments of the city's white citizenry presented in abundant detail, yet he persisted in his dissent.

Sometimes he and Black would argue the matter, and Cable would press home his logic until Black would declare heatedly, "I'll have you understand this is a Democratic counting room, sir!" Whereupon, Cable said, "I always took up my hat in silence and walked downstairs and out into the street, loving him still, but burning with indignation, and taking all too much comfort in the knowledge that my dear friend was suffering more than I." [20]

In September of 1875 an incident occurred in which Cable for the first time publicly arrayed himself on the side of the Negro freedman in a question involving racial integration. Cable describes the event in "My Politics." The New Orleans public schools were integrated, but a mob had proceeded to evict from the girls' grammar and high schools all students who could not prove they were of indubitably white blood. A mass meeting was held in Lafayette Square to support the action and to denounce the integrated educational policy, and the city's newspapers, in particular the New Orleans *Bulletin,* joined in the denunciation. Cable thereupon wrote a letter to the *Bulletin,* signing it "A Southern White Man" but informing the editor of his identity, in which he maintained that segregation by race was unnecessary, since "there is sufficient antagonism between races to keep them, in the main, pure, without the aid of onerous civil distinctions." The editor, Page M. Baker, published the letter, but prefaced it with a lengthy rebuttal, in which he ignored the logic of Cable's argument. Cable then produced a brief but incendiary written reply, which the editor refused to print. [21] This was not to be Cable's only difficulty with Page Baker.

After the incident, Cable made no more public pronouncements on the racial attitudes of New Orleans for some ten years. His own position, however, as expressed not only in the public letter but obliquely in "Bibi," " 'Tite Poulette," and "Posson Jone'," was clear. Later, when Southerners accused him of having adopted Northern sentiments on the race issue in order to further his literary success, he was to point to his action in the school dispute of 1875, long before he had published a book of his own, to show that he had stated his convictions as strongly as he was ever again to state them, while still "in my native New Orleans, where dwelt ninety-nine hundredths of all my friends and acquaintances; opposed point-blank to their sentiments and to the sentiments of almost the whole white population; with the whole people in a frenzy of political agitation and on the verge of an armed and bloody revolution. . . ."[22]

Meanwhile he had begun work on a novel. Edward King had urged him to do so several years before. A New Orleans physician, J. Dickson Bruns, likewise encouraged him.[23] A native of Charleston, South Carolina, Bruns had in the 1850's and 1860's been the friend of William Gilmore Simms, Henry Timrod, Paul Hamilton Hayne, and others of the Russell's Bookstore group there; something of a poet himself, he was a great talker, and Cable valued his opinion. Richard Watson Gilder had also made some suggestions about the possibility of a novel.

Then in late February, 1877, came a letter which played a large part in Cable's decision to put aside everything else and concentrate on an extended work of fiction. The letter was from Hjalmar Hjorth Boyesen, a professor at Cornell University, and author of several novels as well as much poetry and criticism. Educated in Norway, Boyesen had come to the United States in 1869, worked as a teacher and a newspaperman, and begun publishing extensively in the *Atlantic* and then in *Scribner's Monthly*. Boyesen informed Cable that on a visit to New Orleans some seven years ago he had been struck by the golden opportunity awaiting a novelist there, and that now, having read "Belles Demoiselles Plantation" in *Scribner's Monthly,* he was sure that the opportunity was being utilized; ". . . since I read this sketch," he declared, "I have never missed an opportunity to praise you in public as in private. I have lectured about you to my students . . . and have made many ardent converts among the coming generation of critics." He urged Cable to call on him if he could be of service, for "I only wish to hasten the day when our whole public shall recognize your exceptional merit,—your genius. . . ."[24]

Elated, Cable replied at once, sketching for Boyesen the plot of the novel he contemplated, which would eventually become *The Grandissimes*. Boyesen's response was all the encouragement that Cable could have asked:

> The magnificence of the material for your novel quite dazzled me,   •
> and your little parenthetical remarks, sprinkled through the main
> narrative, convinced me that you see both your dangers and your
> exceptional advantages as clearly as any novelist I ever knew. You

have a superb grip on reality—that is what I have always admired
in your sketches and still you are so far removed from being a
mere dry, materialistic photographer of actual events. You will
soon know me well enough not to suspect me of flattery, and it
is my opinion that there is not a man living in the U. S. at present
who is more finely equipped as a novelist than yourself. . . . Yours
is going to be the kind of novel which the Germans call a
"Kulturroman," a novel in which the struggling forces of opposing
civilizations crystalize and in which they find their enduring
monument. This is rather awkwardly expressed, but you know
what I mean.

Boyesen closed with the suggestion that Cable offer the novel to
Scribner's Monthly for serialization before book publication, and told
Cable that he would soon be going to New York City and would
let magazine editors there know what he thought of Cable's
work.[25]

Boyesen was as good as his word. While Cable worked away
both before and after his hours of employment at the counting-
house, with the result that he underwent a spell of ill-health that
kept him from writing for a time, Boyesen on his visits to New
York continued to sing Cable's praises, while to Cable he wrote
additional words of encouragement. He wished that he could give
Cable some of his own superfluous vigor, he said. "You hardly
know down there in the literary Sahara of the South how many
hearty friends and warm admirers you have here in the North,"
he told him. "I mean no disrespect to the South, but I have been
there and know how uncongenial its atmosphere must be to a
true artist."[26]

So touched was Cable by Boyesen's interest and understanding
that on January 3, 1878, he wrote Boyesen a long letter in which
he unburdened himself of his cares and ambitions. His endless
hours of work at the Cotton Exchange had all but brought his
writing to a standstill. He held 3 jobs, he said, so that finances
were no longer a problem. "And yet, my dear Mr. Boyesen, I have
just that discontent—I keep up just that champing of my bit that
you, I know, would want me to indulge in. I ought to be writing.
A man ought to keep invested the talents of gold that God has
given him as well as the talents of silver. I can write better than
I can do anything else. Business is distasteful to me. I love litera-

ture; I'm no Samson in it, it's true; but so much the more it doesn't follow that I should have my eyes punched out & go to grinding corn in this Philistia of a country." After his house had been paid for, he planned a much more vigorous sally in the direction of authorship. Until then, he had "really nothing to complain of. If it wasn't for one single thing I should be altogether comfortable—the black sheep in my flock is my ambition. I drug it with every possible opiate; I get it to sleep, I jog along with it muffled up in my bosom, I think I have peace, when—here comes a letter from Gilder or yourself, and—it takes me weeks to get the brat quiet again." Cable ended his letter by urging Boyesen to come down to visit him, and declaring that as for himself, "I yearn toward the North. To me *that* is the South. There is the sunlight and flowers and fruits—there is Boyesen." [27]

Even as Cable wrote, Boyesen was at work in New York making possible what Cable had long desired and had given up any hope of accomplishing for the present. He convinced Charles Scribner that Cable's short stories should be published in book form. His letter containing the news crossed in the mails with Cable's. "I shall rejoice with all my heart to see those delightful stories as a book," Boyesen declared. "It is the first genuinely artistic contribution to our literature which the South has given us and may it be the forerunner of much more to come." [28] But what Boyesen did not tell Cable, and Cable learned only later, was that so confident was Boyesen of Cable's genius that he had personally guaranteed to indemnify Scribner for any loss he might sustain in publishing the stories. [29]

One remark in Boyesen's letter disturbed Cable, however. Boyesen had said that he thought he could sell at least 100 copies among his students. The suggestion made Cable acutely uncomfortable: " . . . one thing I want you to promise me," he wrote; "you mention your students in connection with 100 copies—I shudder—; if you love me don't offer *anything* that I *ever* do to *anybody* except on its intrinsic merits. You will excuse me for appearing to suspect such a thing; it's such a common occurrence down here, and therefore—besides all better reasons—because I am a Southerner—I would like the handful of people that make up my little world to be assured I am nobody's widow." [30] When the letter from Scribner's arrived, Cable found that no conditions were proposed. A royalty of 10 per cent was to be paid after sale of 1,000 copies.

In accepting Scribner's offer, Cable proposed that the title of the collection of stories be *Jadis*. "It touches the Creole *electrically* just where he has a soft spot common to all mankind," he declared.[31] In another letter he suggested alternative titles: *Prose Idyls for Hammock and Fan, Half-Hours for Hammock and Fan, The Old Regime, Creoles et Creoles, A Peculiar People, Creoles, Creoles du Vieuxtemps, Hammock and Fan,* and also proposed that each story be prefaced with lines from some old Creole songs he had collected.[32] Finally the publisher proposed *Old Creole Days*, which as Arlin Turner notes was a fortunate choice in that "it hints at the time, the place, and the people of the book without giving it away as a collection of stories."[33]

Boyesen assured Cable that he had no intention of promoting his work on any other than literary merit. "Never fear my recommending you against my conscience," he wrote. "You must allow me the privilege, as a friend, to talk you up among men of letters—I have no hesitation in doing so; because you only need to be known in order to be loved." He continued his encouragement, saying: "it is time now that the South should be represented in our literature by a genuine author, a genius *par la grace de Dieu*. And you are the man."[34] Later in the same letter he gave Cable his views on the writing of fiction. "The plot should be merely a frame-work so arranged as to bring the problem of the story into the strongest possible relief," he asserted. Improbable, exaggerated plot complications should be avoided. He urged Cable to read the stories of Turgenev: "their uncompromising pessimism is a personal trait of the author's which need not affect you; but which nevertheless in his case adds a stronger spice of interest to his books."[35]

Cable expressed his agreement with Boyesen's view of the secondary importance of plot in fiction, and he also reported his uneasiness with highly didactic and moralistic fiction: "What do you think of one of those novels that smell of the moral like very small houses do of the dinner that is cooking in the kitchen? Don't they make you restless? Everybody eats dinner, and dinners ought to be cooked in every house; everybody ought to be moral, and novels ought to have a moral effect; they ought to nourish the soul as viands do the body; maybe you don't believe it but I believe it. However, I don't propose to permit any novelist through the medium of his novel, to hold me on his lap and spoon his morals down me to the limits of distention!" In the light of Cable's later difficulties with Gilder about the didactic aspects of his fiction, his views here are interesting. He also assured Boyesen that he shared his opinion of the excellence of Turgenev. "Gilder set me on that track two years ago. Yes, sir, he is a Titan. That is why he is a pessimist. And I must study him more." [36]

In late May, Boyesen, who was about to be married, wrote to Cable that he was planning to leave for Europe on July 13, and urged Cable to attend his wedding. "It will be a fine and select affair, no crowd, but almost all men of letters and personal friends. W. D. Howells, Chas. D. Warner, Gilder, G. P. Lathrop, etc. . . . Your book, in whose fate I continue to be deeply interested, will benefit by it. Therefore consider it as a literary investment and come." [37] But, hard at work on *The Grandissimes* and occupied with his cotton house duties, Cable could not accept the invitation.

While Boyesen was journeying in Europe, however, Cable was encountering far weightier personal problems than the writing of a novel. Yellow fever had once again struck New Orleans. At first the city authorities had attempted to suppress the news, but when at length the extent of the disease's spread became known, thousands of citizens fled the city. Business came to a standstill. Medical authorities had no knowledge of how to combat the fever: quinine and castor oil were prescribed, lime was spread in the streets and gutters, sheets saturated with carbolic acid were hung in rooms and in yards, barrels of tar burned, cannons fired in the streets. More than 4,000 deaths were officially reported, and many others went unreported. [38]

The Cable household did not go unscathed. Cable wrote to Charles Scribner on October 17 that "death has been thinning the ranks of my kindred and of my own family and household." [39] To Gilder, and later to Boyesen, who had learned of the epidemic while in Germany and had written to express his concern, Cable wrote at length. His wife, his four children, the family of his sister Nettie, and the families of his wife's two sisters had been attacked. Nettie's husband, James Cox, had died "a horrible death, leaving a wife (my sister) and three little children without a farthing in this world." His own son George died, and was buried "by *stealth* 15 hours after his death," to avoid having the other children learn of it. "My dear friend," Cable declared to Boyesen, "may you never in any house that you may call home hear the moaning and crying and screaming of three children all 'burning up inside' at once." Finally the Cable family was out of trouble. "And I, I hardly know how, have still some strength left, though not much. It looks as if we had had trouble; but I assure you, such is the terrible behavior of this fever in some houses that we are, by comparison, subjects of congratulation, and can, ourselves, sincerely say, 'God has been good to us.' " [40]

The experience left a deep scar on Cable's mind. It was to be reflected at least a half-dozen times in his later writings. Cable was furious at the city's failure to take common-sense precautionary measures. For business reasons, quarantine of incoming ships was not enforced, and newspapers and health authorities had kept news of the spread of disease suppressed until too late. Open drainage ditches and sewage outlets, together with the pools of stagnant rainwater left about the city because of inadequate runoff facilities, had increased the unhealthiness of the humid climate.[41] Cable began, too, to see a relationship between the city's business and political corruption and its attitudes toward race and democracy.

Cable had now to assume financial responsibility for his widowed sister and her family. He installed them in a house across from his own, and his mother moved in there, thus giving Cable, for the first time since his marriage, a room he could use for a study.[42] Apparently, too, there had been difficulties between his wife and his mother, which the removal of his mother to Nettie's house would ease. To his sister Mary Louise, who objected to the new arrangements, he wrote, "the one child of Ma's with whom she loves to live is Nettie. We have found her a comfortable room and she shall not want for anything that we can get her. But I hope, and wish to see whether or not, I have found an issue safe and fair out of the strife that has tormented me for 9 years." [43]

On May 17, 1879, *Old Creole Days* was published. Sales were good; within a month, 250 copies had been sold in New Orleans alone. After three months, the first edition of 1,000 copies was exhausted and a second printing was under way. The reviews were full of praise for the stories. The Boston *Courier* stated: "We not only have no hesitation in pronouncing their author a genius with special captivating endowments, but we feel it an imperative critical duty to so declare him." Writing for *Scribner's Monthly*, Charles DeKay, Gilder's brother-in-law, said of "Jean-ah Poquelin" that "the man who can write such a story is no mere talented writer; he is a genius in his way." The *Christian Intelligencer* noted an inventive genius, "which ranks the author among the best of our modern writers." The *Atlantic Monthly* found that the stories compared favorably with those of Bret Harte, said that Cable's "mastery over mongrel dialects is something marvelous," and that the stories "one and all have an ardor, a spontaneity, a grace of movement, a touch of fire, which are severally present as elements, and summed up in that rarest of endowments, an original and delightful *style*." The New York *Times* thought that for a writer so young, Cable showed great skill at plot conception and development. Everywhere delight was expressed. Cable's use of dialect, his character delineation, his probing awareness of social forces, his introduction of realism into Southern literature and life, were variously noted.[44]

The New Orleans newspapers, with one exception, were highly laudatory. The *Times* compared Cable with Hawthorne, and not to his disadvantage. The *Picayune* remarked on the quaint delicacy of style, the faithful delineation of Creole speech. The single harsh note came from the French-language newspaper *L'Abeille,* which had been critical of the stories when they appeared in magazines and now renewed its attack. But the *Times* in its review defended Cable's treatment of the Creoles, declaring that Cable "gives us the Creole, not perhaps as the upper crust think Creoles to be, nor as the upper crust would like them to be, but just as they are, just as you, I and a hundred others have met them on rue Royale, in the Cathedral, at the French Market and elsewhere in the old town. So true is the author to this idea that some of the pictures sting, and, with the sting, draw forth the critic's remonstrance, which remonstrance is the true criticism of the merits of the picture. . . ." And Cable lost no opportunity to portray "all the noble and chivalrous traits for which the Creoles are distinguished," the *Times* insisted.[45]

The reception of *Old Creole Days* in New Orleans and elsewhere heartened Cable as he plunged ahead in the task of completing his first novel. Early in 1878 Gilder had proposed its serialization, and by mid-August of that year Cable had submitted the manuscript for three installments of *The Grandissimes*. *Scribner's Monthly* announced the forthcoming publication of the novel in its October, 1878, issue; and on March 4, 1879, Gilder approved Cable's revision of the early chapters and sent him an advance payment of $500. Serialization began in November, 1879.[46]

In order to get the novel written, Cable had once again arranged to hire an assistant in the countinghouse to perform his routine duties there. In December, 1879, however, his senior employer and longtime friend William C. Black died. Cable wrote to Scribner's: "He leaves his wife his executrix, but both the settling of the estate and the continuance of the business will fall principally upon me. I feel as though I had been suddenly driven apart from my New York friends and shall be partially so for a portion, at least, of the present season."[47] Cable now thought seriously of giving up his clerical and financial duties and devoting full time to writing. He wrote his publisher to ask for advice, and was told that though *Old Creole Days* had made "an unusual beginning," it had still earned only $20 in royalties after six months. Robert Underwood Johnson pointed out that even if Cable earned as much as $2,500 a year from his writings, that was still no more than what it cost Johnson's family of three to exist in New York, and Cable's much larger family would surely require more. Cable finally decided to stay on for awhile at the cotton house, with its annual salary of $1,400, and it was announced by Robert Y. Black, his dead employer's partner, that Cable would continue in charge of "the finances and general affairs of the counting room."[48]

Early in 1880, as *The Grandissimes* was appearing serially in *Scribner's Monthly* and Cable was at work on the long story to be entitled *Madame Delphine*, Colonel George E. Waring, Jr., visited New Orleans to collect material for the Tenth Census of the United States. On the train trip south he had read *Old Creole Days,* and upon arrival he sought out Cable and appointed him local assistant. Cable soon afterward began forwarding data to Waring's home in Rhode Island, and for fourteen months earned an average of slightly less than $100 a month for this. The work of gathering information on commerce, industry, drainage, sewage disposal, and yellow fever interested Cable, and he was pleased to find that Waring's views confirmed his own opinions about the need for sanitary reform in the area.[49] Waring, an internationally prominent agricultural and sanitation engineer and author of a number of books, admired Cable. Oddly enough, the two had been cavalrymen in opposing armies in Mississippi in 1864.

In September, 1880, Cable left New Orleans for a second visit to New York. He was tired, weakened from overwork, in need of a vacation. With *Old Creole Days* an assured success, and *The Grandissimes* completing its serialization and soon to appear in book form, he was very much a rising man of letters, and his stay in New York was a succession of receptions, dinners, entertainments, and visits with leaders of the literary world. He met Boyesen for the first time, visited the Gilders on Staten Island, saw his friend the artist Allen C. Redwood, was entertained by Robert Underwood Johnson and Roswell Smith, met the poet and essayist Maurice Egan, attended "the finest concert I have ever heard in my life," at which music by Wagner, Liszt, Gounod, and others was "rendered by an orchestra one of whose features was twenty violins," and generally enjoyed himself. "They say I look better every day. This is a wonderful atmosphere for holding a man up," he wrote his wife; "He can do anything."[50] Cable's second taste of the life of a literary man in New York thus proved even more attractive than his first. Thereafter he returned to New York and the Northeast at least once each year until 1884, when he moved his family permanently to New England. But in 1880, as *The Grandissimes* appeared in book form, he was still very much a citizen of New Orleans, and he waited anxiously to see what the local response to his first novel would be.

VI

The Grandissimes

Richard Watson Gilder sailed for a year in Europe not long after Cable began delivering the manuscript of *The Grandissimes.* He had read the introductory chapters, praised them, and even complimented Cable on his views of the controversial political matters expressed, saying that he thought they would lead to better understanding. Assigned to the task of editing *The Grandissimes* for serialization in *Scribner's Monthly,* Robert Underwood Johnson, Gilder's chief assistant, began a lengthy correspondence with Cable. If anything, Johnson was even more cautious and prudish than Gilder, and more inclined to edit the novel closely. It was apparently Johnson's first major editorial assignment, and he took both himself and the assignment very seriously. "You must remember that my reputation as an editor is involved as well as yours as a writer," he even wrote Cable on one occasion.[1]

Johnson had two assistants, both of them Southerners. Irwin Russell, a native of Mississippi and author of the dialect poem "Christmas Night in the Quarters," offered extensive criticism, often questioning the appropriateness and authenticity of Cable's material.[2] Russell was apparently much more sympathetic with conventional Southern racial attitudes than was Cable. At one point, Cable had his Creole Raoul Innerarity declare: "I don't care if a man are good like a h-angel, if 'e har not pu'e w'ite, *'ow can* 'e be a gen'leman?" On the reverse of the page of manuscript bearing that statement, Russell wrote: "This will scarcely do. No man in that part of the country ever for one minute entertained the idea: that a man with the least tinge of Negro blood could be a gentleman—or recognized as an equal by the commonest white man. Mr. Raoul would never have thought of uttering such a truism (from his standpoint)." Cable would not accept the criticism. "The above is a mistake," he replied. "The old false beliefs of pro-slavery were only sustained by these incessant reiterations. I heard them myself from my earliest childhood, up."[3] Cable soon afterward made Russell's acquaintance, and disliked him at once.

Another editor at *Scribner's Monthly* was Mrs. Sophia Bledsoe Herrick, daughter of the Confederate pamphleteer Albert Taylor Bledsoe. She made far fewer objections, and generally accepted Cable's story as written. When the editing assignment was finally over, Johnson was highly satisfied with the results. "I admire every brave word you have said in the Grandissimes about slavery and I often think how much it must have cost you," he wrote Cable, declaring that he was proud to have been its editor.[4]

In an important sense, *The Grandissimes* may be said to be the first "modern" Southern novel. For if the modern Southern novel has been characterized by its uncompromising attempt to deal honestly with the complexity of Southern racial experience, then *The Grandissimes* was the first important work of fiction written by a Southerner in which that intention is manifested. In this respect, Cable opened up the path along which Ellen Glasgow, William Faulkner, Thomas Wolfe, Robert Penn Warren, Eudora Welty, William Styron, and others would follow. In unmistakable and uncompromising terms, he dealt with that most pervasive of all Southern social issues, the race question and the role of the Negro in society. If the loss of the Civil War had at last freed the Southern writer from the need to defend Southern racial attitudes, it was Cable who first took advantage of the new freedom.

"I meant," Cable wrote later, "to make *The Grandissimes* as truly a political work as it ever has been called. . . . I was still very slowly and painfully guessing out the riddle of our Southern question." And again, "I wrote as near to truth and justice as I knew how, upon questions that I saw must be settled by calm debate and cannot be settled by force or silence; questions that will have to be settled thus by the Southern white man in his own conscience before ever the North and South can finally settle it between them. This was part of my politics and as a citizen

I wrote." [5] But Cable's novel was more than a disquisition on race; it was also the picture of a society in transition, very much a *Kulturroman,* as H. H. Boyesen had said. And although set in 1803, just after the Louisiana Territory had been purchased by the United States from France, its implications were very much for post-Civil War Louisiana.

What is most striking about *The Grandissimes* is its rich social texture. Though the story had its romantic elements, in particular the conventional love story plot of the day, more than almost any other Southern novel of its time it was, to use the distinction set forth by Hawthorne in his Preface to *The House of the Seven Gables,* a Novel, as opposed to a Romance, in that it presumed to deal with the "probable and ordinary course of man's experience" rather than the fanciful, the "Marvellous." Not of course that it is a work of Howellsian realism, and still less does it resemble the kind of faithfulness to everyday life of Sinclair Lewis or Sherwood Anderson. But its essential fidelity is to the here and now. The dynamics of the story arise from the problems of caste and class, and human beings are portrayed to a remarkable degree as they exist in everyday life. Cable's chief concern is with social problems, and the weaving of a dense social fabric, in which what transpires among the characters is presented as part of a complex community existence, is absolutely necessary to the meaning of the novel. We see Creoles, *Américains,* quadroons, Negroes, at work and at play, in their homes and on the streets, at balls, receptions, feasts, eating meals, making love, in illness and in health, jesting, talking, quarreling, scheming, going about their lives from day to day. There is plenty of adventure and excitement, of course, and not a little violence—a riot, a lynching, a murder, several stabbings, even a suicide. Yet such events arise out of the patterns of community life for the most part, and exist not for their own sake alone but as the heightened representation of the ultimate tendencies of community life.

To readers of the day, for whom Creoles, quadroons, and existence in a semitropical city in the early years of the century were strange and fascinating, the life depicted in *The Grandissimes* doubtless seemed romantic and exotic indeed. In particular, the dialect that Cable's ordinarily French-speaking Creoles used when talking to Americans was singularly droll; [6] not only Mark Twain but others of Cable's literary friends zestfully savored its quaintness and delighted in talking to each other in Creole English. Cable was intensely interested in language, and his recreation of Creole speech was the product of close observation and considerable literary labor. When the Boston *Literary World* had criticized the way that the Creoles talked in "Jean-ah Poquelin," Cable had written to protest that he thought the accusation "does me real injustice. If I may do so I assure you that scarce a day has passed since the publication of 'Jean-ah Poquelin' that I am not told by persons who have been accustomed to hear the 'dialect' from their earliest days, and many of whom speak it, that I have rendered it capitally. . . . "[7] Cable was quite careful to have his Creole characters speak in such fashion only when talking with Americans. Their conversation among themselves was rendered in mostly flawless English. This did not, to be sure, satisfy all of the Creoles, some of whom vigorously objected that Cable had made them sound like semiliterates, but one guesses that the real Creole objection to Cable was not his representation of Creole dialect but his attitude toward the speakers. But of that, more later. For now it should only be noted that in his careful attention to the way in which his people talked, and his considerable reliance upon dialogue to develop his story, Cable resembled another American novelist whose work he had perhaps never read at the time, Henry James. And at its best, Cable's representation of the social scene, with its texture of dialogue and description, is reminiscent of James's fiction.

The events of *The Grandissimes* take place within the space of no more than a year. The novel opens at a ball given in September of 1803, and closes in September of the year following. Its central character is Joseph Frowenfeld, a young German who has come to Louisiana to make his fortune in the very year that the territory has been sold by Napoleon to Thomas Jefferson. Frowenfeld sets himself up as a pharmacist, and begins to learn the ways of the Creoles and of the few *Américains* who are in the city. He becomes acquainted with the proud and powerful Grandissime family, whose ancestry dates from the earliest days of the province and from Bourbon France before that. The family's leader is Honoré Grandissime, a vigorous and thoughtful man in his thirties. Old Agricola Fusilier, Honoré's uncle, is proud, martial, the epitome of Grandissime pride and an exemplar of the Creole temperament at its most fiercely passionate and atavistic.

Frowenfeld is befriended by old Agricola, however, and also wins the friendship of Honoré, with whom he discusses the problems of caste and class and of Creole adjustment to the coming of American hegemony. He also makes the acquaintance of his landlord, likewise named Honoré Grandissime, and finds out that the two Honorés are half-brothers, sons of the same father but one by a white mother and the other by a quadroon. The two had attended school together in Paris, and it was to the quadroon Honoré that most of the father's considerable wealth had been left. Because the older Honoré, known as "f.m.c."—free man of color—is of mixed blood, however, he is not recognized by the family, and is considered beyond the pale by white society. The clash of the close blood ties of the two Honoré Grandissimes with the separation by race that the society requires constitutes the main dramatic struggle of the novel.

There is, however, a love plot, which Cable has woven into the problem of caste. Among Joseph Frowenfeld's clients are Aurore de Grapion-Nancanou, in her thirties and still very attractive, and her daughter Clotilde. Aurore's husband had gambled with Agricola Fusilier, lost his plantation, fought a duel with Agricola, and been killed. Their plantation now owned by the Grandissimes, the Nancanous live in genteel but extreme poverty. Honoré Grandissime has long been in love with Aurore, and Frowenfeld soon falls in love with Clotilde. But Honoré is loved by a quadroon, Palmyre Philosophe, and she in her turn is loved by Honoré's brother, Honoré Grandissime f.m.c.

The resultant overlapping triangle is further complicated by the passionate hatred borne by Palmyre for Agricola Fusilier, which goes back to the time of Bras-Coupé, a Negro slave. It was the episode describing Bras-Coupé, then titled "Bibi," that Cable had first shown to Edward King in 1873, and that King had sought in vain to market for him. Apparently with little change the "Bibi" narrative was incorporated into *The Grandissimes* as a story within the story, and as such it represents an effective thematic presentation of the issue of Negro slavery that is at the novel's heart. An African prince, Bras-Coupé had been brought as a slave to the plantation of a Spaniard, Don José, and betrothed to Palmyre by her owner, Agricola Fusilier. Palmyre already detests Agricola, and his willingness to give her to the huge African, whom she admires but does not love, only infuriates her the more. The wedding, which the Creoles all consider a joke because it involves Negroes, takes place as part of the ceremony in which Bras-Coupé's owner Don José is also being married to Honoré Grandissime's sister. But it is not consummated, for when Bras-Coupé, drunk on wine, is refused another drink by Don José, he knocks him down and runs away. The huge slave lives in the swamps, all attempts to capture him failing, while the voodoo curse he has placed on Don José's establishment is followed by Don José's taking sick and dying and his plantation and crops deteriorating. Finally, Bras-Coupé is captured while drunk and dancing in Congo Square outside the city. He is whipped, mutilated, and hamstrung at the order of the dying Don José, just as the law decreed for a slave who struck his master. Before he dies, however, Bras-Coupé lifts the curse on Don José's child. Then, asked by a priest: "Do you know where you are going?", the huge slave murmurs: "To—Africa," and dies.

Palmyre Philosophe's continued hate for Agricola Fusilier leads her to try to put a voodoo curse on him, and she employs a Negro cake vendor, Clemence, to place various voodoo talismans about Agricola's house. Meanwhile, Honoré Grandissime, whom Palmyre loves in vain, has decided to make recompense to Aurore de Grapion for the loss of her plantation to Agricola. In doing so, he endangers his financial well-being, and therefore that of the Grandissime family. Both because of that and because of his decision (in which he is encouraged by Joseph Frowenfeld) that the caste system that sets him and his brother asunder is wrong, he enters into a business partnership with Honoré Grandissime f.m.c., to be known as Grandissime Brothers. In thus officially recognizing his kinship to his half-caste brother, he earns the dismay of the family and the outrage of Agricola Fusilier.

Meanwhile the cake vendor Clemence is captured as she goes to Agricola Fusilier's house to place a voodoo fetish there, and she is taken out by the whites and shot to death. Then, as Agricola Fusilier talks with Joseph Frowenfeld in the druggist's shop, Honoré Grandissime f.m.c. enters. The enraged Agricola orders him to remove his hat, and when the half-caste refuses, attacks him, whereupon the half-caste stabs Agricola, who dies shortly afterward. Honoré f.m.c. and Palmyre flee to Paris. But, still in love with the white Honoré, Palmyre refuses the f.m.c.'s hand, and the half-caste takes his own life by diving into the harbor at Bordeaux. As for the white Honoré, he is accepted in marriage by Aurore de Grapion, while Frowenfeld himself marries the daughter Clotilde.

The elaborate family relationships of the Grandissimes are unraveled only slowly by Joseph Frowenfeld, as he comes to learn the nature and customs of New Orleans society, and it is his deepening discovery of the situation, with its overtones of caste, injustice, and clashing concepts of honor, that constitutes the narrative development of the novel. Of German parentage, but reared in America, Frowenfeld represents the coming of the Anglo-American ways to Creole Louisiana. A scientist, without prejudices of caste, Frowenfeld is characterized by an innocence that enables him to judge the attitudes and the ways of Creole society objectively. Though he is made out as somewhat naïve and rather too quick to view complex questions of custom, caste, and habit in terms of abstract moral principles, it is plain that Frowenfeld's opinions represent Cable's, and that his lack of commitment to Creole society renders him able to judge it by superior moral standards. Honoré Grandissime, who recognizes this, instinctively turns to Frowenfeld for advice and support in his problems, and the counsel he receives from Frowenfeld is always disinterestedly moral.

But if *The Grandissimes* was designed to be a *Kulturroman*, a novel of the clash between two societies, it must be noted from the outset that Cable's own conscious position in the matter is *not* as a disinterested artist bent on showing the accommodations forced upon both sides and the values inherent in the opposing social ideas. For although Cable makes a few gestures to the effect that Frowenfeld is naïve, overly given to theory, too innocent of human perception, and so forth, there is really very little attention paid to Frowenfeld's own liabilities. What Frowenfeld must learn is never any new moral perspectives, but only a more detailed knowledge of the society he has come to join. Nothing that Frowenfeld does find out about the society serves to change in any way his views or the judgments he makes; what he discovers only confirms and clarifies his principles, which he never questions, and which the author also never questions. Thus Cable's viewpoint is not so much *of* Frowenfeld as it is *through* and *with* Frowenfeld.

Arlin Turner noted the relevance of the novel to the problems of post-Civil War New Orleans, and the probability that Cable was well aware of this.[8] The Creoles of Louisiana, at the time of its acquisition by the United States, faced the necessity of coming to terms with a government imposed upon them not of their own choosing, and they saw in that government a threat to their own institutions and rights. Similarly, the New Orleans of the years following the Civil War had a government imposed upon it by force, and pledged, in theory at least, to political and social principles very much at odds with those of the society thus subjected. In both instances, what was being forced upon New Orleans from the outside was, as Cable saw it, a government based upon ideals of liberty and attitudes of progress which ran counter to established prejudices and which demanded new and more enlightened responses. And in making the problem of race and caste the central theme of his novel of the Louisiana of 1803, Cable was dealing with the single most controversial and inflammatory issue of post-Civil War Louisiana life.

It will be remembered that Cable's original impulse for writing the story entitled "Bibi," which now became the Bras-Coupé episode, had come from his encounter with the provisions of the old *Code Noir*. Cable transferred this concern to the larger scope of the novel, and the episode of Bras-Coupé is made into the principal thematic motif. The violation of the Negro's humanity involved in his enslavement is dramatically symbolized by the depiction of the tall, handsome African prince standing regally among the Creoles, and the curse he pronounces upon his owner's plantation when he is mistreated signifies the blight that the South brought upon itself and its lands by the moral crime of human slavery. The callous willingness of the whites to flout Bras-Coupé's dignity and integrity by staging the mock wedding of the slave with the unwilling Palmyre is a measure of the white South's insensitivity to the Negro's humanity. Equally, the acquiescence of the Catholic priest who performs the ceremony in the violation is emblematic of the failure of Southern Christianity to perceive the moral wrong of slavery and caste. Properly treated, respected as a human being, Bras-Coupé could have been of tremendous help to the whites in their agricultural enterprise—and Cable makes a point of showing how the material advantages even of slave life exceeded anything that Bras-Coupé had known in his African savagery. But by their inhuman, unfeeling exploitation of him, Bras-Coupé was converted into an implacable enemy by his Creole owners, and his vengeance causes the death of his owner even while he is himself dying. His final words, in which he expresses his yearning for his African home, signify his desire for freedom above all else. The inescapably brutal nature of the whole transaction, the savagery whereby the African is subdued and forced into the status of slave, constituted a powerful indictment of the injustice and suppression which lay at the base of New Orleans—and Southern—society.

The wrong done to Bras-Coupé is emblematic of the basic corruption that runs through Creole New Orleans, and it is precisely the same attitudes that could acquiesce in the enslavement and mutilation of Bras-Coupé that permit the humiliation of Honoré Grandissime f.m.c. Significantly, it is Agricola Fusilier who plays a leading role in both transactions. That fiery, passionate old Creole had been willing to give Palmyre to be Bras-Coupé's bride, had resisted all the efforts of the white Honoré to bring about a reconciliation between Bras-Coupé's owner and the slave who was hiding out in the swamp, had insisted upon the whipping and mutilation of the captured Bras-Coupé in accordance with the provisions of the *Code Noir*. It was he who refused to recognize his nephew Honoré's acceptance of his half-brother the f.m.c. and who, by assaulting the f.m.c., had brought about his own death and the flight of the f.m.c. to France. In his terrible pride, his furious insistence upon purity of race at the expense of justice and of blood ties, his invincible belligerence, and his championing of Creole rights and Creole virtue, Agricola Fusilier typifies the unreasoning atavism of the Creoles, and by inference, of the white South.

Yet such are Cable's insight and artistry that the basic characterization of the fiery old Creole is by no means totally unsympathetic. For Cable recognizes the pathos and dignity of the proud old man, the heroic quality of his misguided loyalty to Creole tradition and his zeal in a miserable cause, and the warmth of his friendship as well as of his hatred. The deathbed scene, in which the mortally wounded old Creole struggles for words with which to imbue his kinsmen with his own lifelong prejudices and loyalties, is one of the most moving in the novel. Feeling his grasp slipping on a world in which his own fixed principles and goals seem to be commanding less and less respect, he tries to rally the young men to their defense. "Oh, Honoré," he pleads with his nephew, "you and the Yankees—you and—all—going wrong—education—masses—weaken—caste—indiscr—quarrels settl'—by affidav'—Oh! Honoré." To his friend Frowenfeld he says, "Joseph, son, I do not see you. Beware, my son, of the doctrine of equal rights—a bottomless iniquity. Master and man—arch and pier—arch above—pier below." Then, at the very last,

> "Agamemnon! Valentine! Honoré! patriots! protect the race! Beware of the"—that sentence escaped him. He seemed to fancy himself haranguing a crowd; made another struggle for intelligence, tried once, twice, to speak, and the third time succeeded: "Louis—Louisian—a—for—ever!" and lay still. They put those words on his tomb.

Here, as indeed throughout the novel, the literary artistry of Cable takes precedence over the politics and is responsible for much of the success of *The Grandissimes*. For it is impossible, more so perhaps than Cable had consciously intended, not to admire the old man's conviction and his resolution. If, as is likely, Cable intended Agricola Fusilier to represent not simply a passionate old man, nor merely the embodiment of Creole virtues and vices, but those of the South itself, then his very name, signifying the planter and the soldier, is quite appropriate. For Cable himself, the onetime trooper of the Fourth Mississippi Cavalry, C.S.A., had long since come to feel that he and his countrymen had fought bravely and well for a cause that was unjust, and that the South's passionate bellicosity, however heroic in battle, represented a primitive, unreasoned defiance of the moral imperatives of the nineteenth century.

In any event, it is what Cable was able to do with Agricola Fusilier that makes his novel so compelling an examination of his society. For it enabled him to portray Creole society with considerable fondness and sympathy even while he was engaged in searching out its essential defects, and to save his story from becoming a didactic censuring of Creole deficiencies alone. There was no conscious doubt in his mind as to where, between the Creoles and the newly arriving Anglo-Americans, the chief virtues lay. With the notable exception of old Fusilier, Cable's Creoles were generally portrayed as possessing important positive virtues only to the extent that they were atypical of their race.[9] Honoré Grandissime is seriously disturbed over the racial views of a society that would force him to deny his kinship with his half-brother; he will not adopt the shortsighted policy of refusing to take part in the new American government imposed on New Orleans; he does not share the Creole contempt for mercantile pursuits; and he places justice above both expedience and pride by restoring to the Nancanous the value of the plantation that Agricola Fusilier had won in a game of chance.

Agricola's own refusal to give up the Nancanou plantation had been dictated not by its financial worth, but by the imputation that he had won it unfairly. He had written to the widow and offered to restore the estate, if she would only state in writing her belief that the stakes had been won fairly; if not, he would be compelled to retain the plantation in vindication of his honor. It is Honoré's salvation that he perceives the emptiness and falsehood of what even Charlie Keene had considered necessary Creole honor. And in the letter in which he restores the property, Honoré Grandissime appends these words: *"Not for love of woman, but in the name of justice and the fear of God."*

In contrast to the idealistic Frowenfeld, however, Honoré is aware of the difficulties involved in reforming conditions in New Orleans. In an early conversation with Frowenfeld he remarks, gesturing toward a path in the fields, "Now, Mr. Frowenfeld, you see? one man walks where he sees another's track; that is what makes a path; but you want a man, instead of passing around this prickly bush, to lay hold of it with his naked hands and pull it up by the roots." To which Frowenfeld replies, "But a man armed with the truth is far from being bare-handed." *

Quite expectedly, Honoré's conduct—in the affair of the

*In a passage that did not finally appear in the printed version of the novel, Cable had Honoré display considerable skepticism about the likelihood of Louisiana being reformed merely because of its new union with the United States of America. The changeover would only mean that New Orleans would become

Nancanou estate, in his willingness to cooperate with the American governor Claiborne, and in his public recognition of his kinship with the half-breed f.m.c. implied in his use of the name "Grandissime Brothers" for his firm—arouses intense hostility among his family. Their dilemma is cruel, because in gaining for his firm the considerable financial resources of the f.m.c., Honoré has rescued the family fortunes from considerable imperilment. As Raoul Innerarity, Frowenfeld's devoted clerk and member of the Grandissime family, tells Doctor Keene, "H-only for 'is money we would 'ave catch' dat quadroon gen'leman an' put some tar and fedder."

Except for Honoré Grandissime, the Nancanous, and perhaps Agricola Fusilier, most of the other Creoles in *The Grandissimes,* like those in *Old Creole Days,* are portrayed, on the conscious level at least, with a mixture of condescending good humor and moral scorn. The best of them is Raoul Innerarity, who as Frowenfeld's clerk comes to admire and trust him, even though he does not understand his odd opinions on race and society. Innerarity is attractive and amusing because of his quaintness, vanity, and hedonism. It is he who proposes that Frowenfeld exhibit and sell for him in his store window the painting of "Louisiana rif-using to hanter de h-Union!" which so amuses and appalls Frowenfeld, and becomes for him the symbol of Creole dilettantism in the fine arts. Raoul is one of Cable's prime comic characters, the best perhaps of all the minor portraits that adorn the rich texture of Creole life which, just as in *Old Creole Days,* contributes so much

a mercantile instead of a military community, he said, and "that will nevva suit you, Mr. Frowenfeld; an unmixed mercantile community will never give rhoom to innovations of any sort, howevva, perhapsa they may be, fasta than there-h is a mawket faw them. To a man who would advocate prhoghressive moves for their-h own sake, the merchants and capitalists will be thawns and brhiers to his feet everhy step of his way. They think, my de-sir, they *must* take a commersshal view of things. They are-h against all rhevolution. Sthrife, they say, is expensive. They oppose—conscientiously—whatevva hurts the mawket; and when passion does move them they move with their customers. Give them only a steady *thrade wind* and they will sail for-h a centurhy over-h a stagnant sea and sweah, with the water-h in their mouths, that it is sweet and chear-h and good, all because they are-h afhraid you will rhaise the waves." Whether because of its didacticism, a too-overt attempt to relate the story to post-Reconstruction Louisiana, or, as is likely, because the episode was too wordy, this passage was excised.[10]

to the charm and the firmness of Cable's literary art. As for most of the other Creoles, they are vain, boastful, sensual, and given to violence. Enraged over Honoré's "betrayal," incensed at the presence of the American governor and his agents, harangued by Agricola, they go off in a rage and take revenge on the first convenient object, which happens to be Frowenfeld's store; holding back the loyal Raoul Innerarity so that he cannot interfere, they sack the druggist's establishment. Again, having trapped the cake vendor Clemence at midnight as she creeps through the woods to do Palmyre's bidding and plant another voodoo talisman on Agricola's property, they form into a lynch mob and prepare to hang the terrified old Negro woman. As if in mercy, they remove the noose, and tell her to run for her life; as she scuttles off, one of them shoots her in the back.

Thus in *The Grandissimes* Cable joined to the unflattering picture of the Creoles as seen in *Old Creole Days* a direct castigation of their racial attitudes. The Creoles now are depicted not only as being sensual, backward, morally lax; they are strident racists as well, and they embody the spirit of the lynch mob. Through the person of the old cake vendor Clemence, Cable delivers himself of some direct criticisms of racism. He shows how Clemence must pick her way warily among the whites, and masquerade her opinions in order to keep from starving to death. He demonstrates the fatuity of white assumptions about Negro attitudes. When someone tells her that "you niggers don't know when you are happy," she replies, "Dass so, Mawse—*c'est vrai, oui!* . . . we donno no mo'n white folks!" And she tells Charlie Keene, "white folks is werry kine. Dey wants us to b'lieb we happy—dey *wants to b'lieb* we is. W'y, you know, dey 'bleeged to b'lieb it—for' dey own cyumfut. 'Tis de sem weh wid de preache's; dey buil' we ow own sep'ate meet'n-houses; dey b'leebs us lak it de bess, an' dey *knows* dey lak it de bess." Her independence, her ostensibly good-humored insolence, do not go unnoticed, however, and when the opportunity comes, as it does when she is trapped while bearing Palmyre's voodoo fetishes, Creole revenge is swift. The scene in which the old Negro is killed is one of Cable's most effective; the very lack of didactic intrusion makes it a powerful indictment of lynching.

It should be noted that Cable's dislike and disapproval of the

Creoles does not extend to their women. Though occasionally he enters a sarcastic remark, as for example about the compassion of the Creole women being shown in their desire that the Negro woman Clemence be given only "a sound whipping" for having been caught bearing the voodoo objects toward Agricola Fusilier's house, Cable generally portrays Creole ladies as soft, tender, and financially impractical. The essence of their femininity comes in their innocence of the real world; the Nancanous are wholly incompetent to take care of their financial problems, and are easily led. Whatever they lack in business acumen, however, they more than make up for in their beauty and their devotion to true love. What in male Creoles would be portrayed as faults are for Creole ladies part of their charm. The Nancanous, for example, are highly superstitious, but their faith in charms and folk remedies is made into an emblem of an impracticality that adds to their femininity. Their inability to comprehend the philosophical pronouncements of Frowenfeld only increases their feminine appeal. As women, they feel rather than think; their emotions are their chief concern, and they live for love.

In portraying the Nancanous, of course, Cable was creating his heroines in the accepted stereotype of the romance form, and since their chief function in *The Grandissimes,* as in most of his other fiction, is to advance the love story, they are circumscribed by the needs of the story line. But Cable's males, in *The Grandissimes* at least, are not thus limited by their roles in the love story, and so it will not do to explain the limitations of intellect and the general recessiveness of Cable's female Creoles as being due to plot function alone. Rather, they are indicative of the kind of attraction that the sensuous and the voluptuous held for Cable; that he conceived of Creole women as so very feminine, and so sensuously appealing in their helplessness and impracticality, is an index to his ambivalent attitude toward them. Quite obviously Cable's heroines are not cast in the heroic mold of his own mother, whose force of character, high moral rectitude, and Presbyterian disapproval of all forms of indulgence seem mirrored in her son's strictures on masculine Creole laziness and unprogressiveness. But again, Cable's own conscious disapproval of so much that the Creoles stand for is accompanied by a considerable delight in their sensuous, languorous ways; as an artist he is drawn to their impracticality, their hedonism, their love of ease, and their addiction to creature comfort. This comes out not only in the style in which Cable designs his heroines, but in numerous other ways. However much his Calvinist training may have taught him to regard dancing as a sin, for example, his delight in describing the masquerade ball that opens the novel is clear. His depiction of the Grandissime women gathered together for their *fête de grandpère* shows a connoisseur's eye for feminine beauty:

> Turn the eye to the laughing squadron of beautiful girls, which every few minutes, at an end of the veranda, appears, wheels and dissappears [sic], and you note, as it were by flashes, the characteristics of face and figure that mark the Louisianaises in the perfection of the new-blown flower. You see that blondes are not impossible; there, indeed, are two sisters who might be undistinguishable twins but that one has blue eyes and golden hair. You note the exquisite pencilling of their eyebrows, here and there some heavier and more velvety, where a less vivacious expression betrays a share of Spanish blood. As Grandissimes, you mark their tendency to exceed the medium Creole stature, an appearance heightened by the fashion of their robes. There is scarcely a rose in all their cheeks and a full red-ripeness of their lips would hardly be in keeping; but there is plenty of life in their eyes, which glance out between the curtains of their long lashes with a merry dancing that keeps time to the prattle of tongues. You are not able to get a straight look into them, and if you could you would see only your own image cast back in pitiful miniature; but you turn away and feel, as you fortify yourself with an inward smile, that they know you, you man, through and through, like a little song.

Nor is Cable's awareness of female loveliness restricted to pure-blooded Creoles; as in *Old Creole Days,* he is adept in his description of quadroon beauty. And if the Nancanous are soft and helpless, not so the beautiful Palmyre Philosophe. She is sensual, svelte, predatory; Cable uses the word "feline" to describe her appearance and her disposition. The scene in which Joseph Frowenfeld goes to her quarters to tend her wound in place of the ill Doctor Keene, and administers to her as she lies in her bed, is full of a repressed sexuality made only more smoldering by Cable's claim that Frowenfeld, almost alone of the men she knows, does not look upon the quadroon woman as a sexual object. The description of Frowenfeld's emotions upon leaving Palmyre Philosophe is striking:

It was many an hour after he had backed out into the trivial remains of the rain-storm before he could replace with more tranquillizing images the vision of the philosophe reclining among her pillows, in the act of making that uneasy movement of her fingers upon the collar button of her robe, which women make when they are uncertain about the perfection of their dishabille, and giving her inaudible adieu with the majesty of an empress.

In such scenes, and in others such as the several descriptions of Aurore and Clotilde Nancanou in their bedroom at night, Cable clearly exhibits both his talent for and delight in the voluptuous.

But if an eye for sensuous beauty is very much a part of Cable's art, it is emphatically not made into an aspect of Joseph Frowenfeld's character. That young man is almost unbelievably high-minded and out of touch with the baser realities of the world around him. In the passage just quoted, in which Joseph leaves Palmyre Philosophe, it is unlikely that Cable meant consciously to imply that Frowenfeld was attracted by the physical beauty of the quadroon; what ostensibly disturbs the pharmacist is the plight of the woman, who because of her Negro blood is automatically considered "as legitimate prey" for all Creole males. Frowenfeld's moral rectitude pointedly differentiates him from almost all the Creole males, and it is depicted as an aspect of his Northern European, which is to say, his German (in effect his Anglo-American) Protestant nature. So much so that it comes with something of a shock to realize that an important part of what, after all, takes place in *The Grandissimes* concerns this high-minded, shy, studious young immigrant who within a single year of coming to New Orleans has not only become a highly successful business-man but has won the hand of a lovely Creole heiress in whose veins flow, as Charlie Keene put it early in the novel, the "best blood of the Province; good as the Grandissimes." For someone who disapproves of ancestry worship, social caste, and sordid materialism, Frowenfeld would seem to have done quite well for himself both socially and financially. If it is an inner grace that Frowenfeld possesses, then in true Calvinist fashion the outward sign would seem to have been made manifest in his acquisition of the things of this world.

To suggest such a meaning to *The Grandissimes* is startling, to say the least, for none of the rhetoric of the novel seems to run in this direction. The design of the book, after all, is to show the triumph of non-Creole virtue and the evils of racism and caste. But the fact that its hero, having come to see the pervasive cruelty of Creole racial attitudes and the emptiness of Creole boasts of social caste, should end by marrying a Creole heiress, would seem an odd way to confirm what he has learned. It might tend to suggest a very different conclusion, to the effect that true success consists of securing a high place in just that Creole society that has ostensibly been so condemned.

In the letter Cable had written to the editor of the Boston *Literary World* in 1875 defending the authenticity of his Creole dialect in "Jean-ah Poquelin," he concluded his defense with a strange claim: "Though it does not absolutely prove anything I will add that I am a creole myself, living today in sight of the house where I was born."[11] That this lie was told for the purpose of convincing the editor of the authority with which he portrayed Creole dialect seems clear; but even so, it is an interesting matter. To assert, in private correspondence with a Boston editor who would surely not know the claim was false, membership in a society of which he is publicly so censorious, and of whose many differences from his own society he was so very conscious, would seem to indicate less actual disapproval of Creole society than Cable appeared to feel. And when we remember, too, that Joseph Frowenfeld, who is so clearly Cable's surrogate in the novel, is rewarded by winning the hand of a Creole heiress of high social position, and we keep in mind the obvious unconscious attraction that Creole life and Creole ways actually held for Cable, we might well question just what his attitude toward the Creoles of New Orleans was. It would seem to be rather more complex than one might at first glance suspect.

Certainly Cable was sincere when he castigated Creole lethargy and smugness, and there can be little doubt of his strong conviction as to the cruelty of Creole racial attitudes; within the next few years, he was to brave the censure of not only the Creoles but the entire white South in order to speak the truth as he saw it. Yet, all the same, cannot one perhaps detect evidence of a certain amount of envy of the Creoles as well—the desire, surely not consciously held, for a place in the very Creole society he professed to disapprove of, and which might, because suppressed, manifest itself in an intensified zeal for denouncing the attitudes and pretensions of that society?

If this were so, it would surely be most understandable in a man of George W. Cable's sensibilities, with his delight in social situations, his gregariousness, his affection for the rich textural fabric of experience. Is it not odd, after all, that one who as an artist so relished and rendered the savor of Creole ways, and so convincingly portrayed them, should in all his conscious social and political thinking so thoroughly and consistently disapprove of the Creoles? But if this is so, it must be emphasized that whatever secret attractions Creole ways may have held for Cable were almost entirely unconscious. Nothing that Frowenfeld says, and very little that he thinks, would indicate the presence of such an attraction.

Throughout *The Grandissimes*, Frowenfeld is not a character who is ever subjected to much critical scrutiny by his author. Cable assumes that Frowenfeld's motives are of the highest, and his only sin is a certain amount of näiveté, a tendency to go off into theoretical abstractions and pronounce moral judgments a bit too readily. "My—de'—seh," Honoré Grandissime tells Frowenfeld at one point, "you mus' *crack* the egg, not smash it!" Frowenfeld may at times be somewhat too hasty and tactless, but he is *right,* in Cable's eyes. And the several outrages and harassments that he suffers for his presumption, as Philip Butcher says, constitute "a prediction of the rejection Cable was to experience as successive books and articles traced the course of his wanderings from the prescribed narrow path the South insisted was the high road of virtue and necessity." [12]

But for Frowenfeld there was, ultimately, success, love, the hand and heart of a Creole heiress. We see him out walking along the levee arm-in-arm with Clotilde Nancanou; they exchange confidences, "no part of which was heard by alien ears," and the lovely Creole tells her "lately accepted lover" how long she has loved him. Frowenfeld is indeed an alien no more; he has been accepted into Creole society—insofar as winning the hand of an authentic De Grapion-Nancanou, and having for his closest friend and now his stepfather Honoré Grandissime himself, may be said to constitute acceptance. Yet the novel itself has been, ostensibly at least, unconcerned with Frowenfeld's social mobility, so that when we think about what Frowenfeld has been able to accomplish in Creole society, we are quite startled. Not only has it not been explained, but we have not been made conscious that Frowenfeld *had* any ambitions of this sort. He seems entirely innocent of the whole business. What, one might wonder, would a writer such as Marcel Proust have made of Frowenfeld's ascendancy? And how would Proust, for example, or Henry James, have looked upon the apparently quite inexplicable way in which proud, caste-conscious Agricola Fusilier is made immediately to take up the immigrant pharmacist Joseph Frowenfeld and become his friend and champion?* What is clear is that Cable himself fails completely to study Frowenfeld in terms of the remarkable social mobility that he displays. His *Kulturroman* describes in great depth the impact of Anglo-American culture upon the Creoles, but almost nothing of the reverse of the process. The latter transaction we can only surmise. In place of what might have been a fascinating delineation of the way in which an outsider responds to the attractions of a richly complex, formidable, but ultimately vulnerable society, we are given only the high-minded but wooden and lifeless characterization of Joseph Frowenfeld.

It is this, I think, that prevents *The Grandissimes,* for all its undoubted excellence of social texture and its unflinching realistic dramatization of the evils of caste and of racism, from being a novel of the first rank. In the best of Twain, Hawthorne, Melville, one finds no such area of experience within the novel so completely neglected. Because of this neglect, the love plot of *The Grandissimes* remains a romantic stereotype; and the author's strictures on Creole society, since they are not examined in terms of motive, tend toward didacticism. Cable's editors were quite right in insisting that he cut down on some of the preaching.[13] But what Robert Underwood Johnson and his associates did not recognize, and so could not tell Cable, was that the reason *why* the author was being didactic was that, instead of examining his character's motives, he was letting the pharmacist serve, uncritically and directly, as surrogate for himself. The conclusion is inescapable that for the most part the characterization of Joseph Frowenfeld seemed quite adequate to Cable's editors, and the sentimental (because partly

*As a fictional character, Agricola Fusilier has some lines that are worthy of the Baron de Charlus, as when he declares: "Hah! sir, I know men in this city who would rather eat a dog than speak English! *I* speak it, but I also speak Choctaw."

unmotivated) love plot whereby the story is resolved and in part structured quite acceptable. Both character and plot fitted the requirements, and suited the aesthetics, of popular serialized fiction well enough. Johnson complained only that Frowenfeld sometimes seemed too saintly; he ought to have lost control of himself sufficiently to have knocked Sylvestre Grandissime down when the little Creole slapped him: "As it is, don't you see you are doing just what you don't want to do—making goodness seem unattributable because not mixed with enough humanity—human frailty if you will." [14] But of what the frailty should have consisted, Johnson did not say.

For Frowenfeld to have envied some of the social glamour of the Creoles of Louisiana, to have been attracted at least partially by the sensuality of their ways, to have exhibited, in short, just a trifle of the motivations of a social climber, would have hardly suited a magazine hero of the Genteel Tradition. The result was that *The Grandissimes,* Cable's best novel, a work of social observation of Southern society unsurpassed in its time, and the first book by a Southerner to deal seriously with the relationships of white and Negro, remains even so a deeply flawed novel.

VII
The Man of Letters

The reception of *The Grandissimes,* by reviewers and readers throughout the nation, was all that Cable could have asked. The editors of *Scribner's Monthly* were so pleased with it that they paid Cable a bonus of $500.[1] H. H. Boyesen found that it fulfilled his expectations; Cable, he declared in *Scribner's Monthly* for November, 1880, was "a literary pioneer . . . the first Southern novelist (unless we count Poe a novelist) who has made a contribution of permanent value to American literature." The *Atlantic* said that Cable was "an artist and a man of large imagination," with a "profound sense of the larger laws of history." W. C. Brownell, in the *Nation,* called him "a literary artist of unusual powers" and "a born story-teller." For *Appletons' Journal* the novel was "a picture of an epoch"; the author was "a story-teller of the first rank" who has "literally created a people, an era, and a place."[2]

There was other praise, too, not all of which Cable saw or heard, but which reflected the general approbation of *The Grandissimes.* "Have you read Cable's book, *The Grandissimes?*" the poet Sidney Lanier wrote to his brother Clifford; "it is a work of art, and he has a rare and fervent soul."[3] William Dean Howells wrote to Cable that he found the novel "thoroughly knit and perfectly clear, portraying a multitude of figures with a delicacy and unerring certainty of differentiation that perpetually astonishes me. It is a noble and beautiful book, including all the range of tragedy and comedy; and it made my heart warm towards you while I had the blackest envy in it. Deuce take you, how could you do it so well?" The Creole dialect had intoxicated him and his wife; "we speak nothing else now. . . ." He noted too that

"of course you expected me to like Agricola, too? He is admirable."
And, apparently forgetting that he had once rejected the story
"Bibi" for the *Atlantic,* he now found the "Bras Coupé episode
most powerful"; "the book is full of atmosphere," he concluded;
"you are a great fellow and we all send you homage." [4] To John
Hay, Howells wrote that "there is no more charming creature in
fiction than Aurora Nancanou in *The Grandissimes,*" and that
"Cable himself is the loveliest and loyalest ex-rebel that lives." [5]

In New Orleans, Cable's novel was accorded the highest praise.
"The creations of this novelist," wrote the reviewer for the *Democrat,* "are in reality *not* creations. They were and are living, breath-
ing men and women, transferred from actual life to his pages,
made immortal by their repeating everyday speech and manners,
and the tinge of genius thrown into every character." [6] Other
newspaper reviews were equally laudatory, and the *Item* published
no less than five commentaries on the novel over a two-year period.
Only the Creole newspaper *L'Abeille* failed to praise Cable's
novel.

Mixed in with the praise, however, were certain criticisms which
indicated future trouble. The generally favorable review in the
Democrat, for example, irked Cable by suggesting that in the
characterization of Honoré Grandissime f.m.c., Cable had pan-
dered to Northern tastes in order to find something condemnatory
of the South, and declared that the novel would probably appeal
most to readers of *Uncle Tom's Cabin.* That there was also some
locally expressed hostility may be deduced from the *Item*'s successive commentaries, which were written in defense of the novel.
"Its paintings are not always flattering to native eyes," said the
Item; "its evocation of dead memories will not be found pleasing,"
but "we cannot perceive that the merit of the romance is at all
marred." The Creole characters were true to fact, though it was
doubtful that the radical social views of the white Honoré Grandissime were true to life. [7]

The *Item*'s commentaries on the novel were written by a friend
of Cable's, Lafcadio Hearn. Hearn had moved to New Orleans
in 1877, after a period of several years in Cincinnati, and had
immediately kindled to the exotic, colorful life of the Louisiana
city. It is likely that Cable's story "Jean-ah Poquelin" was in part
responsible for Hearn's decision to come; on reading it in *Scribner's*

Monthly he had been fascinated, and shortly after his arrival in New Orleans he called on Cable.[8] They were an oddly assorted pair. Cable, six years the older, was a very domestic soul, and at that time still holding fairly strict Calvinist beliefs; he had yet to attend the theater and was not given to strong drink. He possessed, too, a considerable public spirit and social conscience, and was becoming increasingly critical of New Orleans social views. By contrast, Hearn was hedonistic, prone to dissipation, a connoisseur of decadence, and with few of the moral scruples that were so much a part of Cable's character. Yet for a period of several years, Cable and Hearn were close friends. They were drawn together not only by their literary interests, but by a common taste for the exotic, a delight in the heterogeneous charm of New Orleans as manifested in folk songs, vendors' cries, local history, and a shared dissent over New Orleans attitudes on race. Though Hearn had little of Cable's reforming urge on the race question, he believed no less strongly than Cable in the injustice of racial discrimination; indeed, so little did he share the local taboos that in Cincinnati he had lived for a time with a Negro woman, though it is unlikely that he voluntarily revealed this fact to Cable. Hearn soon came to spend several nights a week in Cable's company, and when *The Grandissimes* appeared, he defended it loyally.[9]

The reaction of Creole New Orleans to Cable's novel may in part be gathered from the appearance, late in 1880, of an anonymous pamphlet entitled *Critical Dialogue Between Aboo and Caboo on a New Book; or, A Grandissime Ascension.* Supposedly edited by "E. Junius," it was in reality the work of Adrien Emmanuel Rouquette, a Creole poet and priest with whom Cable was well acquainted. In the Preface, Cable is referred to as a scoffer, a banterer, a ridiculer, of "vulgar, jocose,—and I may say,—outlandish ancestry." The dialogue consists of an extended conversation between the ghost of Agricola Fusilier, "Aboo," and one "Caboo," a surviving Creole. During its course, Aboo declares that Cable's novel was written "FOR the prejudiced and inimical North," by "a pert, waggish, flippant, somewhat bold upstart, brazen-faced witling, who supplies the Northern literary market with that sort of unadulterated, but gratifying, stuff." Its sole intent was "the wicked purpose of slur, travesty and ridicule—leeringly—

sneeringly—jeeringly"; the author "reminds us of the chatty magpie, the cold, sheeny serpent, the slime-imbedded alligator, shedding pitiful tears." Aboo and Caboo deplore the praise given by New Orleans citizens to a book which "is an unnatural, Southern growth, a bastard product, *un digne pendant de* 'Uncle Tom's Cabin,'" written by an author who is "a High-Priest of Negro-Voudouism." The piece closes with a lampoon incantation in which Cable is accused, in Creole dialect, of having participated in voodoo dances and of fathering half-breed children.

Cable's friends were incensed by the document; possibly it may have caused the abrupt termination of Rouquette's friendship with Hearn.[10] From New York, Gilder wrote that Roswell Smith was much concerned by the animosity signified by the pamphlet, and added, "if you ever think it wise to come North you know where you will find friends."[11] Joel Chandler Harris cited it, in the Atlanta *Constitution* of February 20, 1881, as an example of the South's inhospitality toward unpalatable truths, and declared that "if the South is ever to make any permanent or important contribution to the literature of the world, we must get over our self-consciousness and so control our sensitiveness as to be able to regard with indifference—nay, with complacence—the impulse of criticism which prompts and spurs every literary man and woman whose work is genuine. We must not forget that real literary art is absolutely impartial and invariably just."[12]

Meanwhile Cable continued his daily work for the New Orleans Cotton Exchange; made an extended trip to the Acadian country of southwest Louisiana to write about it for the U. S. Census; and while there, took extensive notes on Acadian customs, language, anecdotes, history, and character sketches for possible future use in fiction. He began work on a history of New Orleans, also for the census; and completed the lengthy story *Madame Delphine,* which began as a three-part serial in *Scribner's Monthly* for May, 1881. The story was based on the same theme he had used for "'Tite Poulette," in which the marriage of 'Tite Poulette to the Dutchman Kristian Koppig, considered impossible because of laws against miscegenation, had at the last moment been permitted when the quadroon Madame John had produced papers showing that 'Tite Poulette was not her own daughter but the child of a Spanish couple. Cable later said that he had received a letter urging him, "if you have a whole heart for the cruel use of us quadroons," to change the story, because "Madame John lied! The girl was her own daughter; but like many and many a real quadroon mother, as you surely know, Madame John perjured her own soul to win for her child a legal and honorable alliance with the love-mate and life-mate of her choice."[13] Like " 'Tite Poulette," *Madame Delphine* likewise features a quadroon mother and her daughter, with whom a white man is in love. The man, however, is not a Dutch immigrant, but a Creole, Ursin Lemâitre, who after some years of privateering has come back to New Orleans under an assumed name to enter the banking business. The story line is built upon the kind of romantic plot so popular at the time: the daughter, returning from France aboard ship, confronts a pirate who has taken control of the ship, hands him a missal, and bids him read the Apostles' Creed, whereupon the corsair is both ashamed and smitten with love, and allows her to leave the ship unmolested. It turns out, of course, that the pirate is the selfsame Ursin Lemâitre. When the mother, the quadroon Madame Delphine, asks her banker, Vigneville, to help her find a white husband for her daughter, Vigneville presents himself, proposes, and is accepted. But friends of the banker who know that Madame Delphine is of mixed blood threaten to forbid the marriage because it violates the law. So Madame Delphine perjures herself by insisting that she is not the child's real mother. After the wedding she goes to confession, explains her lie, and dies, whereupon the priest looks up to heaven and cries, "Lord, lay not this sin to her charge!"

What saves the story, in part at least, from entire melodrama is the presence, throughout it, of the priest, Père Jerome. Père Jerome is a devout Roman Catholic, and is remarkable among Cable's characters as being one of the very few Catholics who are sympathetically portrayed *as* Catholics. To be sure, he possesses what in Cable's eyes are somewhat atypical characteristics: he is more interested in the Bible than in the dogmas of the church, and is criticized for this by other Catholic clergymen; and he is severely critical of the Creole community's moral and ethical accommodations. He is convinced, for example, that caste and racial intolerance are sins, and does not fail to rebuke his congregation for them. He both implicitly and explicitly criticizes the community for its acquiescence in sin, not only in its treatment of quadroons but in its willingness to profit from the smuggling that Captain Lemâitre had engaged in. "God help you, monsieur, and you, madame, sitting here in your *smuggled clothes,* to beat upon the breast with me and cry, 'I, too, Lord—I, too, stood by and consented,' " he sermonizes. But in his benevolence, his pleasure in good food, his understanding of the foibles of humankind, and his general enjoyment of the relaxed charms of climate and social scene, Père Jerome is a Latin. To a certain extent he might be said to represent Cable's attempt to disarm those who accused him of denigrating Creole morality, by letting the critique of racism come this time from a Creole priest with no Anglo-Americans on the scene to prompt him. As an aesthetic creation, he is one of Cable's few successful moralists. Later Cable wrote to William Dean Howells that he intended Père Jerome to make up for the artistic shortcomings of Frowenfeld in *The Grandissimes:* " . . . it was my chagrin over my partial failure with [Frowenfeld] that determined me to write out a character who should be pious and yet satisfactory to the artistic sense. . . . "[14]

Madame Delphine was well received; Robert Underwood Johnson, reviewing it for the *Critic* and for *Scribner's Monthly,* found it better than *The Grandissimes,* a "direct evidence of genius," and declared, "we do not recall anything outside of Hawthorne that exhibits so many of the literary qualities which go to make for a novelist an enduring reputation." The *Nation* found it "wonderfully true and real." The British reviews were equally appreciative. Edmund Gosse, writing in the *Saturday Review,* remarked its "rich and musical prose," though he felt it was needlessly complicated. The *Athenaeum*'s editor suggested that English novelists might well take as much pains on their work as Cable did.[16]

For all that, however, the story does not, for the modern reader, stand up so well as *The Grandissimes* or some of the stories of *Old Creole Days,* because not even the charm of its setting, the attractiveness of the rotund little Père Jerome, and the urgency of its depiction of the consequences of racism can overcome the melodramatic quality of its central plot. Only Père Jerome of all the characters escapes from the romantic stereotyping of the love story; Madame Delphine is too much the conventional helpless mother, Vigneville is little more than a type, and the daughter Olive is

hardly characterized at all.[16] The story seems never to rise above
the level of quaint local color; the people behave as in a tableau,
and the charm of the Creole patois is not enough to redeem their
woodenness as characters. The racial commentary seems didactic;
there is none of the vividness and human realism that make the
cake vendor Clemence so striking a rebuke to race hatred in *The
Grandissimes,* or that could invest the story with the power and
meaning of the Bras-Coupé episode.[17] The insipidity of the love
story dominates all else. *Madame Delphine* exhibits a dangerous
tendency on Cable's part: a willingness to include side by side
within one story a conventionally romantic love plot in
picturesque setting and an urgent social commentary, without
being greatly concerned about their interaction.

Apparently New Orleans readers were not as impressed with
Madame Delphine as were readers elsewhere. Though Lafcadio
Hearn, in the *Democrat,* declared the story was Cable's masterpiece,
he objected to the overuse of Creole patois. An editorial, again
in the *Times-Democrat,* though praising Cable as an author, declared that writers of the old antebellum society, notably the
Creole historian Charles Gayarré, had produced works that "will
live when the names of even such brilliant writers as Mrs. [Frances
Hodgson] Burnett and George Cable are forgotten." (The editorial
was concerned not with *Madame Delphine* but with an attempt to
show that the antebellum society built upon slavery had produced
a universal, not a provincial, literature.[18]) The linking of Gayarré's
name with Cable's, to the advantage of Gayarré, seems, in retrospect at least, significant. The elderly Creole historian, although
at this stage of Cable's career still ostensibly his friend, was
thoroughly identified not only with Creole culture but with strict
orthodoxy on the racial and sectional issue.

While *Madame Delphine* was being prepared for book publication,
Cable kept busy with the census reporting for his friend Colonel
George E. Waring, Jr. Waring meanwhile had become very much
involved in furthering Cable's literary affairs. In early January,
1881, he secured an offer of $3,500 for serial and book rights to
Cable's next novel, plus a 5 per cent royalty on sales, from the
Boston firm of J. R. Osgood.[19] The offer placed Cable in a
somewhat awkward position; he had realized comparatively little
from *The Grandissimes,* and he was, as always, hard-pressed for

money. He did not wish, however, to injure his relations with *Scribner's Monthly,* in particular at a time when there was division within the magazine firm itself. *Scribner's Monthly* had originally been published as a three-way partnership of the elder Charles Scribner, Josiah Holland, and Roswell Smith. In 1881, Holland and Smith bought out the Scribner interest in the magazine, and at Gilder's suggestion it was henceforth called the *Century Illustrated Monthly Magazine,* after the name of the Century Club.[20] In the process of setting up the new firm, some hard feelings had developed. Cable wished to maintain his ties both with the newly created Century Company and with Blair and the younger Charles Scribner. He wrote therefore to them, relaying the terms of the offer from Osgood, but making it clear that it had been unsolicited by him and that he had made no commitment himself. "I did nothing from first to last out of dissatisfaction with anything," he emphasized.[21]

Eager to visit New York again and anxious to solidify his publishing arrangements, Cable decided in the late spring of 1881 that the health of his none-too-robust wife and his four children would benefit from removal from the summer heat of New Orleans. He made arrangements, therefore, to board his family in the White Mountains of New Hampshire, and on June 1 established them there.[22] He then returned to New York to spend several weeks in the city and in Massachusetts and Connecticut. Very much a literary celebrity now, he was introduced to numerous figures of the literary establishment of the day. The Century Company had engaged Abbott H. Thayer to do his portrait, and he sat for it. From the Century Club he wrote his mother that he was posing "sitting a few feet away from the corner where Thackery [sic] used to sit. If God wills it I may one day even venture to go and sit down there." He had met Edward Burlingame, John Hay, Augustus St. Gaudens, and Richard Henry Stoddard— the last-named he did not care for, for "he gets red in the face, poor man, and calls me his dear boy more than once too often for good taste." Then he added hastily, "I'm sorry I wrote this."[23] He visited William Dean Howells at Belmont, Massachusetts, and on June 11 went to Hartford, Connecticut, to visit his wife's relatives, the Bartletts. There he met the novelist and journalist Charles Dudley Warner, and his brother George. They telegraphed to their fellow townsman Samuel L. Clemens to come back from "somewhere beyond New Haven" for the occasion, and Olivia (Livy) Clemens came along as well. Cable and Clemens promptly formed an intense friendship that three years later would result in their memorable joint reading tour.[24] "We all lunched together," Cable wrote his wife, "& 'Mark' & Mr. Warner were ever so funny." In the evening Cable met the Reverend Joseph Twichell, General Josiah Hawley, and others of Hartford's elite. He also had "a long, & to me delightful," talk with Harriet Beecher Stowe about the South.[25] Just turning seventy, and not yet in the mental decline that marked her last years, Mrs. Stowe still represented to most Southerners the embodiment of fanatical abolitionism, as the recent remarks in the New Orleans *Democrat* about Cable's characterization of Honoré Grandissime f.m.c. showed. His own increasingly aberrant position on racial matters being what it was, Cable doubtless viewed Mrs. Stowe as a prophet rather than fanatic; in any event, it would not be long before not only New Orleans but other Southern newspapers would be likening Cable's attitudes on race to those in *Uncle Tom's Cabin*.

Earlier, Cable had visited Colonel Waring at Newport, Rhode Island, and there had met the publisher J. R. Osgood. He now went back to New York, with an offer from Osgood to bring out his next novel at a 22½ per cent royalty and a $1,000 advance upon completion of the manuscript, but with the proviso that either Scribner's or the Century Company could have the book by equalling Osgood's terms. Neither was able to do so, however, and Scribner's in particular resented Cable's new book having been promised to Osgood; but there was an agreement that his future books would be committed to Scribner's. Cable also contracted to enlarge his census history of New Orleans as a seven-part serial for the *Century,* followed by book publication by the Century Company; when this came out in 1884, however, it too was published by Scribner's.[26] "Well, the greatest holiday of my life is about over," Cable wrote to his wife on June 22 en route homeward to New Orleans, posting his letter at Atlanta, Georgia. "It was a little dashed with the necessity of doing business with friends (always an awkward task), but it is all done & I believe without losing the kind feeling of anyone."[27]

With his family comfortably in New Hampshire, Cable settled down in New Orleans to work. His Cotton Exchange duties required only an hour or two each day. He busied himself with his census history, and completed a term as secretary of a grand jury.[28] Lonely for the family, he kept a steady stream of letters en route to New Hampshire. On July 2 he was able to report that a "handsome little red, cloth-bound volume" containing *Madame Delphine* and three of the *Old Creole Days* stories had arrived from Frederick Warne & Co., London.[29] He described his occupations: he taught Sunday School, saw his friend the Baron Ludwig von Reizenstein—a noted entomologist who had named a newly discovered moth *Smerinthus Cablei* in his honor[30]—spent long hours with his friends Marion Baker, James B. Guthrie, and George Henry Clements; and reported steady progress on his history. He missed his wife and family tremendously; he read over the letters Louise had written him before their marriage, got out photographs of her and carried them about with him. "Yes, I hate my bed," he wrote on July 17. "I do not sleep until I weary of tossing. I tried very hard to give attention to the sermon tonight & to the conversation of those with whom I talked after church; but I had no thought but—thee. Louise, Louise!"[31] "I am terribly lonely," he wrote again on August 21; "I hunger and thirst for your letters and they seem very far apart. Nobody is any company to me."[32] Finally, on September 20, Louise and family left for New Orleans.

Cable had decided at last to end his connections with the Cotton Exchange and the countinghouse, and to undertake the risk of supporting himself and his family by literary effort alone. The contract with Osgood for his next novel, the income from his census work, the serialization and book plans for his history of the Creoles all gave him some assurance that his future might be reasonably secure. Several magazines asked for new work. Charles Dudley Warner, editor of the American Men of Letters series, invited him to write a study of William Gilmore Simms, and he agreed tentatively to do so. His books were appearing in England and, in translation, on the Continent. So on October 1, 1881, he resigned from the Cotton Exchange, the resignation to take effect December 1. On December 2, the board of directors of the Cotton Exchange adopted a resolution commending his long services.[33] "Nothing now for offense or defense but my grey goose quill!" he wrote to William Dean Howells.[34]

Within two weeks after he left the Cotton Exchange, Cable put aside the manuscript of his new novel and began revision of his history of New Orleans. The Century Company was ready to begin illustrations for the history, and in January Joseph Pennell, then only twenty-one years old but destined to become a leading American magazine illustrator, came down to New Orleans to begin work. Pennell filled his sketchbooks with views of the French Quarter, including twelve of the houses described in Cable's stories. Except for Charles Gayarré, however, he saw little of the Creoles themselves, for Cable had no access to them: " . . . alas I am entirely barred out," he wrote, "for Cable the only 'Américain' down here who knows them is the most cordially hated little man in New Orleans, and all on account of the Grandissimes; and so he can do nothing with the better class." Pennell wanted Cable to visit the West Indies with him to collaborate on an illustrated travel account for the *Century;* but Cable decided not to go, and proposed Hearn in his stead. Eventually the project fell through.[35]

On April 28, 1882, Samuel L. Clemens arrived in New Orleans, with James R. Osgood and a stenographer in tow. Howells had planned to accompany them, but had taken sick and could not come along. Clemens was engaged in a return trip along the Mississippi River, where once he had worked as a steamboat pilot. Now, with Cable as his guide, he happily toured the city, finding it changed, mainly for the better. "The party," he wrote in *Life on the Mississippi* a year later, "had the pleasure of idling through this ancient quarter of New Orleans with the South's finest literary genius, the author of *The Grandissimes.* In truth, I find by experience, that the untrained eye and vacant mind can inspect it and learn of it and judge of it more clearly and profitably in his books than by personal contact with it." They visited Lake Pontchartrain, and dined on pompano, "delicious as the less criminal forms of sin." [36] Such was his regard for Cable at the time that Clemens even attended church with him along with Joel Chandler Harris, who arrived from Atlanta to join the group. It was worth the trip to New Orleans just to hear Cable sing, Harris wrote later.[37] The three writers held forth at Cable's house in the Garden District and at the home of James B. Guthrie. According to Clemens, Harris's appearance disappointed a group of children who had come to see him: "Why, he's white!" they said of the creator of Uncle Remus.[38] So shy was Harris that he refused all requests to read aloud from his work, so Cable and Clemens read some of the Uncle Remus stories as well as extracts from their own writings. Clemens noted how well Cable read aloud from his work, and it may well be that it was on this occasion that he formed the idea of a joint reading tour.

It was a notable moment. There, at one and the same time, were gathered the three nineteenth-century Southerners who wrote most memorably and indelibly about the Negro in the South. In his Uncle Remus stories, the shy, introverted Harris was creating for all time the picture, the stereotype perhaps, of the "old-time darky," wise in his knowledge of the ways of the animals and fowl of the plantation, and acute in his judgment of the ways of the white folks. Twain would soon be returning home to complete *The Adventures of Huckleberry Finn,* with its immortal characterization of the runaway slave Jim. As for Cable, he had already, in *The Grandissimes,* produced some of the most trenchant criticism of racism ever to be written by a Southerner.

Harris returned to Atlanta and to his editorial desk on the Atlanta *Constitution;* he would never directly challenge the South's racial shibboleths of his day. Clemens likewise managed somehow to refrain for the most part from open hostility; his superior artistry kept his best work from being read as a tract, and whatever ill feelings his comments on Southern provincialism in *Life on the Mississippi* occasioned did not linger for very long. But Cable was shortly to enter into full hostilities; already *The Grandissimes* had ruffled Southern tempers, and *Dr. Sevier* would do so even more directly, until finally Cable would engage in direct polemical writings about the Southern treatment of the Negro and thus expose himself to the full onslaught of Southern outrage and denunciation. Of the three writers, it was Cable who would deal most openly and fearlessly with the single most important and controversial issue of Southern life: the race question. He was to pay a very high price for doing so.

VIII

Reformer

Now that he was living on his literary earnings alone, it was important that Cable maintain a steady productivity. Both the novel and the history of the Creoles demanded his attention. Instead of using his new-found freedom to increased literary advantage, however, Cable soon became involved in a project for prison reform that took much of his energy and time. As secretary of the grand jury the previous year, he had inspected prisons and insane asylums in New England on his visit there, and the contrast between what he found there and the conditions of similar New Orleans institutions profoundly shocked him, so that his report to the jury had castigated local indifference and neglect. With his friend James B. Guthrie and two others, he secured passage of a city ordinance setting up a nonpolitical Board of Prisons and Asylums Commissioners.[1] Then in December, 1881, Cable was asked by Major E. A. Burke,* manager of the *Times-Democrat,* to write a series of articles on behalf of prison and institutional reform; he would be paid $20 for each article, and would have the right to approve or disapprove publication of any other material on the subject of prison reform by the *Times-Democrat.*[2]

*Burke himself was hardly a model civic reformer. Of dubious origins, he became active in New Orleans politics during the Reconstruction. He was involved in the working out of the Compromise of 1876 whereby Federal troops were withdrawn from the South and Rutherford B. Hayes was declared winner over Samuel J. Tilden in the disputed presidential election of that year. Later Burke became engaged in mining and shipping interests in Honduras, and it was then discovered that he had been involved in bond frauds of almost $2 million while state treasurer of Louisiana. He refused to return to Louisiana to stand trial, and continued in his Central American operations until his death. For a sketch of Burke's career, see C. Vann Woodward, *Origins of the New South, 1877–1913* (Baton Rouge, La., 1951), pp. 70–72.

Cable set out, with the *Times-Democrat*'s assistance, to organize a large civic group to support the commission. In a series of articles, he detailed the appalling conditions existing in New Orleans prisons and asylums, and laid the blame to public indifference. On March 7, 1882, the Prisons and Asylums Aid Association was founded, with a membership including many of the city's leading business and professional men. Cable, as nonsalaried secretary, was instrumental in the association's success in securing a number of important reforms.[3] Other reforms were defeated, however, and in the process of investigation Cable became convinced that deplorable prison conditions existed elsewhere in Louisiana as well as throughout the South, and that these were being ignored by the people of the South, who were thus permitting widespread atrocities in state prisons and penitentiaries.

Cable discovered that under the aegis of penal correction, convicted lawbreakers were being forced into cruelly hard labor under shocking conditions. They were leased to private parties and corporations engaged in mining, lumbering, railway tunnel construction, road building, and other such activities, where they worked under brutal conditions, with primitive housing and sanitary facilities. The result was an appalling mortality rate among convicts; a prison sentence meant in effect that a prisoner would very likely die before his prison term expired, or at best would emerge from imprisonment seriously crippled or sick.

In September, 1882, Cable was invited to address the National Conference of Charities and Correction at its meeting in Louisville the following year. His speech, made in 1883, was aimed squarely at the South. For state after state, from Virginia to Texas, Cable cited statistics and gave details of what was going on. Relying for the most part upon actual statements reported by prison officials themselves, his evidence was overwhelming and his logic devastating. That it was very much a sectional indictment was clear, for Cable was careful to cite comparable figures for Northern and Western states to demonstrate a highly unfavorable comparison between prison mortality and severity of sentences in the Southern states, all of which employed the lease system.

Cable's Louisville address, which took two hours to deliver, was heard with undivided attention, and when he was done he received an ovation. He was elected a vice-president of the National Prison

Association. Editorials in newspapers throughout the country praised him. There were, however, some demurrers from the South, and they were repeated when Cable's address was published in the *Century* in February, 1884. Not only had Cable held up every one of the Southern states to a highly unfavorable comparison with the North, but it was obvious that the leased prisoners Cable was talking about were for the most part Negroes. Jailed often on very slight pretext, given lengthy prison terms for what frequently were no more than simple misdemeanors, they were in effect being sold into bondage again, under working conditions that equalled or surpassed the very worst that antebellum slavery had to offer. Without actually saying so, therefore, Cable was by implication attacking the South's treatment of Negroes. Though the states of the former Confederacy had ostensibly acquiesced in the abolition of human slavery, Cable implied, widespread involuntary servitude was nevertheless still being carried on under the guise of penal correction.

Cable was confident that when the best people of the South realized what was being done by their state governments, they would no longer tolerate it. But in presenting his case as he had done—and there was hardly any other way in which he could have presented it—he had come close to making the issue one that involved sectional pride and sectional racial attitudes. Yet it was difficult to fault Cable's facts or his logic, and any kind of humane defense of the convict lease system was obviously all but impossible. However much, therefore, Southerners may have resented Cable's attack on the lease system, and however uncomfortable its racial implications may have been, there was relatively little public criticism of Cable's action. And in New Orleans itself, the association of which Cable had served as secretary and for which he had provided the principal direction and leadership had after all been composed of many of the city's leading citizens, including more than one prominent Creole. There were thus no legitimate grounds for attacking Cable—yet.

But the time would come; Cable surely must have known that. For, en route to Louisville to deliver his address, something had happened that left Cable furious with rage and shame, and determined to attack, not merely the convict lease system, but the whole shameful business of racial segregation and mistreatment of the Negro in the South. A year later he described it in his paper on "The Freedman's Case in Equity":

> One hot night in September of last year I was traveling by rail in the state of Alabama. At rather late bedtime there came aboard the train a young mother and her little daughter of three or four years. They were neatly and tastefully dressed in cool, fresh muslins, and as the train went on its way they sat together very still and quiet. At the next station there came aboard a most melancholy and revolting company. In filthy rags, with vile odors and the clanking of shackles and chains, nine penitentiary convicts chained to one chain, and ten more chained to another, dragged laboriously into the compartment of the car where in one corner sat this mother and child, and packed it full, and the train moved on. I returned to my own place in the coach behind, where there was, and had all the time been, plenty of room. But the mother and child sat on in silence in that foul hole, the conductor having distinctly refused them admission elsewhere because they were of African blood, and not because the mother was, but because she was *not,* engaged at the moment in menial service. Had the child been white, and the mother not its natural but its hired guardian, she could have sat anywhere in the train, and no one would have ventured to object, even had she been as black as the mouth of the coalpit to which her loathsome fellow passengers were being carried in chains.[4]

It was hideously wrong. Yet it was tolerated, in the name of the Separation of the Races. And, Cable later said, he then and there determined that he would not keep silent any longer. He would await the proper occasion—not in the North, but in the South— and he would speak forth. He must have guessed what would happen when he did.

Cable's work on both his novel and his history of the Creoles went badly at first. The report he had sent to Colonel Waring for the census project had been published in late 1881, in considerably shortened form. Before his historical material was deemed acceptable for subsequent publication in the *Century,* however, it went through several revisions. Even then, it was only after Colonel Waring had turned up an offer from J. R. Osgood to publish the material as it was that the *Century* came to terms with Cable. The difficulty, as Arlin Turner declares, was due primarily to Cable's desire to emphasize completeness and historical accuracy, when what the magazine wanted was the same kind of picturesque local

color material that characterized Cable's fiction. Cable was willing
to compromise, and eventually six articles appeared during the
first seven months of 1883, illustrated with drawings by Joseph
Pennell. For book publication the next year, Cable restored much
connecting material and added additional sections. He did not,
however, restore the meticulous documentation of his sources that
Colonel Waring had removed from the manuscript for census
publication.[5] These would have shown that he had used more than
thirty authorities in preparing the history, as well as periodical
and newspaper files. Not only Charles Etienne Gayarré's historical
work on Louisiana, but that of Charlevoix, Dumont, and Marbois
were drawn on, along with books of travel and official reports,
city ordinances, state laws, and other historical documents.[6]

Shortly after an installment entitled "Plotters and Pirates of
Louisiana" appeared in the *Century* for April, 1883, Cable was
attacked for his assertion that General James Wilkinson had
connived in the 1780's to deliver part of the territory of the United
States to Spain. A descendant of the general, one James Wilkinson,
denounced the statement in the *Times-Democrat* for April 15. Cable
replied on May 13, supporting his position chiefly by references
to Gayarré's four-volume *History of Louisiana.* He described Gayarré
as "that accomplished Creole gentleman and Spanish and English
scholar," who had written "the best history of our state extant."
When Wilkinson rejoined, accusing Gayarré of having shown the
"greatest bias and prejudice in his work," Gayarré entered the
dispute himself. In two long articles, on May 20 and June 3, he
cited extensive evidence from Spanish documents to prove his
claim.[7]

In his first article, however, Gayarré struck out at Cable as well.
"Why wait before taking offense," he asked, "until Mr. Cable has
copied my statements and republished them as his own?" Cable
was considerably perturbed, and he hastily wrote to his friend
Marion Baker, literary editor of the *Times-Democrat,* possibly
delivering the letter to him in person so that Baker could show
it to Gayarré. Surely his friend Gayarré could not have intended
the inference that the remark seemed to imply, he said; "a magazine article setting forth facts of history simply as such is not
expected to make acknowledgement of its authorities unless they
are new and unknown." The original manuscript, he declared,

was "positively loaded with foot-note references to authorities in which no other name appears so often as that of 'Gayarré,' " but the government editor had struck them out as unnecessary. He hoped that Gayarré would, in his second article, "indicate in some subordinate and incidental way that I am not reproached by him as making unjust use of his writings." [8] Apparently Gayarré was temporarily mollified, to the extent of making the wording of his next article read that Cable had quoted rather than copied;[9] but the original remark was not specifically retracted.

Gayarré's clear hostility came as a shock to Cable, for he had considered the elderly Creole historian his friend. Gayarré had loaned Cable some letters from William Gilmore Simms when Cable had contemplated a biography, and Cable had given Gayarré letters of introduction to editors in New York and had written to Charles Scribner's Sons on his behalf.[10] Cable had recommended Gayarré to write the essay on New Orleans for the *Encyclopedia Britannica,* even though he himself wished to undertake it.[11] Gayarré again had several times sought Cable's help and advice in finding a publisher, had invited him to his home to attend a series of lectures on the French Revolution,[12] and had apparently been a guest in Cable's home as recently as February, 1883.[13] To have the distinguished old Creole turn upon him almost overnight, as it were, was most disconcerting.

In retrospect, however, the development would seem to have been quite understandable. Gayarré was in his late seventies at the time, and living in considerable poverty. A onetime lawyer, judge, and legislator, he had been well known as Louisiana's most distinguished man of letters for many years. His *History of Louisiana,* written first in French and then in expanded form in English, was a standard work, which even today is relied upon by historians. He also wrote a biography and other works, including several novels. Already fifty-five years of age when Louisiana seceded from the Union, he had invested a large part of his considerable wealth in Confederate bonds, which by 1865 had become worthless. There followed a steady decline in his fortunes, so that ultimately he had been forced to sell most of his household belongings and his collection of family pictures and paintings; the novelist Grace King, a friend of the Gayarrés, had described a "tombola" held by Gayarré to raffle off his paintings.[14] Living, therefore, in very straitened circumstances, unable to find a publisher for his writings, it must indeed have been a source of chagrin to find the young George W. Cable—who was not even a Creole but an *Américain*—not only becoming the leading literary figure of postbellum Louisiana but gaining a national reputation as *the* authority on the Creoles. When, therefore, Cable actually began publishing historical narratives of Creole Louisiana in the *Century,* earning what to the impoverished Gayarré surely represented considerable money in the process, and in so doing drew liberally and without public acknowledgment on the fruits of Gayarré's laborious researches in the archives of Louisiana and of France and Spain, the old historian's resentment could no longer be contained, and he lashed out. In *Times-Democrat* articles in June and August of 1883, he attacked first the claims of all novelists to be considered as historians, and next the use of Creole Negro patois and Acadian material in books which were derogatory of the South; such books, he declared, would sell very well. He did not mention Cable, but the inference was clear; the writer of such books, he declared, would be a traitor to his country.[15]

Cable must then have realized that further efforts to pacify Gayarré were useless, for when the book version of *The Creoles of Louisiana* was published in 1884, not only did he not allude to his use of Gayarré's researches, but he made no mention of Gayarré's writings in the text.[16] For all the provocation, Cable's failure to acknowledge his debt to Gayarré's writings was exceedingly ungenerous, since there can be no question that he had drawn extensively on the historian's researches throughout his book.

As a work of history, *The Creoles of Louisiana* is an interesting volume. It is well researched, even if undocumented (and meticulous documentation was hardly expected of such works in the nineteenth century). Cable later wrote that when asked to expand his census work into an illustrated volume, he had "consented, well pleased to write historically of a people whom I was accused of misrepresenting in fiction. . . . "[17] The successive revisions of the work show, as Arlin Turner notes, a deliberate effort not to be unjust and unkind, and Cable balanced the faults of the Creoles carefully against those of the Anglo-Americans.[18] I question, however, whether Turner is right when he states that "a Creole not over-sensitive might find, actually, that Cable came closer to violating accuracy through sympathy than through severity,"[19] for there are numerous interpretative passages throughout the book which, as Kjell Ekström points out, are hardly flattering to Creoles. These were almost certain to have caused resentment, while "here and there, there is something in his style that makes even an entirely neutral reader suspect that Cable took a certain pleasure in exposing them."[20] He described the first Louisianians as "unrestrained, proud, intrepid, self-reliant, rudely voluptuous, of a high intellectual order, yet uneducated, unreasoning, impulsive, and inflammable. . . . "[21] Only a few of them, he said, were persons of rank and station; many had been jail inmates in France. All of which was undoubtedly true, just as it was true of the First Families of Virginia, and even Gayarré himself had documented the facts; but it was another matter for an *Américain* like Cable to point out and insist upon it. And Cable's basic approach, which was to show how the Creoles had steadily improved themselves over the decades until from lawless and low beginnings they had evolved into "a proud, freedom-loving, agricultural, and commercial people," was surely not calculated to flatter such an ancestor-conscious race.

Of the Creoles at the time of the Louisiana Purchase, Cable wrote that they were "said to have been coarse, boastful, vain; and they were also deficient in energy and application, without well-directed ambition, unskillful in handicraft—doubtless through negligence only—and totally wanting in that community feeling which begets the study of reciprocal rights and obligations, and reveals the individual's advantage in the promotion of the common interest." Moreover, "with African slavery they were, of course, licentious, and they were always ready for the duelling-ground. . . . "[22] The remark about the slaves touched upon a raw nerve. Several other times in his narrative Cable did not fail to suggest similar inferences.

Cable devoted a considerable portion of the history to explaining why New Orleans had failed to keep pace with the other leading cities of the United States in its development. "Why Not Bigger Than London?" he entitled one chapter, and went on to explain that the presence of slavery, the climate, and general Creole complacency had served to stifle the progressive tendencies of the age. It was, he made clear, the Anglo-Americans, not the Creoles, who introduced whatever progressive moves and new ideas had been accepted. The successive epidemics, floods, and pestilence that had ravaged New Orleans were the result, he implied, mainly of Creole backwardness: "He has ten good 'cannots' to one small 'can'—or once had. . . . "[23] And while he also censures the Anglo-Americans, it is primarily for their adoption of Creole attitudes.

The fact is that the improvement that Cable cites in the Creoles, and that he praises in his final chapters, came precisely because the Creoles had increasingly adopted American ways. There were Creoles, Cable noted, who now took the lead in reform, in finance, in business, in the professions. They no longer opposed drainage; they supported education; they joined eagerly in civic projects. But all such innovations had come, he makes clear, by virtue of an increasing disposition to accept the *Américains* and to do things their way. And he concludes his book with a discussion of Creole speech, ending with a compliment, but one that is a trifle left-handed:

> There are reasons—who can deny it?—why we should be glad that the schoolmaster is abroad in Louisiana, teaching English. But the danger is, that somewhere in the future lurks a day when the Creole will leave these lovable drolleries behind him, and speak our tongue with the same dull correctness with which it is delivered in the British House of Lords. May he live long, and that time be very far away![24]

It is, in short, regrettable but inevitable that the quaint distinctiveness of Creole speech must eventually disappear; ultimately, the once-proud Creoles of Louisiana will have vanished.

Cable's history of the Creoles was generally well received when it appeared, though most of the national notices were brief. Those in the New Orleans newspapers were largely favorable. A *Times-Democrat* editorial, probably by Marion Baker, declared that Cable understood his native city thoroughly, "not only its history, but its social life, its people and all its peculiarities." The *Picayune* asserted that "reading this book one cannot doubt the fondness and affection, whether returned or not, of Cable for the Creoles." And Edward Everett Hale, writing in the *Critic* for September 12, 1885, said that "if [Cable's] Creole friends are not satisfied this time, both with the historian and the history, they must be hard to please." [25]

While Cable was at work on *The Creoles of Louisiana* and *Dr. Sevier,* he delivered several public addresses on the subject of literature in the South, in which he stated his position on various matters of the day more boldly than ever before. He had been invited to give the commencement address before the literary societies of the University of Mississippi, and on June 28, 1882, he spoke to them on the future of literature in the South. What he had to say was widely reported; he was, by then, the South's best-known writer. He reviewed the history of the demand for an American literature, and contended that in antebellum times the South had been unable to play its proper role in the creation of such a literature because of its allegiance to slavery and caste: "Our life had little or nothing to do with the onward movement of the world's thought." Because the South then had no middle class, it was estranged from the democratic literature of the rest of America. The demand for a distinctively Southern literature had meant a literature defending the institution of slavery, and had thus been sterile. [26]

Now, however, there was no need for such literary provincialism; Southern writers could be national, not separatist, in outlook. He noted the achievement of recent Southern writers. The continuing failure of the South to support and honor its best writers, he declared, was due to a failure to believe in "those writings which hold the freshest, the best, and the most beautiful thoughts of the nation. . . . " Allegiance to the past, therefore, would not do. "When the whole intellectual energy of the southern states flew to the defense of that one institution which made us the South, we broke with human progress. We broke with the world's thought." Now the South must reunite with that thought, and when it does, "there will be no South. We shall be Virginians, Texans, Louisianians, Mississippians, and we shall at the same time and over and above all be Americans. . . . Let us hasten to be no longer a unique people."

He did not, he said, favor the idea of a New South. "What we want—what we ought to have in view, is the No South! Does the word sound like annihilation? It is the farthest from it. It is enlargement. It is growth. It is a higher life." He scored the "plantation idea"—by which he meant the sharecropping and tenant farming that had grown up in the post-Reconstruction South. Coming as close as he could to an attack on racism without actually uttering the words, he excoriated the principle of caste and class. A century and a half of the practice of slavery had left its marks on the Southern community, and hence there was need for a searching of Southern views and tempers for flaws. "And who should we expect to do this? Certainly not outsiders. Certainly ourselves," he said, in a concluding plea for toleration of Southern writers who ventured to criticize the region.

It was a call for self-examination and for a democratic society, and it might be expected that the speech, in particular its demand for an end to Southern uniqueness and for a "No-South" instead of a New South, would have been widely attacked in the Southern press. Yet the address, though reported throughout the country at length, seems not to have come under much fire. There was even commendation. The Memphis *Appeal,* for example, thought that Cable "speaks with the independence of a brave thinker and pleads eloquently and sensibly. . . . Conceived in the right spirit—a thoroughly patriotic one— . . . [the speech] will encourage merit and rebuke assumption and ignorance." [27]

At the University of Louisiana in New Orleans, on June 15, 1883, Cable renewed his appeal for Southern acceptance of a literature which dared to question some of its beliefs and attitudes. This time he was quite specific. "Are we going to demand . . . that [the Southern writer] shall bow down to our crotchets and whims?" he asked. Will he "be expected to practice certain amiable and cowardly oversights and silences in order to smooth the frowns of sections and parties and pacify the autocratic voice of ruling classes and established ideas?" Literature, he asserted, "must be free; free to study principles for themselves; to present and defend truth; to assert rights; to dissolve and sublimate and re-crystallize all that is best of old and new; to rectify thoughts, morals, manners, society, even though it shake the established order of things like an earthquake." He urged that the South throw the entire spectrum of its life "wide open" to "the criticism and correction" of its writers, "reserving the right to resent only what we can refute." [28]

That he had the reception of his own work in mind there seems little doubt, both in reference to the reaction thus far and to what he feared might be the reaction to the novel he was then writing. He must have realized all too well that he was drawing ever closer to a direct attack on that most controversial and vital of all issues, the treatment of the Negro. His research into the convict lease system was leading him toward the expansion of the issue from one involving the treatment of Negro convicts into a general critical scrutiny of the white South's treatment of the Negro. He hoped that the South would hear him out, and respect his critique as well intended and well said, despite its sensitiveness toward any attempt to criticize its racial practices. Thus, when he insisted upon the need for the Southern writer to be national rather than sectional in his outlook, to write for the entire nation and not merely for the comfort of his fellow Southerners, he was surely thinking of himself, for he was the first important Southern writer to dare to write about Southern racial and social attitudes in terms other than those of praise and defense.

Meanwhile, as Cable worked toward the completion of his next novel, a new prospect had begun to open up for him, one that might well secure a considerable income without his having to turn completely away from his literary work. He had gone to New York once again, in the early autumn of 1882, to confer with Richard Watson Gilder about the new novel. Installing himself in a room on West Twenty-second Street for a month, he had found that he could turn out his writing at an increased rate while free of the family and social distractions of New Orleans. His financial situation, however, was critical; at the price of considerable anguish, he had been forced to ask the Century Company to make regular advances against future royalties. Then in late September Gilder took him down to Baltimore to meet President Daniel Coit Gilman of Johns Hopkins University, and Gilman invited him to give a series of lectures there in the following spring, for a fee of about $1,000.[29]

Lecturing and reading from one's own work was an accepted and widespread practice among American authors during the latter half of the nineteenth century. Almost all writers of note took to the lecture platform occasionally, and of these none was more successful, or more famed for his speaking, than Cable's new friend Samuel L. Clemens. For close to two decades Mark Twain

had been renowned as a public entertainer; indeed, his fame as
a performing humorist probably exceeded that as an author.
Apparently during or just after his meeting with Cable and Joel
Chandler Harris in New Orleans in April of 1882, Clemens had
conceived the idea of a grand lecture tour, in which he would
be joined by Cable, Harris, William Dean Howells, Thomas Bailey
Aldrich, and Charles Dudley Warner. They would rent a private
railway car, hire a chef, and set forth on a luxurious and triumphal
tour of the country; he himself would be the entrepreneur, paying
the others fixed salaries.[30] To the morbidly shy Harris, of course,
any such venture was out of the question; he had not even been
willing to read from his own work before friends and admirers
in New Orleans. Cable, however, was interested, and his speech
at the University of Mississippi that June was apparently in the
nature of a trial run, to see whether he could perform in public.
"I am said to have scored a decided success," he wrote Clemens
on June 29. "The house was full—crowded except in the gallery—
& probably contained 800 people. I spoke for an hour & three
quarters with frequent interruptions of applause to the end. Only
under the low badly constructed galleries at the far end of the
room was I not heard, though I made no special effort." He was
thus disappointed that Clemens's plan had proved unworkable:
" . . . I am the more regretful that the menagerie has to be given
up."[31]

President Gilman's invitation reopened for him an enticing
prospect. His friend Roswell Smith of the Century Company was
also enthusiastic about the possibility of Cable's lecturing. He
asked James R. Osgood to arrange an engagement for Cable at
the Lowell Institute in Boston, and suggested to Cable's friends
in Hartford that they also sponsor an experimental lecture. Such
plans for the future helped make Cable's visit to New York, which
lasted into November, a decided success despite his money worries.
Gilder and Smith vied in making his stay a pleasant one. He met
Edward Eggleston, Mary Mapes Dodge, Brander Matthews, John
Burroughs, Noah Brooks, Helena Modjeska, and Joseph Jefferson.
He spent some pleasant hours with H. H. Boyesen. On three
occasions he and the operatic soprano Clara Louise Kellogg had
a great time together, with Cable singing Creole and Negro songs
while Mrs. Kellogg sang operatic arias and Negro melodies. In

Baltimore, Cable met Basil Lanneau Gildersleeve, Herbert Baxter Adams, Innes Randolph, and Severn Teackle Wallis.[32] A visit to Hartford and Boston was notable for a stag dinner at which Clemens, James R. Osgood, John Boyle O'Reilly, Charles Fairchild, and Thomas Bailey Aldrich all held forth, "properly fortified" as Clemens wrote to Howells. Clemens was greatly taken with Cable; "Cable has been here, creating worshipers on all hands," he told Howells. "He is a marvelous talker on a deep subject. I do not see how even [Herbert] Spencer could unwind a thought more smoothly or orderly, and do it in a cleaner, clearer, crisper English."[33] Apparently Cable, however, found some of the humor at the stag dinner a bit gross, to judge from a remark in a letter to his wife on a later occasion.[34]

Despite his busy social rounds, Cable was able to make real progress on the new novel while in New York, and to work out an agreement with Gilder. This was doubtless a considerable relief, for things had been going badly for a time in that respect. When Cable had sent his first draft of the new novel to Gilder the previous winter, Gilder's response had been dismaying. "I wish the Fates had not placed me in a position where I must 'judge' my betters. But so it is, and so I suppose it must be," Gilder had written. "Now, about 'Bread.' To me it is the least good work you have ever done. And yet it has in it some of your best work, and it is free from your greatest fault, namely confusion." Declaring that he had no objection whatever to "the inculcation of morality, religion or any kind of spiritual truth," in fiction, Gilder insisted that such material must however be well done, and that in "the present story (if it is a story) your heart has got the better of your head. The story to me fails of its end because the motive is too apparent." He complained that the characters were being run through an almost endless procession of misfortunes so that Cable could preach about them. Citing Hawthorne and Turgenev as examples of writers who had handled didactic material with artistic grace, Gilder assured Cable: "my dear fellow, I care more for your work than for that of any other writer of fiction who has written for the magazine," and expressed his fears that Cable's literary career would be jeopardized unless he could suppress his growing tendency toward sermonizing in fiction.[35]

How much of Gilder's unfavorable response to the new novel

was due to its didactic tendencies, and how much to its inclusion
of what for the editor of the *Century* was surely some very unpleasant and controversial subject matter, is difficult to say. Even
as finally printed in 1884, the novel (by then entitled *Dr. Sevier,*
although at first it had been given the title "Bread") contains
considerable moralizing, but it is not the prison scenes or the
depiction of the yellow fever epidemic that make it what in
retrospect seems a very poor work of fiction. Its faults lie elsewhere.
For now, however, it will suffice to say that Cable was seriously
taken aback by Gilder's reaction. Because his financial well-being
depended so strongly on his writing, he was disposed to accept
Gilder's criticism for the best, and was soon at work on a revision.
Meanwhile Roswell Smith, who as president of the Century
Company ordinarily gave Gilder a free hand with the editorial
problems, stepped in to interpret Gilder's criticism so as to give
Cable encouragement. A strong believer in idealistic reform himself, Smith did not attempt to steer Cable away from social
betterment.[36] Thus when Gilder received Cable's revision, he wired
Cable, "Richard's himself again," and followed with a letter in
which he said that "if you keep on at that rate you will have
a fortunate journey and a capital book. Such fine artistic work
warms the cockles of an Editor's heart."[37] No doubt, too, Gilder's
eagerness and enthusiasm were not entirely unconnected with
Cable's letters to him and to Robert Underwood Johnson to the
effect that he was considering another publisher, and that Albion
Tourgée had offered to pay $7,500 for a serial novel for his new
weekly, *Our Continent.*[38] In any event, matters were smoothed over,
and Cable proceeded with his work.

Returning home in early November, Cable remained in New
Orleans until the end of February, 1883, writing on his novel and
preparing his Johns Hopkins lectures. These, on the general topic
of "The Relations of Literature to Modern Society," began on
March 5. The first, entitled "The Necessities from Which Literature Springs," was given to a crowded house in Hopkins Hall.
Cable reported to his wife that "I never did quite so poorly,"
though apparently he held the attention of the audience throughout.[39] The second, on the influence of literature on daily life,
pleased him much more; it was "an emphatic success," he wrote
home. "People turned away. Audience interested, attentive, sym-

pathetic. The lecturer the only idiot in the house. Both the public generally & the higher students—the young doctors of this & that & 'tother expressing their pleasure on every hand." [40] The other lectures proceeded on schedule, the only untoward development coming during the sixth lecture when a lady fainted in the audience. So well did Cable do that President Gilman invited him to stay over for a public reading of his work. If the lectures were a distinct success, the reading was apparently a triumph. Before a packed lecture hall, with men and women standing in the wings, Cable kept the house "in almost incessant laughter" as he read his Creole sketches. When he was done, the demand for more was so insistent that at Gilman's behest he read a selection from *The Grandissimes.* Afterwards he dined upon "the famous Baltimore dish—terrapin" at the home of Severn Teackle Wallis. "Woke this morning with a faint impression that one of the terrapins had died during the night," he reported.[41]

He had thus proved, to his own satisfaction and that of a discriminating audience, that he could not only lecture successfully, but provide an evening's entertainment of readings from his own work that would amuse and delight, and he was greatly reassured. The local press had been highly laudatory, the Baltimore *Sun* declaring that his lectures were equal in caliber to those delivered earlier by James Russell Lowell and Sidney Lanier. "Since the days when Charles Dickens read his own droll stories," the Baltimore *American* said of his reading, "it is doubtful whether any novelist has appeared before an American audience so well prepared to interpret his own writings as Mr. Cable." [42]

Cable now proceeded northward, arriving in Hartford, Connecticut, for his reading at Unity Hall. On April 3 he had an engaging visit with "dear old Mark Twain," in which he saw his friend at his explosive best. His reading was held the next evening. On the stage were Osgood, Gilder, and Charles Dudley Warner; Roswell Smith and Colonel Waring were in the audience, and Clemens presided. Apparently the reading was not completely successful, in that even though Cable held the attention of the audience, his voice, which was cultivated and precise, did not project clearly throughout the large auditorium. Cable sensed that Clemens recognized this, and was "not satisfied." Since it was Clemens who had first broached the idea of Cable's entering the public reading business, this was discouraging. Cable also felt at first that the "huge horse fun" of Twain's grandiloquent introduction had been in part responsible for his partial failure. He changed his mind by the next day, however, and asked his friend to introduce him again for a reading before the Saturday-Morning Club. This time, before the much smaller audience at the residence of Mr. Charles Perkins, the reading was a distinct success—"the greatest success I have ever made in my life," Cable wrote to his wife; "The whole company was completely enraptured." Twain told him afterward, Cable reported, that he had done better before the club than had Bayard Taylor, Howells, Henry James, and Bret Harte: " . . . never before had he seen them so worked upon & drawn out.—'Why they *forgot* themselves, that's what they did!'" Gilder, who was also present, was equally enthusiastic; Cable must give a New York City reading, he declared. Afterward there was a dinner in Cable's honor at the Hartford Club, "the maddest, merriest three hours—the wittiest uproar that *ever* I heard in my life." The lecture netted Cable $125. "Light is breaking, sweetheart," he told Louise.[43]

Riding the train up to Newport, Rhode Island, to spend the weekend with Colonel Waring, Cable felt exhilarated both with the prospects for the future and with his welcome in New England. "Winter is in its dying throes," he wrote to his mother from his seat on the train. "The patches of snow are thin & small & the land soaked by the falling rain has withal a look of spring promise. As I write this the valley opens far ahead & the river spreads & stretches southward for miles between [sic] its huge dark leafless hills. My visit to Hartford has been full of pleasure & of profit. A new future appears to be opening before me. To *us* the brown winter of the past seems just ready to give birth to a green & roseate spring, and if it be so I rejoice that you have been spared to see it." [44] While there is no way of knowing, it seems possible that it was at this time that Cable may have first considered seriously the idea of moving from New Orleans to New England. A week earlier he had met Mrs. Francis Bacon, of New Haven, wife of a distinguished surgeon and active in hospital and charity work and reform, who had begged him, after hearing him talk about prison reform work in Louisiana, "O, Mr. Cable, come to Connecticut & teach us how to reform!" Cable thought enough of the remark to have reported it to his wife exactly.[45] Surely the life of a man of letters in the Northeast, close to the publishing centers of New York and Boston where he was so recognized and honored and where people seemed so eager to pay to have him read aloud from his work, must have seemed tempting.

If Cable was to take advantage of the possibilities of platform lecturing and reading, however, it would be necessary to improve his delivery so that he could project his voice as effectively in large halls as he was obviously able to do before small groups. He therefore undertook a course of voice training in New York under Franklin Sargent. A matinee reading at the Madison Square Theatre was attended by his friends at the Century Company, who reported that in his effort to be heard his voice lost much of its richness of tone and variety of inflection. Newspaper reviews echoed their verdict. So he bent every effort to improve his delivery, and lost no opportunity to test himself before other audiences.[46]

Before leaving for New Orleans, Cable had a profitable meeting with the banker and reformer Morris K. Jesup, whose sumptuous mansion he found quite dazzling. He also attended a meeting of the Authors Club with Gilder, where he met various literary notables, including Henry James, then on an extended visit to America from England. James interested Cable. "I wish I could see more of Henry James Jr.," he remarked to Gilder the next day. "Well, you never will," Gilder replied. "Nobody ever does. My wife has known him 20 years & knows him no better today than you do." Cable reported the remark to his wife; "this disappoints me much," he added.[47] On April 16 he met James again, this time at a conference of authors on the copyright problem. "Henry James very odd," Cable wrote to his wife. "Stammers, hesitates, but never misses his grammar & never says anything foolish—from a worldly point of view. His manners are very refined, gentle, reserved, cautious, negative." Cable recognized an essential polarity in outlook and attitude between James and himself, for all his personal fascination with James. "James & I took opposite grounds in the [copyright] debate; I think we could hardly ever fail to do that. But he seemed sincere & to believe me so."[48] Many years in the future they would meet again, in England, and would become strong friends.

He returned home in late April, 1883, resumed his writing of the novel, and prepared his address on the "Due Restraints and Liberties of Literature" for the Louisiana University commencement. In September he went to Louisville to deliver his address on the convict lease system. After touring the Louisville Exposition with James B. Guthrie, he left for Chicago and then for New York again. He intended to stay only for a few weeks this time, but the visit was extended until mid-December. If at the time Cable was already considering a move to the Northeast, he had apparently not decided in favor of doing so, for in his letters to his wife he discussed plans for remodeling his house and wrote of his intention to purchase some bamboo shades. Meanwhile he settled in for more voice training work with Sargent; on several occasions he went to the Madison Square Theatre and, with Sargent seated in the rear of the empty hall, "I blaze away," he reported to his wife, "at the empty seats. . . ." [49] He also worked away at his writing, completing *Dr. Sevier* and beginning some Acadian sketches. The Century Company accepted his convict lease speech for publication; apparently Gilder was not especially eager to publish it, doubtless because of its unpleasant subject matter, but Roswell Smith intervened. Scribner's agreed to bring out new editions of all his work; for that of *The Grandissimes* Cable removed some of the dialect. Again he was caught up in New York literary and cultural life. At Gilder's home he met Andrew Carnegie and Matthew Arnold. "Mr. Arnold is tall, commanding, kindly, intellectual in expression, with great breadth of forehead," he reported to his wife. "There is a certain brokenness of surface in his white brows that give them a look of tremendous thinking power and immense strength of conviction. You would say a bull, butting it, would crack his own skull." [50] He also met the musicologist H. E. Krehbiel, music reviewer for the New York *Tribune*. A friend of Lafcadio Hearn's from their Cincinnati days, Krehbiel had long been interested in Cable's work with Louisiana folksongs. Apparently rumors soon reached Hearn that Cable was collaborating with Krehbiel on a volume of such songs, for Hearn, morbidly jealous, began filling his letters to Krehbiel with warnings against Cable and with exaggerated abuse.[51]

On a previous visit to New York Cable had met the actor Joseph Jefferson and had been agreeably surprised by Jefferson's gentility and goodness. By virtue of his Presbyterian upbringing, Cable had always considered the theater a sinful activity, and had supposed that all actors and actresses were immoral. There had been an active professional theater in New Orleans, of course, for many decades—Jefferson had played there on several occasions—but Cable would never have thought of attending it. His mother was strenuously opposed to the theater, and so were his wife's parents. But Cable's experiences in the literary and social life of New York City were making inroads on his narrow Calvinist views—though not so deeply as to prevent Mark Twain the next year from railing to his wife and to others about Cable's religiosity. In any event, the theater was forcing its attention upon him. No sooner had he arrived in New York than he had been approached about writing a play for the Madison Square Theater; apparently his wife remonstrated when he wrote her about it, because he hastily assured her that he would write no play without discussing it further with her.[52] Walking along Broadway one day, however, he again encountered Jefferson, who was then appearing in *The Cricket on the Hearth.* The actor was delighted to see him, and reported he had been reading the stories of *Old Creole Days* with great pleasure.[53] A friendship swiftly developed.

Cable soon found that all his preconceptions about actors and the theater were being endangered. On October 21 he wrote his wife saying he wished "mother would get into shape anything she can bring forward as an argument against the theater";[54] apparently he felt he was in peril of succumbing to its lures. His resistance did not last for long; his friend Roswell Smith persuaded him to attend a play, and then Cable went all the way—he attended a performance by Jefferson. Anticipating the objections that would be forthcoming from New Orleans, he explained his decision at some length. He had consulted with ministers about the theater, had met and talked with theater people. "When mother says the theater is bad," he declared, "I must admit it generally is. When she says it is wrong—that is, cannot be right—I doubt her ability to show it." He had been invited to go and see Jefferson in the company with "a pious man," who had originally studied for the ministry, "full of noble motives, a man of family & the author of a play, soon to appear on the boards, the intention of which is to impress upon the hearer's mind the loveliness & sanctity of home." So he had gone to see *The Cricket on the Hearth.* "And if there is anything worse in that—no, I'll not put it that way—If it isn't as pure & sweet & refreshing & proper a diversion as spending the same length of time over a pretty, sweet, good story-book, then I'm a dunce." He closed by declaring: "I feel this morning as if I had had a bath in pure, cool water. I am fitted anew for working & loving & doing good. I thank God for the pleasure I have had—let me see if I cannot make some feeble return for it before this rising sun goes down." [55] Thus did a New Orleans Presbyterian and mission school superintendent justify his first foray into the world of footlights and painted faces.

Louise Bartlett Cable was worried not only about her husband's theatergoing, but about finances. Cable was in the habit of sending checks to her for the payment of bills, and apparently this proved a laborious burden. At one point Cable wrote, "My darling you must not complain that I manage all money matters through you. You can do that much for me & I am *too busy* to divide the matters here. Give M[ary] L[ouise] what she has to have, & keep me posted & to how you stand [sic]. No details —only how much you will have to have & don't let me allow you to run short & get embarrassed. Soon, soon, I trust, we shall see a more open path, an easier road. It seems to be very near. I hope to make $1000 at reading before I get home." [56]

The income Cable anticipated was to be the result of a series of readings he was arranging to give before starting back to New Orleans. His friends were active in his behalf. Confident that the vocal training he had received would enable him to read from his work effectively before large houses, he prepared to make appearances up and down the East Coast. Finally, on November 19, he set forth. After a visit with Mark Twain in Hartford, he gave his first reading to an audience of 120 persons in Springfield. It was, he reported, "a great success." [57] After being entertained by Samuel Bowles, editor of the Springfield *Republican,* he continued on to Boston. There, for two weeks during which he gave three readings, he met the literary luminaries of that city. Francis Parkman, Thomas Wentworth Higginson, Charles Francis Adams, Jr., Philips Brooks, Oliver Wendell Holmes, Edward Everett Hale, Thomas Bailey Aldrich—all came to meet him. Especially notable was a visit paid to him by the aged John Greenleaf Whittier. "He talks the tender old Quaker talk," Cable wrote to his wife. "Said—'I've read all thy writings. I've read every line thee ever wrote, and I knew thee would be a great writer as soon as I saw thy first productions.' No wonder I thought he was a sweet old man."[58] The actor Edwin Booth came to hear him; Matthew Arnold was also in the city, and they renewed their acquaintance. William Dean Howells gave a reception for him.

There was no question that Cable's readings were successful. The newspapers vied in praising him. The *Evening Transcript* was most laudatory of all: "It is absolutely exquisite. . . . We cannot say it equalled or surpassed something else, because we have never had anything at all like it, and in itself it was simply fascinating. If we insisted on a comparison, indeed, we should be obliged to go back to the actors of the Shakespearian era. . . ." He was, the *Transcript* said, "the most unique case of indigenous literary genius America has yet produced," and his only peer—not his superior—was Hawthorne himself.[59]

The Boston *Herald* published an extensive interview in which it described Whittier's visit with Cable in detail. "It was the singer of New England, whose verse is as representative of our men and women as our rockbound coast is of the country it protects, welcoming his younger brother from the low shores of the Mexican gulf to the good will of the eastern states folk," the reporter claimed. "It was one of the fathers of our literature hailing one of her youngest sons":

> "I am glad to see thee, friend," Mr. Whittier had said, as he strode into the room and stretched out his hand. "I have read all thy stories, and I like them very much. Thee hast found an untrodden field of romance in New Orleans, and I think thee the writer whom we have so long waited to see come up in the South. I did not expect to find so young a man as thee. But why did we not hear of thee before?"
>
> "Circumstances were against me," responded Mr. Cable. "I had to go out into the world at a very early age. I had a widowed mother and sisters to support, and a boy can hardly maintain a family with his pen. But I have at last

Launched Into a Literary Life

> and am trying to do what I can in pursuance of my favorite plans."

"Thee hast done a great deal in a short time, then. If thee can do as well in the future as thee hast done in the past, thee should be satisfied. The publishers will be always after thee now, and urge thee to write continually."

"They have already tried to force me," said Mr. Cable, "but I refuse to listen to their demands. I do not believe in forcing the growth of the young tree." [60]

Cable also had words to say about the South:

"I have been treated very handsomely here in the North. Do you know, though, that I heartily dislike those sectional terms 'North and South?' I am tired of hearing people talk about the 'southern mind,' the southern this, that and the other. I have wiped the word 'South' out of my vocabulary, and have publicly exhorted people to do the same. Our boundaries are state boundaries, not sectional. I like the grand and comprehensive term 'our country.' " . . .[61]

Before Cable left Boston, he had been engaged for two return readings. He read there and then in Baltimore, New Haven, Cambridge, Springfield, and Brooklyn, before leaving for home. Everywhere he met with stunning success. "O no," he wrote to Louise. "We don't like attention, do we? It makes us pout, eh? We're not vain, and so it displeases us. And when we're waltzed out to the long supper table at the head of the column & when men stand around in groups and stretch their ears to hear what we say, of course it's very unpleasant, and all that sort o' thing." Help me, he urged her, to remember that however pleasing such public attention was, "it's not the *main thing.*" His forthcoming prison reform article was what mattered much more to him, he insisted.[62]

He reached home four days before Christmas; it would be the last Christmas the Cable family would spend in the city whose life and customs he had already made world-famous. His new novel was finished, as was his Creole history. Money was still scarce, but lecture plans were promising; he had engaged Major James B. Pond, who was impresario to Mark Twain and other celebrities, to manage his readings, which would begin the next month. He was indisputably the South's leading man of letters, and save for the hostility of the Creoles and certain others, he had been praised throughout the region. Yet he must have known that in the months ahead, he would be saying things in print that would challenge many of his native region's most zealously guarded beliefs, and it remained to be seen whether his immunity from attack would continue. The December *Century* had contained the second installment of *Dr. Sevier,* and there were remarks in the forthcoming installments, for example, on the commencement of the War Between the States, that went much further than ever a Southern writer had gone before. The prison reform speech would be published in February. What would the reaction be when all this material appeared?

IX

Dr. Sevier

Dr. Sevier was the first product of George W. Cable's days as a professional novelist, dependent upon literary endeavor as his principal means of earning a livelihood. He had written *Old Creole Days* and *The Grandissimes* while still employed at the Cotton Exchange. It was in order to gain the leisure to concentrate fully on his fiction that he had broken loose from his clerical duties. But, as we have seen, he immediately became involved in prison and hospital reform and then in public reading and lecturing. The latter he did in large part because of the urgent need of income, which the writing of fiction could not fill. Yet it will not do to ascribe Cable's inability to concentrate his full-time efforts on his fiction entirely to financial needs alone. When the counting-house occupied much of his time, he had yearned for freedom from his duties. But when the day came that he could resign his job, he became immediately caught up in reform work. Then the public reading platform beckoned. As we shall see, no sooner did he move northward and finish his lecture tour with Mark Twain than he became involved in the Home Culture Clubs, an activity that lasted throughout the rest of his long life. His growing interest in civil rights consumed much of his time and energy from the mid-1880's through half of the next decade, and when that subsided he continued with charitable and religious activities.

It is clear that the writing of fiction, by itself and for its own sake, was not for Cable an enterprise sufficient to occupy his full energies. He was not by nature a recluse; he did not thrive upon seclusion. Like many writers before and since, he needed to be "doing something" as well as writing, if he was to write at all.

When *Dr. Sevier* was published, it was widely reviewed and highly praised. Even before it had finished its serialization in the *Century,* Lafcadio Hearn had previewed it for the *Times-Democrat,* saying that no other novel in America or in England could compare with it, that it combined realism and idealism, and that its nearest comparisons were the novels of Alphonse Daudet and the Goncourts.[1] The response of the national media was almost as gratifying. The New York *Times* thought Cable showed more inborn talent than any other American writer of romance; the Chicago *Dial* declared he was doing "perhaps the most valuable literary work done in this country at the present day."[2] "There can be but one opinion of 'Dr. Sevier,'" the *Critic* wrote: "it is a beautiful story, told with an exquisite art of which the greatest charm is the simplicity."[3] Elsewhere the praise was high. There were, however, reservations. Several reviewers objected to the plot, others to the realism of setting and description: "Mr. Cable can devote ten pages to an unsuccessful hunt for lodgings, and a whole paragraph to a gesture," the *Nation* complained.[4] Other reviewers again found the novel too didactic. The *Atlantic*'s critic said that though Cable's interest in delineation of character had already been demonstrated in his short fiction, in the new novel, "he discloses the fact that over and above all this he is absorbed in the contemplation of the struggle which is going on in the world. In this he shows his kinship with the great moralists." But, the review continued, he had failed to harmonize his fictional artistry and his ethical concerns, and the novel suffered from the conflict between them.[5]

Dr. Sevier is Cable's first fiction not importantly grounded in the familiar trappings of local color, as Arlin Turner points out. There are several quaint New Orleans characters, to be sure—in particular a Creole, Narcisse, clerk to the middle-aged Anglo-American physician Dr. Sevier—as well as a quadroon landlady, an Italian, Rafael Ristofalo, an Irishwoman, Kate Riley, a German, the baker Reisen, and a Mississippi backwoodsman who guides Mary Richling through the Confederate lines from the North late in the novel. Each of these comes equipped with a distinctive way of speaking the English language, and for readers who enjoyed Cable's skill at dialect, there was considerable variety. Yet they are all minor characters, and the book's principal characters are

Americans who exhibit no regional quaintness and no picturesque qualities to speak of. The scene is set in antebellum and wartime New Orleans for the most part, and Cable is concerned with business life, yellow fever, the condition of prisons and hospitals, the wartime South, and with problems of poverty and wealth. Cable based his novel on a story told him by Dr. Warren Brickell, his family's physician, and he changed the name of his young couple, the Richlings, from that of Ritchie, when Brickell suggested that the real Mrs. Ritchie might still be alive. Dr. Sevier was Brickell in many of his mannerisms and attitudes.[6] In making John Richling, for a time at least, a bookkeeper, Cable was drawing on his own experience; and much of what occurs in the novel is set in places familiar to Cable—New Orleans and its environs, and the terrain of his wartime cavalry service in north Mississippi.

There are other interesting associations with the events of Cable's own life and that of his family. Certainly the main theme of *Dr. Sevier*—poverty and its consequences in a city devoted to trade—is one that was hardly foreign to his own early years. When the Richlings come to New Orleans to start anew, they are in the same situation as Cable's own parents had once found themselves. And when Mary Richling is sent home with her child to stay with her parents while John Richling seeks to establish himself, she is doing what Rebecca Boardman Cable had several times been forced to do while her husband remained behind in New Orleans. In making young Richling, by marrying his Northern-born wife, defy his wealthy planter-father and refuse to concede to "simple sectional prejudice" even when it made him an outcast and forced him to leave home penniless, Cable was dealing with a situation not unlike what was already incipiently his own relationship to his community.

Dr. Sevier's first sentence announces its chief concern: "The main road to wealth in New Orleans has long been Carondelet Street." It is on this street that Dr. Sevier lives, and on its sidewalks that the city's commercial life flourishes, where "congregated the men who, of all in New Orleans, could best afford to pay for being sick, and least desired to die." Dr. Sevier is wealthy, but not because he has worshipped money; he is generous with his time, and "laid his left hand on the rich and his right on the poor;

and he was not left-handed." But because he has never himself been poor, he tends to consider poverty, other than of the temporary sort, the result not of misfortune but* of laziness. "If he wants work he will find it," he says of the poor man. "As for begging, it ought to be easier for any true man to starve than to beg." In the course of the story, through what happens to young John and Mary Richling, Dr. Sevier learns otherwise. He learns how "to feel tenderly for the unworthy, to deal kindly with the erring . . . a double grace that hangs not always in easy reach even of the tallest." Or so he is supposed to have learned; but just exactly what the misfortunes of the Richlings mean, either for Dr. Sevier or for the reader, is never really made clear.

The Richlings have come to New Orleans to make their fortune; we learn, after numerous melodramatic hints, that John is the son of a wealthy Kentucky planter and had been raised in luxury, had traveled abroad, and been taught to do everything except make a living. When he fell in love with Mary, a Milwaukee girl of refined but impoverished origins, his father had disinherited him.

We first encounter Richling when he comes to Dr. Sevier and asks him to visit his wife, who is ill. Richling is proud, and the doctor gruff, but a friendship is begun which continues throughout the novel. Richling goes out to seek work, but is unsuccessful; the couple move to cheaper housing, economize as best they can, but their fortunes still decline. Richling temporarily secures work as a clerk, but is not reemployed; his basic disinterest in making money and in trade communicates itself to his employers, who do not therefore continue him in his job. Then Mary Richling turns up in a charity hospital as Dr. Sevier is touring the ward; he had lost contact with the young couple. He sees to her recovery, and asks her to send her husband to see him at once, with the intention of helping him. But the doctor falls sick himself, and while ill he loses touch with the Richlings, believing they have gone home to Milwaukee.

It is not until Mary Richling comes to his office with word that her husband is now ill in the charity hospital that Dr. Sevier regains touch with the couple. This time he insists that Richling accept the loan of a sum of money, to be used until he can take care of himself. The young man reluctantly does so, and for a while he is hopeful, but the money goes with no upturn in his fortunes, and when he steels himself to go to the doctor for more help, the doctor is not at home. Weak and feverish, he falls asleep on the street, is arrested by a policeman who beats him savagely about the head when he attempts to resist, and is thrown into jail. He is sentenced to thirty days in prison, beaten by a trusty when he refuses to wash the cell, and in this condition is found by an Italian friend, Rafael Ristofalo, who is also in jail. Ristofalo, who knows how to manage such things, gets word to Mary Richling, who goes to Dr. Sevier. They secure Richling's release, and nurse him back to health. At this point Dr. Sevier persuades Richling to send Mary, who is expecting a child, back to Milwaukee until things are better for him, and Mary reluctantly departs.

Now Richling's material fortunes begin to improve. He secures a job with a German baker, Reisen, and becomes so valuable that when Reisen falls ill and dies he is entrusted with the business, which prospers exceedingly. Finally, he can send for Mary. Unfortunately, the war has begun, and Mary, with their newly born child, Alice, finds it difficult to come South. She goes to New York, hoping to take a ship, but none is available; while there she meets the widow of the German baker, who is bound for Hamburg. Mrs. Reisen has closed out the business and left Richling 100 barrels of flour, which are so valuable that he is secure from want. Mary returns to the Midwest and attempts to make her way through the lines; it is an involved, perilous business, and she is a long time getting through. Eventually she manages to reach a point opposite the lake from New Orleans, which is in Union hands, and she waits for a schooner that will take her across to the city. But Richling, who has never completely recovered from his ordeal in prison, has been growing ever weaker, and is now failing fast, despite Dr. Sevier's every attention. Finally, Mary and the child make their way to the city, but within a day of their arrival, Richling dies.

In the last chapter of the novel we find Mary and her child, some years later, living contentedly and spending much time with Dr. Sevier, who worships them both. Why doesn't he marry her? someone asks. "—'they love each other; they suit each other; they complete each other; they don't feel their disparity of years; they're both so linked to Alice that it would break either heart over again to be separated from her. I don't see why'—" But his wife shakes her head: " 'It will never be.' " And the novel ends.

Originally Cable had concluded his novel with the marriage of Mary and Dr. Sevier, but Richard Watson Gilder had objected strenuously. "Why on earth," he demanded, "should that woman keep away from her husband during the year of his prosperity, and then—worse than all—why spoil everything by making an infidel of her—an infidel to the true love of her life? Her marrying the Dr. seems to me under all the circumstance, a most wanton and cruel infliction upon the sympathies of the reader."[7] Cable changed this, but even so it was a poor novel that he had written, and there seems little doubt that Gilder was right all along when he objected to it. His first reaction, that the characters were being dragged through a seemingly endless succession of misfortunes in order to enable Cable to sermonize, was generally true. The Richlings are subjected to one disaster after the other, and yet there is no buildup, no progressive enlargement or depth resulting from the experience, that would have given the novel a development, either of theme or of characterization. What development there is is entirely one of narrative chronology; Richling eventually suffers a sufficient number of disasters to cause him to die, whereupon he does so. Mary's lengthy adventures in getting back south through the lines have absolutely nothing to do with the meaning of the story; they are there only for purposes of narrative melodrama.

It is not enough to say, however, as Gilder did, that the novel fails because it is designed to enable Cable to preach, that it "fails of its end because the motive is too apparent." The difficulty is rather that the novel is not didactic enough, in that it is not at all clear what Cable's purpose was, or what the story is supposed to mean. Was it designed to be a treatise on poverty and the need for charity, as its first title, "Bread," and Cable's remarks about poverty in the first chapter indicate? If so, then the moral would seem to be nothing more than that the Richlings would not have suffered all they did if Dr. Sevier had been sufficiently generous and concerned to have forced them to accept his aid from the start, and had seen to it that the young man got a decent job. But the novel is *not* mainly about that; it is not primarily about what Dr. Sevier thinks or does at all. There is no extensive psychological portrayal of Dr. Sevier as he watches the Richlings suffer from poverty, until he learns what he should have done. The doctor remains a secondary character throughout. If he sins, it is through omission rather than commission, and this is not enough to focus our primary attention on him and on his role.

The chief dramatic emphasis is rather on the fortunes of the Richlings. Though Cable attempts to show that Richling is wrong in being too proud to ask for Dr. Sevier's help, Richling's main problem is not one involving his relationship with the doctor. Rather, it has to do with his relationship to the society in which he finds himself. He cannot get work. He cannot enter into the spirit of moneymaking and of getting ahead which seems necessary for success, and so he fails and eventually dies. But why? The reason is obscure. Richling does not scorn trade. Eventually, when he gets his chance with the baker Reisen, he does extremely well at it. He is not a lonely poet, for example, his every thought focused on Beauty, seeking in vain to discover a way to make ends meet while pursuing the Muse. Rather, he merely fails to fit in and to prosper, presumably because of his personality. Again, it is difficult to understand just why this should be so. Cable tells us that Richling cannot get and keep a job; he shows him failing to do so; but he presents no convincing reason for Richling's failure except that of continuing bad luck. This reason may do for an episode or two, but when Richling's failure to get employment continues for chapter after chapter, we become reluctant to ascribe the reason to bad luck alone. Yet nothing is suggested in its stead. It seems that Richling is virtuous and the world sinful, so he must inevitably be rejected, though precisely in what manner the world sins against Richling is left unexplored. The result is a failure of structure that ruins the novel, for since what happens to the chief character is not explained, the novel cannot very well make much sense either.

It is not until almost the very end of the novel that we find a real clue to the explanation for what it is that sets Richling apart from his society, and then only by inference. On his death-bed, Richling is talking to his friend Dr. Sevier, and he finally tells the doctor something about his past. "You know I'm a native of Kentucky," he says. "My name is not Richling. I belong to one of the proudest, most distinguished families in that state or in all the land. Until I married I never knew an ungratified wish. I think my bringing-up, not to be wicked, was as bad as could be. It was based upon the idea that I was always to be master, and never servant. I was to go through life with soft hands. I was educated to know, but not to do." When he met Mary, and proposed to marry her, his family disinherited him, for no reason except "simple sectional prejudice."

This explanation in itself is obviously not what is wrong with Richling, because the fact is that he has in the course of the novel shown no reluctance to work hard if given the opportunity, and no assumption that it was his lot to be master rather than servant. It is not Richling's aristocratic Kentucky origins as such that account for his difficulties. We have rather to ask ourselves what lies behind that past that might conceivably account for such a schism. The answer is, though as a theme it plays no part in the novel at all, *Negro slavery.* In other words, not only does Richling espouse a Northern girl; at one point we are told that when the war came, he wanted the North to win. The issue that separated North and South was Negro slavery. The *only* issue that could really account for Richling's suffering what he does, and being so cut off from his society, is the Negro issue. *But the novel says nothing whatever about the Negro issue.*

What I am getting at is that what Cable did was, through imaginative extension, to give his protagonist the net results of *his own* incipient estrangement from Southern society, without at the same time going into the causes of that estrangement. It was the Negro issue, and nothing else, that was steadily isolating Cable from Southern society, and that in his own life constituted a very clear, credible reason for and explanation of that isolation. Cable put John Richling in something of the same position as his own *vis-à-vis* New Orleans, but said nothing whatever about the Negro. Instead, he attempted to make it into a matter involving a general other-worldliness, a lack of aptitude for practicality and success, and the result is unconvincing. Had he portrayed Richling as an opponent of slavery, critical of the injustice of the South's attitude to the Negro and its treatment of Negroes, then Richling's break with his father, his failure to get anywhere in New Orleans, his endless misfortunes would all have been quite believable.

Save for a quadroon landlady, there are no Negroes in *Dr. Sevier.*

That fact of itself is very odd. A contemporary Southern critic, W. M. Baskervill, who as we shall see came to disapprove of Cable's treatment of the Negro question and the South in his fiction, made this point in 1897:

> The artist cannot be a suppresser of truth, or an ignorer of facts, and the omission of the negro, so curious and marked that it must have been of deliberate purpose, leaves a noticeable blank in the picture. Was it due to a slavery too dark and oppressive to be painted, or to the fear of portraying the gentler aspects and kindlier relations of master and slave in a way which would seem to soften and condone, that kept this picturesque element out of the story and prevented the author from giving the entire household of Dr. Sevier?

And Baskervill came even closer to recognizing what I think is the hidden problem of the novel:

> But the chief defect of the book is the author's treatment of the hero. His trials and his difficulties are real, true to life, though an insufficient reason is assigned for them; for they were in a large measure the author's own experience.[8]

What Baskervill is alleging is that Cable wrote the book in order to criticize antebellum Southern society, and that he omitted mention of slaves because the necessarily benevolent master-slave relationship in such a household as Dr. Sevier's would have spoiled his polemic. This is hardly likely, for Cable had shown no such inhibition in *The Grandissimes*. Yet Baskervill grasped what it was that lay behind Richling's troubles: "It is easy to see that the poor fellow has no chance, that the author intends first to make him a failure, and then to kill him," he claims. "Why these useless efforts, this hopeless suffering? Was it merely that at the close of the story [the deathbed speech to Dr. Sevier about his Kentucky origins] might be put into the mouth of the dying man?"[9] Here again the explanation is oversimplified, for Cable cared much more for his narrative than that. Baskervill perceived, however, that it was Cable's attitude toward the South and the Negro question that accounted for Richling's failure.

The true explanation of Cable's omission of the Negro issue is rather the other way around, though Baskervill, being by that time strongly opposed to Cable's racial views, could not have realized it. Part of the matter would appear to be that Cable must deliberately have omitted the race issue from *Dr. Sevier* in deference to Southern opinion and from a reluctance, when he was writing it in 1882 and 1883, to jeopardize his position in New Orleans by including a direct condemnation of racism. He was as yet unprepared to make the ultimate, irreconcilable break with his community that a sympathetic portrayal of an antislavery adherent's losing struggle with antebellum New Orleans would necessarily have brought on. So what he did was to omit all mention of the Negro, while yet attempting to present Richling's misfortunes as an indictment of the South—as if it were not the Negro issue, but Southern materialism and lack of generosity toward the white poor that was at fault.

It is probably unfair to Cable, however, to suggest that an unwillingness to offend Southern racial views was his sole reason for not portraying Richling as an antislavery man. Cable had lived in antebellum and wartime New Orleans, and he had a strong historical sense. Doubtless he knew all too well that had a man such as Richling expressed antislavery views in the New Orleans of the late 1850's and early 1860's, he would have been ridden out of town on a rail without further ado, and the story as Cable conceived it would have ended then and there.

Of course, Cable could have made John Richling a Southern Abolitionist and had him flee from New Orleans, and subsequently continue his adventures from there. But this would have made it impossible for Cable to have done what obviously he very much wanted to do in the novel, which was to present a picture of New Orleans during the years when war was declared and the city was captured and occupied. The chapters chronicling these events are among the best in the novel, and are obviously drawn directly from Cable's own experience. The description he gives of the scene along the levee as the Federal fleet comes into view closely parallels a similar scene, quoted in part earlier in this book, from the nonfiction article, "New Orleans Before the Capture," published in the *Century* a year after the publication of *Dr. Sevier*.[10] It would have been difficult to use all that material in the novel had John Richling not been there and able to observe it himself—and manifestly Richling would not have been there had he ever dared to express strong antislavery views in New Orleans in the immediate prewar years.

Cable's conception of his novel was so bound in with his memories of the wartime experience that it is improbable that he ever considered making Richling an Abolitionist and having him flee from New Orleans. It must also be remembered that, as Baskervill realized, much of Richling's experience was undoubtedly Cable's—Cable's experience, both immediately before and in the years after the war, that is, in search of a job. The autobiographical linkup is there; and the young George Cable of the immediate prewar and the wartime years was not at all an Abolitionist. To have portrayed Richling as holding and expressing antislavery views, therefore, would have been false to his own experience.

Yet—to continue this speculation on what the novel might have been—if it was somehow necessary that the personality of Richling not violate Cable's view of his own personal identity, there might seem to have been another alternative open to him. Why could he not have portrayed Richling as being in much the same circumstance that Cable himself had been during recent years, and indeed was in at the time of writing, by showing him holding racial attitudes at strong variance with those of the New Orleans community, yet forced to suppress them? Surely this *was* the situation he was in, with reference to the very novel itself. Would not this have given much more substance and motive to Richling's misfortunes? Richling could have remained in New Orleans feeling that the community's political and social attitudes were mistaken, tried to keep his opinions to himself, and found himself unable to get ahead in trade because of his inability to tolerate the racism of his employers. Cable had been in precisely that relationship with his old employee William C. Black, in Reconstruction New Orleans—but in pre-1865 New Orleans he would not have been able merely to go out for a walk when the argument grew too intense, as he had been accustomed to do; he would have had to be careful to keep his thoughts to himself. Could not John Richling have been put in that position?

Here we get close, I believe, to the heart of the matter. For Cable to have developed his characterization of Richling in this fashion, it would have been necessary for him to have examined and understood his own personality in a way that there is no evidence he was ever capable of doing. He would have had to perceive the

logic, the motives, the conflicting drives and attitudes of a man
in such a situation of enforced repression—a situation very much
like his own during the years when he was writing his novel. But
the necessary introspective self-examination that would have been
involved in the working out of such a characterization was beyond
his capacities. He did not view himself in such a light; he did
not recognize the contradictions within his own personality—the
desire for social approval in New Orleans as contrasted with the
desire to protest the injustice being done to the Negro; the desire
for approval by the Genteel Tradition in literature as contrasted
with the desire to deal with the often raw and unpleasant realities
of the life around him; the Calvinist disapproval of Creole sensuality and indolence as contrasted with the sensuous and voluptuous attraction that such attitudes held for him. Much of Cable's
finest writing had come out of just the two-way pull of those
polarities and the resulting dramatic tension it had produced in
his fiction. The polarity, the ambivalence, are abundantly present
in his best fiction; but to judge from his letters and his other
writings, apparently it was only *as fiction*, in the concrete particu-
larity of characters and situations, that he was ever to express
them.

We have already seen an example of this in the characterization
of Joseph Frowenfeld in *The Grandissimes*, where the significance
of Frowenfeld's brilliant social advancement from immigrant to
lover of a Creole heiress, and to friend, even stepson, of Honoré
Grandissime himself, went almost unperceived by Cable, for whom
Joseph was ostensibly virtuous, high-minded, and above any such
considerations. Like John Richling, Frowenfeld represented his
creator, and so in neither instance is there an examination of
motives, attitudes, social and racial ambivalence, and the like. It
is only with characters who are *not* ostensibly like himself that the
attraction of so much of the New Orleans scene for Cable is
allowed to reveal itself. In *The Grandissimes* the fate of the
Grandissime family, in both its white and quadroon branches,
with its attendant stories of Bras Coupé, Palmyre, Clemence, and
the Nancanous, held the center of the stage sufficiently strongly
to prevent the weakness of Frowenfeld's characterization, with its
unexplored areas, from destroying the structure of the novel. But
in *Dr. Sevier,* there is no Grandissime family, no rich social situation

to be developed independently of the autobiographical protagonist; and the author's failure to scrutinize himself, to examine
the complexity of a character representing himself and serving
as his surrogate, becomes a crippling liability. It keeps him from
giving his protagonist sufficient dramatic tension and motivational
conflict, in a story that depends for its success on how imagina-
tively the central character can be made to think and feel.

The absence of race and racial consciousness in John Richling,
therefore, does not simply represent the avoidance by Cable of
a controversial topic; it is a failure in characterization, arising
ultimately out of a failure on the author's part to recognize and
understand—whether consciously or through working it out in
terms of a fictional character—his own complex personality.
Because Cable could not do this he was able, as a novelist, to
create characters of only limited depth and complexity. The result
was that the variety and the profundity of meaning that Cable
could give to his fiction was limited: he could develop the characterization, which is to say the form, of his fiction only so far, and
no further. In dealing with the picturesque folk of *Old Creole Days*
and *The Grandissimes,* that limitation had not been so apparent.
With *Dr. Sevier* it began to reveal itself.

It has been suggested that *Dr. Sevier* was in part a failure because
of the insistence of Cable's editors, in particular Richard Watson
Gilder, that he omit from his story a great deal of unpleasant
material that would otherwise have made the novel into a work
of powerful social protest. Philip Butcher declares that Cable's
"efforts to make the novel a powerful social study were frustrated
because his editors regarded any treatment of an inherently
unpleasant subject as a tract. Had Gilder's squeamishness not
prevented, Cable would have had a villain for his novel:
society." [11] Edmund Wilson is equally censorious of Gilder: "It is
impossible to know what Cable's second novel . . . would have
been like if he had been allowed to publish it as he wrote it,"
he says. "The dreadful conditions in the local prisons were apparently to have played a more important role than they do in
the final version." Wilson, however, does go on to suggest that
Cable too may have been at fault here: "The unsatisfactoriness
of *Dr. Sevier* may be due partly to the soft-pedalling of editors and

partly to the author's desire to show lovable and worthy characters who would appeal to the Victorian appetite for reading about respectable virtue and humble people with hearts of gold." [12]

Now Gilder, as we have seen, was not one to encourage authors to introduce unpleasant subject matter into their fiction. But there is no factual evidence to suggest that in the case of *Dr. Sevier,* Gilder actually made Cable take out any unpleasant material. In fact, the single direct reference made by Gilder to such material in his correspondence with Cable about the novel is to precisely the opposite effect. "I am sure you can make a good book out of most of those characters—though that young couple are, I fear, pretty hopeless," he wrote on February 20, 1882. *"But you can bring in still more about your prison*—and the opening vista of the war is just stunning." [italics mine][13] Thus, instead of wanting less about prison conditions, Gilder was suggesting that Cable add more!

Gilder's strong objection to the novel was not to its social material, but to the way in which Cable sent his protagonist through misfortune after misfortune in order to preach about social conditions. In June of 1883, when Cable was well along in his revision, Gilder wrote him a letter which might be said to sum up his attitude toward the whole matter. "With all its fun and charm," he said, "you must not be disappointed if this story as a whole does not create as pleasant an impression as your others." Note the way he *assumes* that this is what Cable desired. "You have chosen, (for a purpose) the most painful and sordid theme that exists—you have made a careful study of this theme and have interjected into the story a hundred practical and in[?]formatory notions and theories—evolved from your own experience," he continued. "You have garnished this dish—a wholesome dish no doubt—to the best of your extraordinary and unique ability. It may be wholesome—it *is*—but it can never be thoroughly good to the taste. Still it is an interesting and valuable study—at the worst.—But it is your next book that will be in every respect your best." And he goes on with a lengthy lecture on the place of morality in literature.[14]

The notion that Gilder disapproved of Cable's developing attack on Southern racial discrimination because he did not want controversial material to appear in the *Century* must also be severely qualified, at this stage of Cable's career at least. He was, in fact, highly satisfied with "The Freedman's Case in Equity," Cable's first major onslaught against racism. A letter from his assistant, C. C. Buel, written six months after the essay had appeared in the *Century,* informed Cable that although the magazine's usual rate for essays was ordinarily $250, Gilder insisted that the payment for a new Cable essay on the same subject, "The Silent South," be set at $400.[15] And nine days later Buel wrote again to say that Gilder had ordered that another $100 be added to the stipend, so pleased was he with the piece.[16] Thus at this stage of his career, Gilder was actively encouraging Cable to write about civil rights. It was later, in the late 1880's and early 1890's, that Gilder began energetically discouraging Cable's activities on behalf of the Negro.

If Gilder was at fault in his role as Cable's editor for *Dr. Sevier,* it is rather for what he did not do. He must have known how strongly Cable felt about the Negro situation, but he did not apparently object to its being omitted from the novel. It seems he did not connect the lack of motivation for John Richling's quarrel with New Orleans with the omission of the Negro issue. He recognized the lifelessness, the lack of buildup, in the plot of the novel, but he did not, in his letters at least, make any suggestions as to what Cable could do about it. He merely complained about inartistic moralizing, without advancing any hints as to how Cable might make the moralizing artistic. Read Hawthorne, was all he could say. But was there any magazine editor in America, except possibly William Dean Howells, who might have been able to tell him how? And save for Henry James, was there any novelist or critic of the day who could have done so? One cannot imagine Richard Watson Gilder—or for that matter, Robert Underwood Johnson, Henry Mills Alden, Edward Burlingame, J. Henry Harper, the Scribners, Henry Holt, Bliss Perry, or any of the other defenders of ideality who dominated New York publishing in the 1880's and for two decades thereafter—telling George W. Cable that he should introduce any such highly combustible material as an attack on racism into his fiction. Nor can one readily imagine any of them suggesting to Cable that he shore up a sentimental plot and a wooden characterization by providing the kind of psychological subtlety and complexity that Henry James would have produced instinctively.

Cable could indeed edit himself only very imperfectly. He was unable to recognize fully what it was that he was really trying to do, or why he wanted to do it. Faced with dual objectives as novelist and reformer, he had no idea how to bring those two roles into harmony. As a reformer, he moved into the arena of public controversy and took on the entire South in a brave but hopeless battle. As a novelist, he moved toward the Genteel Tradition.

Cable had liked what he found in New York; on each successive trip northward he had stayed longer in the metropolis. His fascination with the literary and cultural limelight, his growing appetite for the role of a leading man of letters of the Genteel Tradition, is a constant refrain in the letters he wrote back home to Louise in New Orleans throughout the early 1880's. Banquets at the Century Club, convivial evenings with Twain and the Warners in Hartford, dinners with Joseph Jefferson, Edmund Clarence Stedman, Brander Matthews, Augustus Saint-Gaudens, lectures and readings throughout the Northeast, praise from Holmes, Howells, Whittier, Horace Scudder—it was a pleasant business indeed.

But with the role and the acclaim, there was an obligation as well. He must *be* a genteel novelist, he must *be* a purveyor of idealism. One could not enjoy the benefits and privileges of the higher literary life of New York during the brownstone era, while at the same time going one's own independent way as an artist. Nor is there any indication that Cable, consciously in any event, was interested in doing so. The truth is that at this juncture in Cable's life it was not at all necessary for Richard Watson Gilder to force him to cut out unpleasant material from his fiction; Cable was quite willing to do so on his own, without being told. To blame the insipidity of *Dr. Sevier* on Gilder is to commit the same kind of error as the late Van Wyck Brooks made in blaming the literary prudishness of Mark Twain on the influence of Livy Clemens and William Dean Howells. Just as Sam Clemens very much *wanted* to be respectable, and so sought out those he thought could excise his barbarities and teach him how to conform, so did Cable want to produce the kind of idealistic, sentimental fiction that Gilder and his confreres admired. What saved him, for a while at least, was his innate taste for the sensuous and the vigorous, and his

Presbyterian moral zeal, which led him to perceive injustice and to desire to right it.

To harmonize those clashing and contradictory impulses would have required a greater artistic talent than his. It would have required, in fact, the skill of Twain, James, or Whitman—none of which he was. Twain was able to avoid the inhibitions of the Genteel Tradition by discovering an area—the past, the Missouri town and the river of his childhood—in which he could fulfill himself, though at the price of omitting from his best fiction one whole dimension of human experience, that of adult sexuality. James was able to do so by going abroad, and through force of intellect and of artistic passion making the very tradition itself into the subject of his fiction: he saw it for what it was, understood his relationship with it, and turned it into art. As for Whitman, his response was simple: he ignored it, deliberately chose unrespectability, remained in Camden, and wrote poems. What was the Century Club as far as he was concerned? Since the price of recognition in his own time came too high, he would wait for posterity.

Had George W. Cable been a greater artist than he was, he too would not have paid the price, for in that case he *could* not have done so. Cable conformed because as a novelist he *could* conform; it is as simple as that. There is in Cable, as there is not in Whitman, James, or Twain, a point at which as an artist he stops, draws back, and refuses to go beyond. It involves a failure of self-scrutiny—whether conscious or unconscious self-scrutiny does not matter. It accounts for Joseph Frowenfeld, John Richling, and all the romantic sentimentality of plot and characterization that to greater or lesser degree bedevils almost all Cable's fiction save some of the stories in *Old Creole Days*. It is, perhaps, the price he paid for the capacity for moral fervor that made possible his heroic championing of the Negro at a time when almost the entire American nation had wearied of the cause of the newly created freedman.

What Cable did as a man and a Southerner in the 1880's was incredibly brave. Joel Chandler Harris, whom one sometimes suspects of secretly seeing what was happening just as clearly as Cable, did not show similar bravery at all. Neither did Mark Twain—as a man. It is impossible, I think, to overstate the moral fortitude and courage of Cable on the issue of racism. Nor should we fail to recognize how much that moral insight contributes to his literary art; *The Grandissimes* and, later, *John March, Southerner* are what they are because of its presence in them. All the same, we cannot ignore the artistic limitations that are at work, and that are, alas, part of the same impulse. Had Cable been able to reflect more, to examine his own motivations, and perceive the contradictions involved therein, it is doubtful that he would or could have taken the kind of unequivocal stand that he did. For the zeal for reform, the determined and unswerving fixing of one's sense of outrage upon external injustice, the injustice of society, can also be a way of refraining from looking within oneself. The fact, commented on earlier, that Cable was unable to write unless he was also doing something else at the same time is an indication, it may well be, of Cable's limitations. That ultimate dedication, that surrender to the demands of artistic creativity at the expense of "life," was not possible to him. Indeed, he would have scorned it.

Ironically, for all Cable's avoidance of the race issue in *Dr. Sevier,* he managed to touch off the fires of Southern resentment. For during his description of Mary Richling's trip to New York and her attempt to secure passage aboard ship to New Orleans, he had portrayed the movement of some Union soldiers through the streets of the city, en route southward to battle, singing "John Brown's Body" as they marched along. Then he added one more paragraph:

> Yes, so, soldiers of the Union,—though that little mother weeps but does not wave, as the sharp-eyed man notes well through his tears,—yet even so, yea, all the more, go—"go marching on," saviors of the Union; your cause is just. Lo, now, since nigh twenty-five years have passed, we of the South can say it.
>
> "And yet—and yet, we cannot forget"—and we would not.

No sooner did that paragraph appear in public print than a denunciation was unleashed in Southern newspapers that did not cease for years to come. The New Orleans *Times-Democrat,* hitherto silent out of personal friendship for Cable, now led the way. "The Union is at peace today," it declared editorially, "and so let it be forever! But no misery of the past, no happiness of the present has ever led, or can ever lead, the Southern people to a confession of treason. They are not before the bar of history pleading for leniency on sentimental grounds." [17] The Southern press followed suit. Cable was mistaken; twenty-five years might have passed since the close of the war, but what he had said could *not* be said with impunity. For the cult of the Lost Cause was now taking form throughout the South, and however much one might accept and even publicly rejoice in the verdict of the war, any admission that the South had in any way been legally or morally wrong in taking up the struggle was not to be tolerated. For all the good that it did him to leave Negroes out of *Dr. Sevier,* Cable might just as well have put them in. The result was the same. Henceforth, in the eyes of much of the South, he was a panderer, betraying his native land for Northern gold.

X

Departure

Within three days after New Year's Day, 1884, Cable was back on the road. Installments of *Dr. Sevier* were appearing each month in the *Century,* and he was fairly well advanced in the writing of his Acadian stories; but the need for money was such that his immediate prospects of revenue from platform reading were what mattered most. Major Pond had arranged an extensive schedule of engagements that would take him as far west as Chicago and Madison, Wisconsin, and to many of the large and small cities of the Northeast. Before his first reading in New York, however, he found time to attend services at the Reverend Henry Ward Beecher's Plymouth Church in Brooklyn. Afterwards he had dinner with the Beechers, with whom he found himself most congenial.[1] Cable's first lectures were disappointingly attended, but when he got to Chickering Hall in New York there was a large audience, and the attendance continued good both in the New York area and elsewhere. On January 21, he read at Northampton, Massachusetts, and was most enchanted with the little college community, despite evening temperatures of 15° below zero. "O the snow, snow, snow! Sleighs and sleigh bells numberless and musical . . .", he wrote Louise. "Make some memorandum to ask me about Northampton when I come home & I'll interest you."[2]

Soon, however, his reading schedule was interrupted. After a performance in Hartford on January 26, he spent the night with the Clemenses, only to awake the next morning with "a slight indiscretion . . . a savage little attack of neuralgia in that part of my face that I make my living by, in short, my lower jaw—the part that wags, and the doctor, in order to make short work of it, has ordered me to keep my bed for twenty four hours." [3] The slight indiscretion lasted for three weeks, which he spent at the Clemens's house, abed for most of the time. Despite reassuring words from the Clemens's physician, and daily expectations of being able to leave for New York the following morning, Cable continued for some days to be quite sick, and for much of the time he was kept well dosed with opiates and quinine. No one was worried except for Clemens himself, who thought that Louise should come up from New Orleans but was overruled.[4] Olivia Clemens and Lilly Warner continued for several days to write out Cable's letters for him. After Cable had recovered sufficiently to be up and about the house, he and Clemens had some enjoyable times talking and speculating about various matters. Meanwhile Roswell Smith wrote Louise to call on him for any money she might need. Cable took pleasure in entertaining the Clemens children with stories of New Orleans.[5] Not until February 16 could Cable write to his wife to say that he was back in New York.

A week later, the true nature of the slight indiscretion was finally identified when all the Clemens children came down with the mumps, and later the nurse who had tended Cable wrote to say that she too had come down. "If I can pick up any other mild contagion about the country anywhere I'll bring it to your house, you seem so pleased to have me give your babies the mumps," Cable wrote Clemens. "Well, never mind; if you ever get the whooping-cough, come and see us down in New Orleans; Mrs. Cable will be delighted to see you." [6]

It is likely that it was at this time that Clemens began developing an impatience with some of Cable's ways that eventually widened into a powerful dislike. For though Cable was clearly unaware of any resentment, in a letter to Howells a few weeks later Clemens mentioned that his daughter Susie had the mumps and "has suffered 13 times more than Cable did (whose pain lasted but 2 days), & yet has not made as much fuss in the 4 days as he used to make in 15 minutes. . . . " [7] And six months later Twain was writing Howells again to say, "I notice that Mrs. Howells mentions Cable. Privately—she mustn't do anything on *our* account . . ."; apparently the Howellses were preparing to entertain Cable, and Clemens wished to make it clear that they should not do so in any mistaken belief that he would desire them to do it.[8] As for Cable, he obviously suspected nothing whatever of any change of attitude toward him on Clemens's part.

Clemens and Cable had discussed a scheme involving the joint writing of a story by five or six authors. For a while it was seriously considered by the two of them and by Gilder, but eventually it came to nothing. It is likely, too, that at this time definite plans began to take shape for the joint reading tour they would undertake during the coming autumn. By mid-summer Clemens would be ready to make a formal offer.

Soon Cable was back on the road again, appearing in Philadelphia, Hanover, Amherst, Concord, Worcester, and Boston, then westward to Buffalo, Ann Arbor, Chicago, Milwaukee, Madison, and down to Indianapolis. Not until April 1 did he head eastward again. "Huzzah!" he wrote to Louise while waiting for the train to leave Albany. "I cross into New England in a little while. The South makes me sick, the West makes me tired, the East makes me glad. It is the intellectual treasury of the United States. Here is cultivation & refinement, & taste."[9]

For six weeks and more he averaged a reading a day, with double performances on some days. Much of the time he was homesick. His letters were full of his longing to be with his family. "I seize a moment to write," he wrote from Philadelphia on February 21. "The day is a busy one. I have more to do than I can get done. No news. I don't feel bright. I am suffering more than a man of good mind & firm will ought to suffer, from homesickness. I don't want you to mention it; but you will not mind it and it's some relief to tell you."[10] "In my loneliness I know not what to turn my mind to for relief," he wrote on February 29. "I have never felt so sadly alone since I was a soldier. The little tastes of domestic life I get at intervals only tantalize me with what I have not got and cannot reach."[11] And on March 24, while en route between Indianapolis and Chicago, "This is one of those days when I would like to drop everything and run to you. I lay awake last night, unable to sleep, until midnight. . . . Do you remember that I used to say I thought it so strange that, loving you so much, I should never, in your long absences from me, dream about you? But now all that is changed. I dream about you often—often! The time is coming when, God willing, we shall not need the consolation of dreams." [12]

Apparently Cable still had no intention of leaving New Orleans permanently, though it was becoming obvious that so long as he maintained his residence there, his need for making money by giving public readings would cause him to be absent from his family for long periods of time. He continued to advise Louise about improvements for their house; for one thing, they planned to install a bath and water closet. He remained interested in church affairs; there was a crisis involving the resignation of a minister and the election of new officers, and he wrote to Louise at length about what he thought should be done. But the advantages that would come from having his family with him in the Northeast where he did so much of his reading were doubtless becoming very clear. "I forgot to say that I still hope we may spend the latter part of the summer in some cool place," he wrote to Louise on February 24.[13] And, despite occasional vexation with its famed weather, the attractiveness of New England was a constant theme in his letters.

Cable found time during his lecture tour to play one memorable joke on his friend Mark Twain. While convalescing at the Clemens house in Hartford, he had noted with amusement his host's volcanic wrath over letters which requested his autograph. So he had some circulars prepared which he sent to some 200 friends of Clemens's, telling them to write letters asking for his autograph, and to post them so that the letters would all arrive on April 1. On the appointed day Clemens was deluged with more than 150 letters, while all day long telegraph boys arrived with telegrams.[14]

It was not until April 25 that Cable arrived home again in New Orleans, following three readings in Louisville. When he did, it was to get back to work on his Acadian sketches, and prepare for two public appearances. One would be on May 15, at Grunewald Hall in New Orleans, in which he would read from his work, just as he had been doing in the North and Midwest, for the benefit of the Southern Art Union. The other would be at the University of Alabama, in mid-June. The two occasions would present him before the South in two roles. The New Orleans reading would be as the city's and the South's most famous man of letters, reading from the fiction that had won him an international reputation, in the city to which he had brought widespread renown. The other would be as reformer—for he had made up his mind at last to speak the truth about race and racism in the South.

The appearance at Grunewald Hall was before an immense audience. He read from *The Grandissimes, Dr. Sevier,* and *Old Creole Days,* and sang several Creole-Negro songs. Though obviously much of the quaintness of the Creole-English that had so delighted his Northern and Western audiences was lost upon his New Orleans audience, accustomed as they were to hearing such language spoken daily, the reading was a success, for many of his audience at least. Cable had hoped that the effect of his reading would be to convince both Creoles and others in New Orleans that what the audiences for his performances and readers of his books throughout the country had enjoyed so heartily was not ridicule of the Creoles, but only the eccentricity of certain comic characters. He wanted his fellow citizens to see that the net result of his work was to convince everyone of the charm and grace of his Creoles.[15]

Not many Creoles were there to be convinced, however; "it seems unfortunate," the *Times-Democrat* editorialized, "that so few Creoles were present to hear Mr. Cable's tribute to them and to the beautiful characters he had drawn and whom he loves." The performance only caused the Creoles to resent him more than ever. One fair-minded Creole who did attend wrote to the *Times-Democrat:* "I confess I was carried away by the great talent he displayed . . . I had never read any of his works, I felt determined to soon make up my neglect . . . I acknowledge the truthfulness of the Creole characters as far as he depicts them. I concede that they are vivid, living; that I seem to recognize the individuals." But he went on to object that Cable failed to write about the noble and heroic Creoles of history, and gave the impression that all Creoles were like those he depicted.[16]

As Arlin Turner has noted, there was really no way that Cable could have pleased the leading Creoles except by making it clear that upper-caste Creoles zealously guarded stratifications of caste, by including their heroes, and by allowing no confusion of the social elite with the others. More than that, as Turner points out,

Cable's very mode of artistry was certain to offend. For despite his
exotic subject matter, Cable was essentially realistic in his attitude
toward his material: he did not confine himself to modeling his
heroes and heroines after the chivalric figures of traditional romance, in the manner of Sir Walter Scott and such American
counterparts as William Gilmore Simms; he sought to show his
people as typical human beings, either unhampered by class re-
strictions or straining against them. Within the general romantic
framework of his time, he worked realistically. But the Creole
aristocrats wanted themselves portrayed in the fashion of high
romance; they were quite unaccustomed to the kind of fiction that
Cable wrote, and could view it only as stemming from contempt,
drawn with the intention to ridicule them.[17]

Nor were they, if the truth be known, entirely mistaken. As has
been shown, Cable *did* view the Creoles as far less than perfect;
his attitude toward them was by no means one of overall admiration. He had not hesitated to criticize their role in New Orleans
life in his Creole history, while in *The Grandissimes* and *Old Creole
Days* he had often portrayed Creole ways quite unattractively.

As for the non-Creole white population, which by that time
was the dominant element in New Orleans, *they* had not been
particularly offended by what he had written thus far. Except in
The Creoles of Louisiana there had been no full-scale criticism of
them, and even there the general effect was to show the non-Creole
population as considerably more progressive than the Creoles. As
Turner points out, Cable had brought renewed fame to New
Orleans, had become a figure of national prominence, and had
led the conservative business community in prison and hospital
reform which the public generally commended.[18] If there was some
unease, it arose not from the Creole protestations, but from some
of the implications of his speeches, which suggested a disbelief in
the white South's racial attitudes. Perhaps, too, there was still the
memory of the incident of more than a decade earlier when he
had protested so vigorously against school segregation in the city.
Doubtless Cable's continued heresy on the race question was
known to many New Orleaneans, but thus far he had been discreet
about it, so far as public mention went. Then on June 18, 1884,
Cable spoke in Tuscaloosa, Alabama, and all was changed.

Assuming that the widely heralded material progress in

Alabama meant that its citizenry would be receptive to progressive
political and social thought, at the University of Alabama he spoke
his mind on the backwardness of the South. The complete text
of the address itself does not survive, though undoubtedly much
of the material was included in "The Freedman's Case in Equity,"
but clearly Cable on this occasion directly criticized Southern
attitudes on race. He contrasted the glowing reports of progress
in Alabama in material gains, the opening of its mineral resources
to mining and the rapid increase in industrialization, with the
failure of not only Alabama but the entire South to rid itself of
the bondage of outmoded racial and social barriers. It was time,
he declared, that the conscience of the South speak out against
racial injustice:

> What our fathers called their 'peculiar institution' tended, when
> it was in force, to promote in us a certain spirit of command—of
> dictation—that made our wills seem to us nearly or quite as
> authoritative as the laws, and sometimes more so. We were a race
> of masters. We were dictators. The main thing to be kept in sight
> was the discipline of the plantation. Hence a most lamentable
> laxness of parental discipline; a similar laxness of that defensive
> discipline by which society lays down its conditions of member-
> ship; and, springing distinctly from these deficiencies, a group of
> outrageous vices: shameless hard drinking, the carrying of murder-
> ous weapons, murder, too, and lynching at its heels, the turning
> of state and country prisons into slave-pens, the falsification of
> the ballot, night riding and whipping, and all the milder forms
> of political intolerance. Now, I maintain, without fear of offending
> any one here whose good opinion I can honestly afford to cling
> to, that we owe it to the parents who, along with all the moral
> evils that naturally found harbor under the institution of Negro
> slavery, have left us still a Christianity that not even slaveholding
> in the nineteenth century could destroy, to rise to such an acuteness
> of moral sense—to acquire and agree upon such a moral stand-
> ard—that from one end of this land to the other there shall be
> lifted against these crimes an outcry of shame and condemnation
> so long and so loud that it shall divide asunder those who wink at
> such things from those who do not, even though it split every
> social circle and every church and every family in the land. We
> have been silent long enough.[19]

Though Cable says that he received numerous private expressions of approval, the public reaction to his remarks in the
Alabama press was uniform. For weeks afterward he was the

subject of editorial abuse. Such phrases as "New England Puritan" were common.[20] Not only was his attitude on the race question denounced, but the attack was soon extended to his fiction. His treatment of the Creoles was, however belatedly, resented as an unjust libel upon a proud and noble people. Even the New Orleans press, though not making an issue of the address, considered it unfortunate. For Cable had at last publicly attacked the white South on the one subject about which it would accept no dissent: race.

What Cable had predicted in his address to the Louisiana University of a year ago was now coming to pass. The South was demonstrating that it would emphatically not tolerate dissent on its racial attitudes, and that Southern writers who ventured to do so would indeed "be denounced as turbulent overturners of order, as mischievous innovators and disturbers of the peace. . . ." The South was clearly not ready to "throw open our society, our section, our institutions, ourselves wide open to their criticism and correction, reserving the right to resent only what we can refute."[21]

Furthermore, from the viewpoint of having much effect upon the thinking of the white South, the time that Cable had chosen for his onslaught against racial discrimination was most unpropitious. Less than a decade had elapsed since the last of the Reconstruction governments had been overthrown and the Federal troops withdrawn. The white South had since begun consolidating its hold. Segregation in schools was widespread. There was little attempt at legal disfranchisement of the freedman—that would come later—but one way or another the white South was reestablishing its almost total control of the machinery of government.

More important, perhaps, the race question was being allowed nationally to die down. Four years of civil war and a decade of unsuccessful attempts to secure for the freedman the benefits of his new-found freedom through political reconstruction had so wearied the North of the race issue that there was a general willingness to let it drop. Civil rights was almost a dead issue. The Compromise of 1877 had only ratified the North's growing desire to let the South take care of the race problem "in its own way." The *Nation*, for example, thought that the Federal government should "have nothing more to do with [the Negro]," while the New York *Tribune* declared that the Negroes had been given "ample opportunity to develop their own latent capacities," but had only demonstrated that "as a race they are idle, ignorant, and vicious."[22] Cable's own friend and editor Richard Watson Gilder exemplified the North's virtual abandonment of the Negro when he wrote in the *Century* in 1883: "The fact is, and the sooner the fact is recognized the sooner we shall be rid of many dangerous illusions, that the negroes constitute a peasantry wholly untrained in, and ignorant of, those ideas of constitutional liberty and progress which are the birthright of every white voter; that they are gregarious and emotional rather than intelligent, and are easily led in any direction by white men of energy and determination."[23] Though Gilder loyally defended Cable against attacks for the racial views in "The Freedman's Case in Equity," which the *Century* published in 1885, he was not himself strongly concerned with the issue, and in his attitude he typified "enlightened" Northern opinion in the years after the end of Reconstruction.[24]

The legal justification for racial discrimination in the South was being established by a group of Supreme Court decisions, the most important perhaps being that of October 15, 1883, 109 U. S., 3 (1883), in which the Court ruled unconstitutional the Civil Rights Act of March 1, 1875, which had made it criminal for any person to deny to any citizen on account of race or color the full and equal enjoyment of the privileges and accommodations of inns, public conveyances, theaters, and other places of public amusement. The groundwork was thus laid for the host of laws passed by Southern legislators during the 1880's, 1890's, and thereafter, which forced almost total racial segregation upon the South. Such measures met with the general approval of the white South, and with the indifference of the rest of the nation.

Thus Cable, in speaking forth as he did and when he did, was threatening (insofar as he could influence Northern opinion and interest) to disturb what was for the South a hard-won stalemate whereby it could, despite the defeat of the War Between the States, continue to enforce white supremacy. That Cable said he was not addressing himself to the North and the West but to the South itself was, in the eyes of the South, no extenuation. For he was a nationally known figure, whose every public utterance was widely reported. To a region which for a half century or more had been subjected to constant attack, culminating in military invasion and occupation, all in the name of justice for the Negro, there was little disposition to tolerate anyone's raising the issue once again.

Philip Butcher is right when he says·that in speaking forth as he did, Cable was making himself "heir to the cause of William Lloyd Garrison, Wendell Phillips, and the others he called 'the great dead' at a time when that cause seemed lost."[25] However much Cable may have comforted himself with the thought that behind the furious bombast of constant Southern proclamations of white supremacy, there was a "Silent South" which believed in justice for the Negro, the fact was that the vast majority of Southern whites did not believe in Negro equality, and strongly favored white supremacy. On this crucial issue there was simply no room for dissent, as Cable speedily discovered. He had unleashed the whirlwind at last.

It was under these conditions, therefore, that Cable went back to New Orleans to prepare for the summer. He had already planned to take his family northward again, to the cool of New England; Louise Cable's health was as always fragile and the prospect of another season spent in the "engine room" atmosphere of New Orleans, as Cable had once referred to it, was not attractive. But September, when it would be time for the family to return, would be precisely when Cable was embarking on another extended reading and lecture tour, so that it made good sense for all the Cables to stay on in New England for the fall-winter-spring season as well. From late September through mid-April of the previous season, Cable had, after all, been able to spend less than three weeks in New Orleans with his family; if Louise and the children were to remain in New England—a much more central location for his lecture operations—such prolonged absences would not again be necessary. So he decided that, for the next year at least, he would settle his family in the North. His New York friends found a house for him in Simsbury, Connecticut, a town of just over 2,000 inhabitants located near the southern extremity of the Green Mountains, about 15 miles northwest of Hartford. Cable's friend Major E. A. Burke leased his New Orleans home on Eighth Street for him for one year, with an option for the second year if it was still up for rent. Though Cable's sister Mary Louise said she was sure her brother would return to New Orleans, Cable's friends speculated on the possibility that the move would be permanent.

On July 1, the Cable family—the novelist, his wife, and five small daughters—left New Orleans for New York aboard the steamer *Hudson*.[26] Cable and his wife must have realized, as the ship moved through the Mississippi delta into the Gulf and then turned eastward, that they were quite probably leaving Louisiana for good. Thus departed from the South its leading author, the first Southern writer who had ventured in his fiction to come to grips with the complex issues of race and caste that have almost throughout the region's history been its most vexing problem. He was going northward, to the center of the American literary and cultural industry, to be near the source of his livelihood, where he was honored and acclaimed. Though he would frequently return for visits, he was leaving the region where he had been born and had lived for all of the forty years of his life thus far, for which he had fought during a war, and which had been scene and substance for his writings, including almost all the work for which he would be remembered. For though Cable's life was not yet quite half done, and he was to write many more books, most of his enduring fiction had already been written.

"Both Cable and his people," C. Vann Woodward has written, "were losers [by his departure]—the writer, of his art, which never fulfilled its rich promise; the South, of a fearless critic and a point of view that could thenceforth be more readily dismissed as foreign." [27] Yet it is doubtful whether, even if Cable had not chosen to leave the South in 1884, his subsequent literary career could have been very different. Given his rigorous logical consistency and the intensity of his beliefs, his position could only have become more beleaguered. And the polemical response which would thus have been engendered would probably have isolated him from the everyday involvement in Southern life that had been the substance of his best work just as effectively as his geographical isolation was soon to do. Probably it is just as well that Cable left when he did; the direction of his ideological concerns would soon have made his continued residence in New Orleans intolerable, and his only ultimate response must either have been flight, or else weariness and eventual capitulation. His fiction would doubtless have become pleasant local color work, devoid of the social protest that lay at the heart of his best art.

This is not to contend that in leaving for the North, Cable was acting to safeguard his right to deal with the Negro question in his fiction. He was not ready for that yet. As a writer of fiction he was moving at this point *into* the Genteel Tradition, and the literature of social protest had no place in such an aesthetic. For the next several years the fiction he would write would be just what Gilder and his associates wanted. Not until late in the decade, when he was faced with the fact that his campaign for civil rights—waged until then on the hustings and in essays and articles—was clearly failing, would he turn to the medium of fiction in a final effort to make himself heard on Southern problems. But that last effort, as the Cable family sailed northward aboard the *Hudson* in July of 1884, lay well in the future.

XI

"Twins of Genius"

Before Cable and his family left New Orleans, Major James B. Pond had forwarded to him a definite offer from Mark Twain to undertake a joint reading tour for the forthcoming winter season. It was to be Sam Clemens's enterprise; Cable was to receive a guaranteed cash stipend, and Pond a percentage of the proceeds for managing the tour. Cable was offered $350 a week, plus his expenses.[1] Pond was careful to point out to Cable the possible drawbacks of undertaking a joint tour: "Once in a double team & well broke in a horse never pulls as well single after that. . . . Think and be wise. Your life is not half spent."[2] Apparently Pond also informed Clemens about Cable's unwillingness to travel or undertake any business on Sundays. Cable seems to have been reluctant to agree to the figure named, for on July 9 Pond wrote to him in Simsbury, raising the offer to $450 a week and expenses, and quoting Clemens as saying he preferred to have Cable at that figure than someone else for less.[3] This time Cable decided to accept; the terms, even with Pond's commission on his stipend, probably equalled what he could expect to make by reading on his own, and the widespread publicity and public exposure that would come from his joint appearances with Mark Twain would surely benefit the sales of his books.

The summer that the Cable family passed in Simsbury was extremely pleasant. Cable wrote at once to Clemens to thank him for having recommended Simsbury: "We have been here two days now and are quite delighted."[4] To his sister Mary Louise in New Orleans he wrote in August, extolling the climate, the setting, and the pleasant neighbors. He went into raptures about a drive through the countryside.[5] On the same day he wrote to his friend Mrs. James T. Fields, widow of the Boston publisher, "Yes, we are in Beautiful New England. What delight we take in its air, fields, hills, streams, valleys and gentle inhabitants would make a long letter." Noting that he was the object of considerable attack in the Southern press, he declared: "And they are so sincere about it! They believe they're aggrieved."[6] From his comfortable Connecticut retreat, he could afford to be philosophical. When the summer was done, he reported to another friend that his family had passed "one of the happiest summers in our experience. . . . We shall hold our present base until next fall."[7]

Before the reading tour with Twain began, Cable had some engagements of his own which Major Pond had set up, and he also wanted some further lessons in elocution, so he left Simsbury for New York. But now he could return to his family almost every weekend. Clemens sent both Cable and Gilder proofs of the forthcoming *Adventures of Huckleberry Finn* so that each could recommend possible passages for inclusion in the readings. Shortly before the opening date for the tour, Cable wrote to Clemens to suggest a variant title for one of the selections. Clemens had included the passage from *Huckleberry Finn* in which Jim bests Huck in debate on the French language, and had entitled it "Can't learn a nigger to argue." Cable thought the wording would appear gross: "in the text, whether on the printed page or in the reader's utterances the phrase is absolutely without a hint of grossness; but alone on a published programme, it invites discreditable conjectures of what the context may be, from that portion of our public who cannot live without aromatic vinegar." In its place Cable suggested "How come a Frenchman doan' talk like a man?", which Clemens accepted.[8] Meanwhile Clemens was deluging Pond with instructions. Portraits and biographical sketches should be sent ahead for publicity in newspapers.[9] It was important that programs distributed at the readings be of a kind that would not rattle. Perhaps they could be printed on cards, but not on cards large enough to be used as fans; that would likewise be distracting. The selection of readings would be experimental at first, and from the lessons learned from audience response, a permanent one-night program could be assembled.[10] Eventually they were ready to begin.

On November 5, 1884, the joint reading tour, billed by Pond as the "Twins of Genius," began at New Haven, with Olivia Clemens in the audience.[11] The program apparently went well enough, but in subsequent performances in the New England area Clemens was forced to modify his platform tactics. Though he had been performing before audiences for some two decades, he had done so primarily as a comic lecturer; the business of reading from his own works was new to him, and he had proceeded on the assumption that it would be quite enough for him to carry his books out onto the stage and read aloud, with appropriate gestures. This, however, did not work at all well, so after a few times he put the books aside and delivered his pieces from memory, with interjections and modifications as circumstances warranted.[12]

Newspaper reports made much of the relative merits of the two readers, and of the contrast between their styles of delivery. Cable was the more literary in his approach; his method was precise and refined, his manner clear and intelligible; he furnished the humor and the pathos. Mark Twain was natural, droll, unstudied, a master of comedy who had his audiences laughing throughout his monologues. To different critics, they had a differing and not always equal appeal. To the reviewer of the New York *Times,* for example, Cable was far the more preferable:

> The management, in its newspaper advertisements, spoke of the entertainment as a "combination of genius and versatility," but neglected to say which of these gentlemen had the genius and which the versatility. Some of those who were present last evening may have felt justified in coming to the conclusion that Mr. Cable represented both these elements, while Mr. Clemens was simply man, after the fashion of that famous hunting animal one-half of which was pure Irish setter and the other half "just plain dog." Mr. Cable was humorous, pathetic, weird, grotesque, tender, and melodramatic by turns, while Mr. Clemens confined his efforts to the ridicule of such ridiculous matters as aged colored gentlemen, the German language, and himself.[13]

The *Sun,* by contrast, dismissed Cable with brief remarks to the effect that he read with much intensity, with awkward gestures, and frequently used the wrong word by mistake. Mark Twain's manner, his appearance, and his selections were described at length and highly lauded. In particular his recitation of the ghost story "The Man with the Golden Arm" was praised.[14]

Cable's literary reputation at that juncture was almost the equal of Mark Twain's, as Paul Fatout has indicated, and in some circles even higher. To "defenders of the genteel tradition" he was "more literary"; his manner was dignified, in line with what was expected of a man of letters; he was more refined, more mannerly.[15] Furthermore, Cable's controversial writings and statements on civil rights were pushing him into the news with growing frequency. When in late January, 1885, as the tour was half done, the *Century* published "The Freedman's Case in Equity," a storm of controversy resulted and Cable became so famous that he was the object of much curiosity and attention. In Arlin Turner's estimate, "certainly in the last six weeks on the road Mark saw himself, not eclipsed, but nearly equaled in popularity both on and off the platform."[16]

The tour lasted four months, with an interruption for Christmas, and carried the two men, with Major Pond or his brother Ozias going along as traveling manager, to dozens of cities and towns from New England to Iowa, Missouri, and Minnesota, as far south as Kentucky, and northward into Canada. While they were en route, both *Huckleberry Finn* and *Dr. Sevier* came out, and the events of the tour were reported in the press throughout the United States, while at each place where they played they were reviewed, interviewed, and entertained.*

Cable was, as always, greatly impressed with Mark Twain, and their four months of traveling together and being constantly in each other's company did not dim his respect. One searches his letters in vain for any adverse criticism of Clemens, any sign of grating personalities or bruised feelings. If Clemens's profanity,

---

*The story of the Cable-Twain lecture tour has been so abundantly and thoroughly chronicled by scholars that there is no need to provide more than a brief summary here. Guy Cardwell and Arlin Turner have both published full-length books on the subject, and it has been extensively described in the various biographies of Clemens, as well as in our specialized studies of both men. Cable's almost daily account of the proceedings may be found in the letters he wrote home to Louise, often scrawling them on the backs of programs while he sat in theater anterooms waiting to go on while his partner was performing. Clemens wrote less about it, but in some of his letters to Olivia Clemens and to Howells and others, he expressed his reaction with customary hyperbole.

his constant smoking, and his pleasure in social drinking and conviviality irked him, there is no indication of it. On several occasions he did object to Clemens's friends. A meeting with "Petroleum V. Nasby" (David Ross Locke) in Toledo, Ohio, on December 15, elicited comments on Nasby's coarse talk, his frequent references to being drunk, and his materialism. "I'm glad he's gone. He's a bad dream," Cable concluded.[17] A similar meeting with "Marse Henry" Watterson, editor of the Louisville *Courier-Journal* and a cousin of Clemens, he also found distasteful. "I had long been curious to see Watterson," he wrote. "He didn't please me. Talks shamelessly about getting drunk &c &c. Strange that the moral distortion can go with a certain large integrity & public honor but it is so at times."[18] For Clemens himself, however, there was only praise and respect. On January 30, Cable wrote Louise of his companion's "fine instinctive art . . . for the platform. He has worked incessantly on these programmes until he has effected in all of them—there are 3—a gradual growth of both interest & humor so that the audience never has to find anything less, but always more, entertaining than what precedes it. . . . My insights into his careful, untiring, incessant labors are an education almost as valuable as that got from Sargent & Henderson."[19]

As for Mark Twain, his private view of the progress of the tour was considerably less complimentary to Cable. In letters to his wife and to Howells, he sounded off vigorously. Though he had been warned in advance that Cable would not travel on Sunday, he fretted over it. The day before the end of the tour he wrote Howells to say:

> [It] has been a curious experience. It has taught me that Cable's gifts of mind are greater and higher than I had suspected. But—
> That "But" is pointing toward his religion. You will never, never know, never divine, guess, imagine, how loathsome a thing the Christian religion can be until you come to know and study Cable daily and hourly. Mind you, I like him; he is pleasant company; I rage and swear at him sometimes, but we do not quarrel; we get along mightily happily together; but in him and his person I have learned to hate all religions. He has taught me to abhor and detest the Sabbath-day and hunt up new and troublesome ways to dishonor it.[20]

He would have raged ever more had he known that some weeks

before, Cable had written Louise, after a day of churchgoing: "I feel sure that [Clemens's] Sunday has not been happier than mine. Oh! how I wish he were a man of prayer & worship. But he has more nobleness of nature & is more to be admired than I knew before now." [21] One feels some sympathy for Mark Twain (and it is difficult to feel very *much* sympathy for his general behavior toward Cable during and after this tour) when Cable writes to Louise that he "entrapped Mark into a discussion of the duty of practicing religion—from his point of view—whipped him off the field & left him, he saying as I went he wished he had gone to church with me. Would to God I might prevail to take him there. Help me with your prayers, beloved." [22] What Clemens might have thought of the idea of Louise in Simsbury and George Cable in the hotel room next door to him praying for his apostasy is not difficult to imagine.

Clemens's objections to Cable, which grew as the tour progressed, were not confined to this religiosity. He became convinced that Cable was utterly parsimonious. In letters to Livy and in outbursts to Pond he castigated Cable's penury. Supposedly Cable had brought back to the tour, after the break for Christmas holidays, all his soiled shirts so that they could be laundered as an item of expenses. He starved himself when paying his own expenses, but was a lavish spender when the price of meals was not coming out of his own pocket. He took stationery from the hotels they stayed in, in order not to have to buy his own.

Cable's general manner of delivery also began increasingly to irritate Clemens.[23] He extended his reading of "Mary's Night Ride," from *Dr. Sevier,* from six minutes to fifteen, and did it on every program; each time it became increasingly unpalatable to Clemens, and one of the climactic lines, "Cover the child," thereafter became in the Clemens household a byword for melodramatic gesture. Coached in the elocutionary practices of the gilded age, Cable apparently read with a great deal of emphasis and formal eloquence, and Clemens considered that his companion's platform manner had lost entirely too much of the charm it had once possessed before Cable had begun taking his speech lessons. Shortly after the tour ended, Clemens wrote to Howells to compliment him on a public reading, saying that Howells had read "far better than Cable could have done it. . . . It had simplicity, sincerity, & absence of artificiality, in place of Cable's self-complacency, sham feeling & labored artificiality."[24] And twenty years later, when he was dictating his memoirs, he declared that Cable "had been a good reader in the beginning for he had been born with a natural talent for it, but unhappily he prepared himself for his public work by taking lessons from a teacher of elocution, and so by the time he was ready to begin his platform work he was so well and thoroughly educated that he was merely theatrical and artificial and not half as pleasing and entertaining to a house as he had been in the splendid days of his ignorance."[25] Newspaper reviews of their readings occasionally echoed this objection: "Mr. Cable is not near as good a raconteur as Mr. Clemens, although he assumes much more of the manner of the professional elocutionist," the Detroit *Post* commented.[26]

Despite such private reservations on Clemens's part, the two men apparently enjoyed each other's companionship fairly well most of the time. Major Pond reported on their compatibility; they would sing together, tease each other, and generally delight in each other's company. Clemens several times wrote in praise of Cable's intellectual capabilities, which he considered very great. Guy A. Cardwell contends that Cable had had considerable influence on the writing of *The Adventures of Huckleberry Finn* several years earlier. Cable, he says, "may have influenced *Huck Finn* significantly with respect to its social and poetic attitudes at points where Twain explores the nature of culture and the nature of men's relationships within a culture," and he declares that "Twain did need help in grasping intellectually through an analysis of the morphology of Southern society what he felt to be its unhealthy moral state."[27] This help Cable could have given him, for however devoted to the literary manners of the Genteel Tradition he was, as Cardwell notes, Cable's ideas on the South's major social problems were well reasoned and quite bold.[28]

On one occasion, Cable did something that had a direct and acknowledged bearing on Mark Twain's future work. They were in a bookstore in Rochester, New York; Clemens remarked that he had no reading matter for the next day, so Cable picked up a copy of Malory's *Morte d'Arthur,* saying to his friend, "You will never lay it down until you have read it from cover to cover," as he remembered later.[29] Clemens bought the book, read it, and was soon immersed in its idiom and its lore. For a time on the tour the two of them, and Pond's brother Ozias, delighted in conversing constantly in Arthurian terms and the language of Malory. The ultimate result was *A Connecticut Yankee in King Arthur's Court.*

Shortly after the tour ended, there was an unpleasant incident in which Cable at last became aware of Mark Twain's ambivalent attitude toward him. The Boston *Herald* printed a story which alleged that when ill at the Clemens's house in Hartford, Cable had lived on champagne for three weeks and had not offered to pay for it; on the tour, he had ordered $5 breakfasts at the tour's expense and generally lived lavishly; he was so penurious that he had refused to give a benefit reading for promotion of the copyright law; and his selfish refusal to travel on Sundays had caused much inconvenience to his traveling partner. The story was widely reprinted, especially in the South. From the nature of the remarks, it was obvious that they had come from Clemens, with some help from Pond.

When Cable heard the report, he telegraphed at once to Clemens: "All intimations that you and Pond are not my Beloved Friends are false and if you can say the same of me do so as privately or as publicly as you like." [30] When no reply was forthcoming, he wrote in more detail, attributing the remarks to scandalmongers and restating his own admiration for his friend. [31] Clemens's response was considerably less than the public denial that Cable desired. He wrote to Cable, "my dear boy, don't give yourself any discomfort about the slander of a professional newspaper liar—we cannot escape such things." The report had disturbed *him* not a bit, he continued. "To take notice of it in print is a thing which would never have occurred to me. Why, my dear friend, flirt it out of your mind—straight off." [32] Since it was Clemens's remarks about Cable, and not Cable's about Clemens, that had been reported in print, this was hardly the reply that might have been hoped for. Meanwhile Cable had written to the Boston *Herald,* denying all the allegations, and had demanded and received a retraction. While at the Clemens home he had drunk only such champagne as a physician had prescribed, and an offer to pay for it would have been "about as proper as an offer to pay for my food and lodging." He had refused a public reading on behalf of the copyright law because of his wife's illness; his zeal on behalf of the law was well known. His hotel accommodations were made by the traveling manager, and he was not consulted in advance. On rare occasions when he had "made small expenditures that the manager would afterward pay back to me . . . it was a standing jest between us that I generally had to prevent him cheating himself." His unwillingness to travel on Sundays had been understood well in advance. "It is true I spend little on myself," he wrote, "and that I would rather not be so poor as I have been; but I give you my word for what it is worth, I would sooner starve than get my living—as your correspondent seems willing to get his—by slandering unoffending gentlemen." [33]

Clemens had inspired the story not by intention, but by sounding off with his usual exaggeration before someone who had thereupon reported his exaggerations as facts to the newspaper correspondent. This was probably what he was referring to when he wrote to his nephew Charles L. Webster on May 10, "I meant to caution you the other day, but it slipped my mind. This: from this out, write nothing in any private letter to friend, relative, or *anybody*, which you do not want published. . . . *Nobody* is to be trusted. Therefore confine your private letters strictly to what you would not mind seeing in print. . . . I have been burnt so often, in my own experience that I feel like warning & saving *you*." [34] Cable seems never to have held Mark Twain seriously culpable for his unflattering remarks. In the years thereafter they saw comparatively little of each other, but Cable on several occasions strongly praised Clemens and his work. In 1895, in reply to a letter, Clemens wrote to him: "Yes *sir!* I liked you in spite of your religion; & I always said to myself that a man that could be good & kindly with that kind of a load on him was entitled to homage— and I *paid* it. And I have always said, & still maintain, that as a railroad-comrade you were perfect—the only railroad-companion in the world that a man of moods & frets & uncertainties of disposition could travel with, a third of a year, and never weary of his company. We *always* had good times in the cars & never minded the length of the trips—& my, but they *were* sockdolagers for length!" [35] Cable spoke in praise of Clemens at his seventieth birthday dinner celebration, and at greater length and eloquently at the memorial service for Mark Twain on November 30, 1910.[36]

That Clemens should have grown increasingly irritated with Cable over the course of a four-month tour in which the two were in each other's company for long hours each day and night is, given Mark Twain's volatile personality, hardly surprising. It is difficult to think of anyone who could have been in his company for so long and not have incurred his displeasure. He was a personality, a prima donna, accustomed to indulge himself, and not very tolerant of the idiosyncrasies of others. He not only enjoyed being the center of attention, he insisted upon it; and he soon grew jealous of anyone else who shared the limelight.

So long as Cable was Mark Twain's protégé, so to speak, a relatively unknown but worthy artist from the provinces, he could relish Cable gaining public attention under his sponsorship. But once any question of real rivalry was involved, he soon lost his benevolence, and began critically comparing Cable's success with the audiences to his own. His own slow start, during which he found that merely reading from a text would not suffice, was not calculated to soothe his competitive instinct; and throughout the tour he worked tirelessly, and apparently to good effect, at improving his performance. His letters to Livy contain hints of the extent to which he viewed the joint performances as contests.

That Cable's reputation, and his approach to platform reading, was of a somewhat more "literary" nature than Clemens's own—as the Genteel Tradition viewed such things—was also something of an irritant. Throughout his life Clemens's attitude toward such matters was ambivalent; he gloried in his "lowbrow" appeal, in the fact that he directed his art not to the head but to the entire body, and he played brilliantly to the gallery. Yet at the same time he resented the extent to which he was known primarily as a "humorist" rather than an artist. It is in this light that we can interpret his lament to Cable, after having kept an audience roaring with delight all evening, "Oh, Cable, I am demeaning myself. I am allowing myself to be a mere buffoon. It's ghastly. I can't endure it any longer." [37] He did indeed feel guilty at times for his uninhibited genius at low comedy, and yet he felt himself— and rightly so—the superior to Cable and to other less "popular" writers. Thus newspaper reports that emphasized Cable's literary gentility and propriety in contrast to his own unrestrained naturalness were doubtless read by him with mixed emotions. The complaints about Cable's "Christ-besprinkled psalm-singing Presbyterian" beliefs can be largely discounted. This was Mark Twain's favorite form of humor; he indulged in it constantly, not only at Cable's expense but throughout his career. Though he was undoubtedly irked at times, especially when Cable's refusal to travel on Sunday caused inconvenience in travel arrangements for the tour, he was not nearly so outraged by his companion's churchgoing as he pretended to be; indeed, at the close of the tour he accompanied Cable to church in Washington.[38] As for his objection to Cable's penurious ways, this is no doubt genuine, but it is well to remember that Clemens was a highly extravagant man, and doubtless his ideas and Cable's about proper expenditures for meals and the like were at considerable variance. Cable *was* poor; his income was not a tenth of Mark Twain's, and for years he had been forced to watch every penny he spent. As an entrepreneur, Clemens was habitually expansive one day and suspicious of being cheated the next. Though the tour was profitable, it was not the huge moneymaker he had envisioned—his net return for the four months was about $16,000 after Cable's total fee of $5,000 and Pond's commission of $3,000 had been paid.[39] In terms of Clemens's finances this was a comparatively small profit for four months of exhausting work (it would doubtless have been enough to support Cable and his entire family for two years and more).

Clemens was also engaged at the time in directing the affairs of his publishing firm, the Charles L. Webster Company, in bringing out *The Adventures of Huckleberry Finn,* and in securing and publishing General Grant's *Memoirs,* as well as being involved in promoting several inventions, filing a lawsuit, and other activities. To do all this by mail and telegram, while traveling thousands of miles and giving four months of public readings, was enough to tax his energies and his patience to the utmost, and to make his relations with Pond and with Cable more than ordinarily difficult.

There is thus little justification for taking Clemens's complaints about Cable as being either literally true or important. His performance after the tour closed, both in the comments he made on Cable and in failing promptly to come to his defense when the newspapers began reporting them in exaggerated form, was not admirable. Paul Fatout's summary of the whole affair is appropriate: "In the troubled combination of genius and versatility, Mark Twain may have had the genius, yet Cable, because he was the more versatile, was the more humane."[40]

Publication of "The Freedman's Case in Equity" in the *Century* for February, 1885, had placed Cable at the center of controversy, as already mentioned. His speech at the University of Alabama the previous June had touched off widespread attacks on him in the Southern press. By carrying his critique of the South's treatment of the Negro onto the national stage in publishing it in the *Century,* Cable laid down the gauntlet. The "Solid South" was anxious to be allowed to handle its racial policies by itself, without interference from others; Cable was instead making a national issue of the matter. By suggesting to the nation that the South was not giving fair treatment and equal opportunities to the freedman, he was threatening to upset the compromise whereby the South had in effect promised that if left alone, it would see to the Negro's best welfare.

In his essay, Cable gave a short history of race relations in the South from slavery days through Reconstruction. The Negro had been freed by the verdict of the war, but he was still far from a free man. "There is scarcely one public relation of life in the South where he is not arbitrarily and unlawfully compelled to hold toward the white man the attitude of an alien, a menial, and a probable reprobate, by reason of his race and color," Cable declared. Scorning the Southern and Northern attitudes that the status of the freedman was unimportant, he asserted: "One of the marvels of future history will be that it was counted a small matter, by a majority of our nation, for six millions of people within it, made by its own decree a component part of it, to be subjected to a system of oppression so rank that nothing could make it seem small except the fact that they had already been ground under it for a century and a half."[41]

In attacking Southern claims that various methods of enforced segregation and disfranchisement were made necessary by the exigencies of the situation, he pointed out numerous inconsistencies in the application of repressive measures to show that the alleged needs obviously did not exist and were simply a method of preserving white supremacy. The various separate-but-equal provisions in public facilities, he said, were quite unnecessary, and were designed not merely to segregate, but to enforce upon the Negro the consciousness of his menial status.

Resuming his argument about the inhumanity of the convict lease system, this time he made the direct charge that it was designed as a method of selling Negro labor cheaply. Taking up the problem of segregation in schools, he declared that while he was prepared to do his part in keeping the race question out of education, he could not fail to say that the argument that integrated schools would bring about social egalitarianism was essentially absurd. "Social Equality! What a godsend it would be if the advocates of the old Southern regime could only see that the color line points straight in the direction of social equality by tending toward the equalization of all whites on one side of the line and of all blacks on the other. We may reach the moon some day, not social equality. . . ." [42] Social gradations are essential to society, Cable said, as if to guard against criticism that he was a leveler, and the consciousness of such gradations will grow in school as well as out of school, so that "it is no small mistake to put [children] or their parents off their guard by this cheap separation on the line of color." [43]

He scoffed at the idea that there was an inherent racial instinct that made enforced separation of the races a natural consequence. If indeed there were any such instinctive basis in human nature, then it was an argument *against* segregation by legal decree, for "it stands to reason that just in degree as it is a real thing it will take care of itself." [44] He had seen integrated education in New Orleans, he declared, and it had worked well. What with the tremendous financial demands that the need for better education was placing on Southern resources, he was opposed to the multiplication of costs and the loss of efficiency of separate school systems for white and Negro throughout the South.

The freedman, he concluded, is not free. The wish to deny him his freedom is a holdover from the old slavery system, and has no place in the present South. To give justice to the Negro "will not cost much. We have had a strange experience: the withholding of natural rights has cost us much blood; such concessions of them as we have made never cost a drop." If politics stood in the way of freedom for the Negro, then politics must go, because "there is a moral and intellectual intelligence [in the South] which is not going to be much longer beguiled out of its moral right of way by questions of political punctilio. . . ." It was the duty of the South to erase all barriers to full freedom for its Negro citizens, "until the whole people of every once slaveholding state can stand up as one man, saying, 'Is the Freedman a free man,' and the whole world shall answer, 'Yes.' "[45]

The response to Cable's indictment was predictable. The *Century* was besieged with letters from Southern readers, protesting against the essay. As Arlin Turner notes, it was the specificity that proved so effective; a more general approach would doubtless "have been given lip endorsement and then ignored." By mid-January the Southern press was firing away and the Northern press reporting the clamor. The *Times-Democrat,* once Cable's defender, quoted nine Southern newspaper attacks on him.[46] No longer could his friend Marion Baker dissuade his brother Page from pitching into Cable. "The papers—one and all are peppering you about the Century article—," Marion wrote Cable on February 5, "the T. D. heading the pack in full cry. You can form no idea of how bitter the feeling is against you,—as bitter as it used to be against Garrison and men of his way of thinking in ante-bellum times."[47]

To head up the assault on Cable, the *Times-Democrat* opened its columns to Charles Gayarré. Resentful of Cable's depiction of the Creoles, jealous of his literary success, Gayarré at last had the forum he wanted. In two articles, on January 11 and 18, 1885, he scoffed at Cable's knowledge of the Creoles and their language, accused him of abusing the South for financial gain, described the *Century* essay as supercilious, conceited, and written to gain its author notoriety. As for the Negro in the South, he must be kept subordinate for his own protection. Gayarré discussed the question of miscegenation as if Cable had supported it, and he denied that public morality was involved in the South's treatment of the Negro. Throughout, Gayarré's mode of address was hortatory, satirical, malicious; he made no attempt to answer Cable's arguments, but merely responded with abuse and condemnation.[48]

Gayarré also declared that when *The Grandissimes* had appeared in 1880, he had been asked to review the novel for the *Times-Democrat,* but "refused from motives of delicacy. Mr. Cable having heard of it and having requested us to change our decision, we replied that we would, if he could name two Creole families with whom he was intimately acquainted. He could not." [49] This, as Turner remarks, seems unlikely. The correspondence between Gayarré and Cable indicates that relations between the two were cordial enough at the time; it is very improbable that Gayarré would have delivered himself of so rude a remark to one whose help he had on several occasions requested. A month after he had allegedly delivered this insult, for example, he was seeking Cable's advice on placing a manuscript,[50] while the next year he was writing to Cable to ask for the address of Cable's brother in Chicago so that he could call upon him when in that city.[51] It is possible that the *Times-Democrat* did ask Gayarré to review *Old Creole Days* in 1879, for there is a note from Gayarré to Cable declaring that "I have reflected on the subject and have concluded to decline. Thanks for having thought of me." The envelope on the back of which the note is scrawled is dated April 23, but no year is given;[52] as Turner says, this would come close to the publication date of *Old Creole Days* in May, 1879, but not of *The Grandissimes* in September, 1880. In any event, if this is the refusal that Gayarré was thinking of, it contained no remarks whatever about Cable's not knowing Creole families.

At the close of his joint reading tour with Twain, Cable went down to New Orleans in March for a brief visit. There he found that, except for Marion Baker, James B. Guthrie, and several other close friends, his old acquaintances were obviously uncomfortable in his company. He continued on to the western parishes of the state to gain more information for his Acadian sketches, then returned home to Connecticut without staying in New Orleans any longer than needed to board a northbound train.[53] His failure to stop over on the way back disturbed Marion Baker, who wrote to express his disappointment at not seeing more of Cable. "I hope you fully appreciate my position on this, to you, beastly paper," he declared. "I came within an ace of handing in my resignation when the attacks began on you, and if I had not known it would have pained Major Burke, who has been so kind to me, I would have done so. It was a great trial to me to remain and see you assaulted so viciously. As far as Gayarré, I show him in every way I can how contemptible I think he is—the old fool and beggar. He charges you with making money by your pictures of the Creoles, and he goes whining around getting women to get up entertainments for him—Creole women, whom he poses before in the light of a knight who has slain the offender, Cable. I warned you against him long ago, and I told you the truth was not in him. Well, as for me, I take a vicious delight in pitching in to your slanderers." [54]

Gayarré was indeed capitalizing on the hostility toward Cable. In a group of lectures given for his benefit by sympathetic New Orleans ladies, he attacked Cable repeatedly. "Mr. Cable's aim," he said in one talk, "is to degrade, lower in the public opinion the reputation of the population of Louisiana, Creole or not, to put it socially, civilly, and politically below the black race, which he considers superior to ours and destined to africanize the entire South." The author of *The Grandissimes,* he asserted, "is as deprived of all moral sense as the crocodile." [55] Marion Baker's comment on this in a letter to Cable was that "old Gayarré is making a pretty good living attacking you. His lecture is out in pamphlet form." [56]

Instead of publishing all the numerous letters that were arriving in opposition to Cable's article, the editors of the *Century* decided to invite Henry W. Grady, editor of the Atlanta *Constitution* and leading spokesman for the New South program of industrial development, to write a reply, which Cable could then himself answer. A close friend and associate of Joel Chandler Harris, Grady was widely respected both in the North and South, and known as a moderate on race relations. His article, entitled "In Plain Black and White," appeared in the April issue of the *Century.* It was a fairly accurate statement of "enlightened" Southern opinion of the day.

Grady took as his premise the fact that "the people of the United States have, by their suffrages, remitted to the Southern people, temporarily at least, control of the race question." By way of undermining Cable's authority to speak on the question, he questioned his use of the expression "we of the South." He did not intend to indulge in personalities, he said, but he could not forbear saying that Cable's parents were of New England origin (which was not true), that Cable appeared to have had little sympathy with his Southern environment, had expressed himself in print as saying that New England was his spiritual home, and was doubtless happiest there. "There may be," he said, "here and there in the South a dreaming theorist who subscribes to Mr. Cable's teachings. We have seen no signs of one."

Grady directed his arguments toward social "intermingling" of Negro and white. The South, Grady said, would not accept Cable's suggestion of the social intermingling of the races; "It can never be driven to accepting it." Besides, "neither race wants it." The principle of race, Grady declared, was inviolable. Forced into mixed assemblies, the races build up an antagonism. "It is instinctive—deeper than prejudice or pride, and bred in the bone and blood." And this was necessary for racial integrity; without race instinct, the "lower and weaker elements" of the races would begin to fuse, and the process of amalgamation would have begun. This, he said, would result in the disorganization of society, and "internecine war" would be precipitated, for "the whites, at any cost and at any hazard, would maintain the clear integrity and dominance of the Anglo-Saxon blood."

The question faced by the South, Grady went on, was not intermingling, which was out of the question, but whether two races could exist equally free yet entirely distinct and separate. The answer was obvious, he said: the South has been existing in just such a fashion for ten years. "No impartial and observant man can say that in the present aspect of things there is cause for alarm, or even for doubt," that it was working well. Thus, Grady concluded, everything was settling into place in the South, and there was peace and content among Negroes and whites. "Each has his place and feels it, and is satisfied." There was no irritation or suspicion. "Nowhere on earth is there kindlier feeling, closer sympathy, or less friction between two classes of society than between the whites and blacks of the South today." (He did not mention that the year just concluded had seen 211 lynchings.) This good feeling was the result of the doctrine of the whites that the "responsible and steadfast element of the community shall control, rather than the irresponsible and migratory." All the

South asked of the rest of the country was patient and impartial judgment, and the rightness of Southern segregated society would be clearly evident to all.[57]

Grady's reply was more temperate and calm than most of the direct abuse that had characterized the usual response to Cable's essay. It had been Richard Watson Gilder's idea to run Cable's rebuttal along with it, but unfortunately Cable was unable to find time on his tour with Twain to write the rebuttal, so that it went unanswered until the September number, five months later. The delay weakened the impact of Cable's rebuttal, which in masterful fashion disposed of most of Grady's arguments. Entitled "The Silent South," Cable's essay was addressed on behalf of what he insisted was a silent but intelligent majority of the Southern people, whose views were not represented by newspapers and politicians, yet who could be expected to act fairly and justly if given the chance.

The Southern hostility to full civil rights for the freedman was based, he said, on the fear that social chaos would result thereby. The hostility to "The Freedman's Case in Equity" was based on that fear. But the essay had specifically ruled out social equality. "The present writer wants quite as little of it as the most fervent traditionalist of the most fervent South." No form of laws, no definition of rights, could bring it about. The South's error was that it was making "the double mistake of first classing as personal social privileges certain common impersonal rights of man, and then turning about and treating them as rights definable by law—which social amenities are not and cannot be." By using the phrase "social intermingling," Grady was simply begging the issue; those opposed to it "beg the question of equity, and suppress a question of civil right by simply miscalling it 'social intermingling'; thus claiming for it that sacredness from even the law's control which only social relations have. . . ." There was not room in the United States, Cable insisted, for any one class of citizens to force upon another class of citizens "a *civil status* from which no merit of intelligence, virtue, or possessions can earn an extrication. We have a country large enough for all the *unsociality* anybody may want, but not for *incivility* either by or without the warrant of law."

Grady had insisted that neither race wanted the Negro to have civil rights—rights, said Cable, for which the Negro "has been lifting one long prayer these twenty years. . . ." Yet it was not a question of what either race wanted, "but of *what the individual wants and has a right to.*" Neither Grady nor others had written a line to disprove the freedman's title to civil rights; instead, the emphasis was on the claim that the Negro race "does not want them and shall not have them if it does." Cable hit this point hard. "Mark the contradiction. It does not want them—it shall not have them! Argument unworthy of the nursery; yet the final essence of all the other side's utterances." The question was based by Grady on a supposed race instinct, which even if it did not exist would be advocated by the whole South. This ignored the whole question of the freedman's case *in equity*—of right and wrong. And yet Grady had promised that the South would solve the problem without passion or prejudice and in full regard for equity!

Social rights are one thing and civil rights another, Cable said. But while social rights guarantee one couple against the unwelcome intrusion of another, they do not give the same couple the right to insist upon the exclusion of another couple from a public assembly merely on the grounds that the second couple is of an inferior race. No one wants to see decency in dress and behavior usurped "by the common herd of clowns and ragamuffins"; but what the Negro does want is "the freedom for those of the race who can to earn the indiscriminative and unchallenged *civil—not social*—rights of gentility by the simple act of being genteel."

The Negro has demanded only separate but equal rights. "This was the demand, this is the supplication of American citizens seeking not even their civil rights entire, but their civil rights mutilated to accommodate, not our public rights, but our private tastes." Has the separate accommodation been equal? "Not one time in a thousand." Because the white South has thought of the Negro as a menial, it has granted him accommodations fit only for a menial. The Negro has learned that "equal accommodations, but separate" means conspicuously ignominious inferiority of accommodations. To say, therefore, that the Negro wants racial segregation, when such segregation "ignores intelligence and decorum," is absurd.

Cable then attacked Grady's assertion that the Negro himself wanted strict civil separation of races; he cited abundant evidence to the contrary, and declared that the claim was made by whites, and for the benefit of whites, and that the Negro's preferences were not considered. Next, Cable took up Grady's statement that the whites had the right to rule because of superior character, intelligence, and property. As a class, he said, the whites clearly were superior; but as individuals, there were many colored men who were "just as responsible and steadfast" as whites, so the assertion of white supremacy was clearly based not on "character, intelligence, and property" but on the color line. America was founded on "the principle that the right to rule is the consent of the ruled and is vested in the majority by the consent of all." The idea, therefore, that the "right to rule" meant "the right of the white man to rule the black without his consent and without any further discrimination between intelligence and unintelligence or between responsibility and irresponsibility" was not a principle that any free man could accept.

Cable also dealt with a letter appearing in the same issue of the *Century* as Grady's reply, which declared that the white people of the South had to remain united and solid politically, because of the fear of black supremacy, so that not until the Negroes were also divided could the white South risk political division. Cable pointed out that the Negroes of the South had voted as a unit in gratitude to the Republican Party and fear of the Democratic Party, and that so long as political domination by the whites meant suppression of civil rights for the Negro, the Negro vote would continue to be solid. The way to remove such solidarity, then, was to show the Negro that the whites were not solid in their desire to destroy his civil rights.

Cable concluded his argument by taking up the question of the "gradualist" position, midway between the two extremes, which held that full civil rights would eventually come to the Negro but only in due time. The same argument, he noted, had been used to justify the continuation of slavery. A hundred years was long enough for such an argument to keep the South from joining in the vanguard of the civilized world. " '*Make haste* slowly,' is the true emphasis," he maintained. The idea that the South could be commercially prosperous (as Grady and the advocates of the New South contended) while avoiding political advance

was false; politics was the means whereby a people safeguarded
its safety, comfort, and happiness. The South's present poverty
and backwardness was due to its previous insistence that "certain
matters in our politics shall be let alone. It was our letting them
alone that brought federal interference, and that interference has
been withdrawn upon our pledge not to let them alone but to
settle them." The piece closed on a note of optimism. The South,
Cable declared, must move on, and it would do so, for the best
minds of the South were learning to reject the mistakes of the
past. Even those now opposed to further political freedom for
the Negro would come round to that objective, because it was
inevitable.[58]

Throughout, Cable's logic was remorseless and impeccable. By
showing that the denial of civil rights in places of public assembly
under the guise of racial segregation was going beyond civil rights
and making personal preference into law, so that the word "separate"
inherently signified "unequal," he was anticipating by
seventy years the verdict of the United States Supreme Court
in the historic 1954 segregation decision. (His very use of the
phrase *"Make haste slowly,"* in opposition to the principle of
gradualism, would find an echo in Chief Justice Warren's "with
all deliberate speed.")

But if Cable's article was prophetic, it would be so only in
terms of the distant future. For the rest of his lifetime—and
decades more to come—the South would move to maintain and
enforce everything that he most censured. His contention that
there existed, beyond the confines of editorial rooms and political
hustings, a silent but potent majority of white Southerners who
wanted the Negro to have his full civil rights and desired an end
to discrimination by race, was delusory, as he would soon find
out.

The time had come for Cable to decide whether he would move
back to New Orleans or make a permanent home for himself
and his family in New England. Every consideration seemed to
dictate remaining in the North. He would have to keep on giving
public readings in order to earn enough money to support himself
and his family, and there was no opportunity whatever for that
in the South. His wife's health had clearly benefited from the

change. The abuse that followed publication of "The Freedman's Case in Equity" had shown him that he faced the hostility of almost the entire Southern press, and the brief trip to New Orleans in March had demonstrated that his position in that city would be very uncomfortable indeed. It would be difficult not only for himself, but for his children as well; they would surely suffer for their father's unpopularity.

"What are your plans for the future?" Marion Baker wrote. "The newspapers say, you will not again make New Orleans your home. Is there anything in this?" [59] His sister Mary Louise hoped he would return. "You may find plenty to do but nowhere are you so much needed as here," she wrote.[60] New Orleans was his home. For all the chorus of newspaper abuse, it was with New Orleans that he was identified. The guidebooks for the Cotton Centennial Exposition of 1885 gave prominent position to his work, and cited his stories repeatedly in identifying landmarks of the city. Whatever the Creoles and others thought, tourists saw the city through Cable's eyes, read his books, used his descriptions in making their way about the French Quarter and the other areas of the city. (Gilder himself had gone down to New Orleans for the exposition the previous winter. When Grace King complained to Gilder that Cable favored Negroes over whites, assumed the superiority of quadroons over the Creoles, and though well treated by the city had stabbed it in the back to please the Northern press, Gilder had replied, "Why, if Cable is so false to you, why do not some of you write better?" It was then, Grace King said, that she resolved to be a writer.)[61]

The decision that Cable made was probably inevitable. Two years before, he had visited Northampton, Massachusetts, and been greatly taken with it. It had good railroad connections, an active cultural life, and Smith College admitted the children of Northampton residents to its classes free of tuition—"no small attraction to a man concerned about educating a house full of daughters," as Philip Butcher says.[62] So early in September, 1885, he located a home, the Red House, and in October moved in with his family, now consisting of six children.[63]

His house on Eighth Street in New Orleans was sold in November for $5,500, of which all but $1,500 was still under mortgage. Before that, however, New Orleans had tried a last parting shot at him. The assessment on his movable property had been raised by $2,500. His friend, the lawyer James B. Guthrie, was outraged; the move was clearly made to penalize Cable for his views. He filed suit at once in Cable's behalf, and succeeded in having the movable property reassessed at a much lower figure. With the $1,500 profit from the sale of the house, plus advances of $1,000 each from Scribner's and Roswell Smith, the proceeds from the sale of two shares of New Orleans Cotton Exchange stock, and a mortgage for the remainder, Cable bought the Red House. The following summer the rest of the Cables—his mother, his sisters Nettie and Mary Louise, and Nettie's three children—left New Orleans and were also installed in Northampton.[64] Cable would live there the full forty years that remained to him.

XII
Northampton

While a resident of New Orleans, George W. Cable had been active in civic reform work and in the affairs of the Prytania Street Presbyterian Church. Moving to Northampton, he soon proceeded to undertake a similar role there. Though limited by the extensive traveling he continued to do as lecturer and reader, he began teaching a Sunday School class at the Edwards Congregational Church, became a member of the Northampton Social and Literary Club,[1] and, becoming interested in the national movement for home study, founded a Home Culture Club made up of four factory girls.[2] Philip Butcher, who has made an extensive study of Cable's career during his years in Northampton, has emphasized Cable's desire for social acceptance in his new home and has interpreted his eagerness to undertake worthy community projects as stemming in part from his wish to win the admiration and friendship of the leading citizens of Northampton.[3] This would seem a harsh interpretation of the activities of a man who had refused to keep silent about racial injustice when he knew well that to speak out would destroy his hard-won prestige in the city in which he had been born and lived all his life. And in a town as noted for its literary and cultural interests as Northampton—which moreover was the home of a much respected college—George W. Cable arrived with enough renown, both as author and as social reformer, to confer perhaps as much social prestige as he could ever have received.

A more likely explanation for Cable's rapid entrance into social and religious leadership is his strong need to participate in community activities. Having transferred from New Orleans to

Northampton, perhaps he did not feel at home until he had established himself in a similar role in his newly adopted community. If there was vanity mixed in with his civic-mindedness, that would scarcely be unusual; the desire for civic distinction and the desire to do civic good customarily go hand in hand, and to attempt to distinguish where one leaves off and the other begins is an impossibly difficult task. What seems more to the point is that Cable was a man of great energy, and throughout most of his career unable to channel this entirely into literary creativity; he needed to be active in social enterprises, and upon moving to a new home he set about at once to create a new forum for such activity. Significantly, he did no more writing in Northampton than he had done in New Orleans; at no time after he gave up his clerical position with the Cotton Exchange did Cable get as much writing done as he had managed to do when working for a salary. If his role as public reader and lecturer was more congenial to his interest in the writing of fiction, it was also more time-consuming.

Cable's finances did not notably improve during his Northampton years either; for thirty years and more following his move there, he remained plagued by debt and able to stay only barely ahead of his creditors each month. With Cable away on his reading tours, it was left to Louise to make income cover expenditures, and this was a difficult task. "How you can reason that it is right to give away so much of your time, when we owe so many bills, is quite beyond me," she wrote in exasperation at one juncture. "I am ashamed to go into the stores to order anything, we already owe so much, & entirely too much mortified to go near Dr. Cooper; and I thought November was to see us quite paid up." [4] To realize a sufficient income from his pen, Cable needed large blocks of time for writing, but he could not afford to give up his income from readings in order to secure that time; that was the dilemma he faced. Yet it is unlikely that even if ample time for writing had been available, he would have used it to good effect; he seems to have been congenitally unable to sink himself into a full-time writing routine for very long.

Cable's Bible classes in Northampton soon became very popular; he aimed his talks at the skeptic and the nonchurchgoer, and when attendance rose to more than 100 he moved the location to the Opera House. In 1887, he was chosen to conduct the Bible study class of the Boston Sunday School Teachers' Union on Saturday afternoon at Tremont Temple. He was paid $35 a week, and his class numbered several thousands in enrollment. After a little more than a year, however, he gave the class up; the commuting was arduous, it was difficult to schedule his platform readings to permit him to be in Boston on Saturday, and his religious opinions were not pleasing to a small but articulate minority of the council of the Sunday School Teachers' Union. For Cable's religious views were becoming increasingly liberal and social, and he was steadily growing away from the more narrow dogma of the Calvinism in which he had been raised. Increasingly he came to feel that religious activity which concentrated upon the letter of the Scripture and on sectarian considerations was ignoring the problems of society, in which religion should play an active role. In articles for the *Sunday School Times* and in lectures he stressed the need for the church to become involved in the chief moral questions of the day; religion, he felt, should be a liberating force, not a narrowing one. In a lecture that he delivered frequently entitled "Cobwebs in the Church," he attacked the commercialism of rented pews and the atmosphere of exclusiveness in churches which discouraged visitors and in effect kept out lower social classes.[5]

Never a literalist in his outlook, Cable throughout the 1880's and 1890's was not only broadening his attitudes toward the proper nature of religious belief, but also relaxing many of the more rigidly Puritanical tenets that he had been taught from birth were matters of morality rather than dogma. We have seen how his longtime opposition to attending the theater was ultimately put aside as he came to know actors and theater people in New York. He had long ago discarded the Presbyterian notion that novels and fiction in general were sinful. Before long he would be consenting to have his books dramatized, and even attempting playwriting himself. It was a far cry from the day when he had given up his newspaper position in New Orleans rather than attend a theatrical production. For some years longer he held out against traveling on Sunday, but eventually he capitulated. In his later years, he was even known to enjoy a drink of whiskey at home with the family in the evening. So that, despite Mark

Twain's vigorous expostulations over Cable's religiosity, Cable was steadily being weaned away from his Puritanism. Late in his life, at the seventieth birthday dinner for Mark Twain, Cable announced: "We have heard that the friend whom we celebrate has said he likes Cable well enough except for his religion. Well I am bound to declare the exception well taken. The longer I live the less I am satisfied with my religion myself." [6]

In the late summer of 1887, Cable went to Monteagle, Tennessee, in the Cumberland Mountains to speak to the fifth session of the Monteagle Sunday School Assembly. Founded by John Moffat, a Scots-born temperance lecturer and onetime commissioner of immigration for Tennessee, these annual Monteagle assemblies had become a Southern version of the Chautauqua movement; lecturers came to speak, noted singers appeared, and various schools and workshops were held. Cable delivered his lecture on "Cobwebs in the Church," and met the Moffat family, who were charmed and impressed by him. In particular he struck up a friendship with Adelene Moffat, a serious, pretty young woman of twenty-five. [7] A correspondence began, which resulted eventually in Miss Moffat's coming to work in Northampton in 1888, where she became his personal secretary and assumed administrative direction of the Home Culture Clubs. [8] She was to continue in this post for almost twenty years, while also pursuing a career as an artist.

The Home Culture Clubs were an organization for cultural self-improvement; the members met to discuss books and ideas. The clubs were not set up along social lines, and Cable saw them as a method of "elevating the masses." Each group had a leader from its own number who would read aloud and then preside over the discussions. The groups would organize themselves, each comprising from two to twenty or thirty members, and would meet weekly for nine months of the year. The first Home Culture Club was formed by four factory girls in Northampton on October 4, 1886; a year later there were six clubs, and by 1889 there were thirty. At the third annual public meeting, Cable announced that the formation of clubs in other communities would be encouraged, and within a year's time there were Home Culture Clubs in Philadelphia, Baltimore, Chicago, Parkville, Missouri, and Orange, Massachusetts. By 1894 there were fifty-four clubs, thirty-five of them in Northampton, and the others in towns and cities from Canada to Alabama. Each club reported its activities to the parent office weekly, and Adelene Moffat circulated a composite report about topics, readings, and activities. In 1888, reading rooms were leased in Northampton. Soon activities were expanded to include music concerts and other events. The work broadened steadily, and would occupy Cable for most of the remainder of his life.[9]

Throughout the late 1880's and the 1890's Cable continued his readings and lecturing, making several trips to the West Coast. The work was arduous and the money came hard. Some of the novelty of his performances had worn off, so that he could no longer fill auditoriums in Boston and the large cities. He gave a series of readings with the poet Eugene Field in 1892 and 1893, and on another occasion made a highly successful appearance in Chicago with James Whitcomb Riley.[10]

In 1892, Cable moved from the Red House to a new home at the edge of Paradise Woods. He called the new house "Tarryawhile," and spent much time landscaping it, laying out walkways, setting out fish ponds, and generally indulging a longtime interest. Whenever a famous person came to be his guest, Cable would have him plant a tree which thereafter bore his name.[11]

Meanwhile, his writing proceeded sporadically. He contributed two long essays to the *Century* in 1886—"The Dance in Place Congo" and "Creole Slave Songs." With H. E. Krehbiel he prepared a volume of Creole songs, but his *Century* editors found it too ponderous. Subsequently, Cable published most of the material in more popular form, transcribing the songs, discussing their themes, their social background, and language, and doing considerable research into music and folk history.[12]

Ever since his work for Colonel Waring and the U. S. Census, which had taken him into the interior of the bayou country west of New Orleans, Cable had been interested in the Acadians, and now his researches there bore literary fruit with the publication of three long stories—"Carancro," "Grande Pointe," and "Au Large"—which dealt with the Acadian people. The stories appeared serially in the *Century* during 1887 and early 1888, and were published in book form in March, 1888, by Scribner's under the title *Bonaventure: A Prose Pastoral of Acadian Louisiana.* Cable had recorded extensive historical and social data about these onetime French peasants, who had lived in Nova Scotia until the late 1750's when the British had expelled them and they had resettled in what was then Spanish Louisiana. Longfellow's *Evangeline* had described their exodus in verse, but until Cable wrote about them, little attention had been paid to them for purposes of fiction.

The Cajuns, as they were and still are known, were simple, pastoral folk, looked down upon by the proud Creoles and until well after the Civil War little noticed; in their mode of existence they had been largely unaffected by the developments of the nineteenth century. For the most part they had not been slave-owners, and many had resisted attempts to impress them into Confederate service during the war. In the 1870's and 1880's they still spoke little English, conversing in corrupted French that Cable studied closely and strove to reproduce in his stories. They possessed little schooling, and were largely illiterate. Cable observed them carefully, learning much about them from his friend Madame Sidonie de la Houssaye, who lived in Franklin, Louisiana. He admired their simplicity and rustic ways, though he deplored their conservatism and backwardness and was appalled by their illiteracy.

The stories that made up *Bonaventure* had pleased Richard Watson Gilder when Cable began sending them to him for magazine publication, though he complained of an occasional tendency toward "Johnsonian tremendousness" in moralizing. "Your fierce editor is very light on you this time, is he not?" he concluded. "Well, it is a beautiful story and will belong to literature." And, he penned in, "There is only one Cable." [13] It is not difficult to see why Gilder found so little to object to in *Bonaventure*. Unlike *Dr. Sevier,* the material is not subordinated to the requirements of a social message, it is seldom controversial, and it emphasizes the quaint pastoral setting of Acadian Louisiana in the best local color fashion. There is none of the unpleasantness, the realistic depiction of squalor, hatred, and prejudice that Gilder had found disturbing in *Old Creole Days* and *The Grandissimes;* the themes of race and miscegenation are absent, and the author's main concern is in depicting the gentle simplicity of Acadian life.

There is, to be sure, some social criticism. Cable's protagonist

in the first two stories, Bonaventure Deschamps, becomes a school-
teacher and struggles bravely to instruct the children of a tiny
village in the English that they will need if they are to improve
their lot, while his pupil Claude St. Pierre in turn works to bring
progress to the back country of his forefathers. Cable devotes some
attention to the impact of the coming of the railroad and the
schoolhouse to the Acadians, and at one point a priest is depicted
as playing upon the prejudices and fears of the simple Cajuns in
order to block the spread of education and ideas. But the Acadians
are too simple and unassuming to allow even their backwardness
to become very menacing.

Each of the three stories revolves around a love plot, and here
Cable is most melodramatic and sentimental. In "Carancro,"
Bonaventure loves Zoséphine Gradnego, who loves the devil-
may-care 'Thanase Beausoleil. Bonaventure has a part in directing
a Confederate recruiting detachment toward the Beausoleil farm,
with the result that 'Thanase enlists and goes off to war. When
'Thanase fails to return, Bonaventure, remorseful, resolves to find
him. He tracks him all across Tennessee and Mississippi and down
to New Orleans, returning home only to witness the wedding of
'Thanase and Zoséphine. Later 'Thanase is killed, and Bonaventure helps Zoséphine to educate her children. Then he goes off.

In "Grande Pointe," Bonaventure reappears as the first school-
teacher in the little settlement of Grande Pointe. Beloved by his
pupils, he works manfully to teach them English and prepare them
for the modern world. Disturbed at a priest's insinuation that if
the children learn English, the railroads and the migration of other
people into the area will follow, some of the elders of the community attempt to block Bonaventure's school, but they are foiled.
Bonaventure wins the hand of the beautiful Sidonie Le Blanc,
and all ends happily.

In "Au Large," the major development of the story is the love
story of Claude St. Pierre and Marguerite Beausoleil, daughter
of Zoséphine and 'Thanase. There is also the courtship of the
widowed Zoséphine by a jovial, goodhearted book salesman,
George W. Tarbox, who is the single non-Cajun of any consequence in the novel. Tarbox—a great talker, reciter of poetry, and
man of good will—seems a laborious version of a character out
of Dickens, with some of William Gilmore Simms's Captain Porgy

thrown in. In a scene reminiscent of the conclusion of *The Grandis-simes,* mother and daughter alike accept suitors. Bonaventure weeps for joy at the wedding and the spirit of true love prevails.

There is scarcely anything in *Bonaventure* that rises above the level of romantic, pastoral melodrama and sentimentality. Cable left out of it almost all the social satire and trenchant portrayal of social injustice that characterized his earlier work and gave it so much of its power. Writing *Bonaventure* at a time when he was doing battle with the racial attitudes of the entire South, he allowed nothing of this to find its way into his story. The charac-terization is simple and usually sentimental throughout. The book received much better reviews than it deserved; there was some hostile Southern criticism of it as being an argument in favor of Federal intervention in the public schools, but most reviewers praised the volume for its simplicity, its idealism, and its charm of description.[14]

Cable's only other nonpolemical publication during the latter years of the 1880's was the collection in book form of the *Strange True Stories of Louisiana,* published in 1889. Cable had been as-sembling these stories for several years. His friend Madame Sidonie de la Houssaye, who had helped him with the Acadian material, provided three of the total. Cable purchased from her one manu-script entitled "The Adventures of Françoise and Suzanne," telling of a trip from New Orleans into the southwestern parishes in 1795; a second shorter manuscript, "Alix de Morainville," which is the account of a refugee from the Revolution of 1798 who marries a commoner and settles in rural Louisiana; and a short, grisly tale of an early captivity—"The Young Aunt with White Hair." Madame de la Houssaye had literary ambitions, but had been unable to sell her manuscripts, most of which came from old family records; and Cable paid her a price appreciably higher than she could have expected otherwise.

When "Alix de Morainville" came out in magazine form, there were several glaring anachronisms which cast doubt upon the authenticity of the manuscript. Gilder was much upset by the development. Cable amended his introductory essay, "How I Got Them," for the book publication to account for these anachronisms; apparently, he explained, the story, though genuine, had been amended slightly in the recopying by some unidentified Creole who sought to dress up the account. Madame de la Houssaye was grateful to Cable for helping her to realize a profit from the publication of the manuscripts, and did not resent his incorporating them as his own.[15]

Not so Mrs. Dora Richards Miller. An impecunious widow, she was happy when Cable bought from her the "Diary of a Union Woman" which she had kept during the Civil War in Louisiana and Mississippi. Cable also helped her to publish an essay of her own, employed her to search historical records for him, and at other times loaned money to her.[16] But when in 1892 Cable published another manuscript, "A West Indian Slave Insurrection," which he had purchased from her after she had failed to find a publisher, she objected strenuously in a letter to the *Times-Democrat*. Cable had stated in his Introduction that he had taken the text exactly from the manuscript of a friend—the Dora of the narrative—and reiterated that it was hers, not his; but he did not list her name as author. When Mrs. Miller's charge that he had appropriated her work without credit was noted by other publications, Cable wrote a reply in which he emphasized the extent of his revision, and suggested that the implication that he had concealed her literary ability was hardly appropriate in view of her failure to sell the manuscript on her own.[17] This story, not included in the 1889 volume, was later incorporated into *The Flower of the Chapdelaines* (1918).

In purchasing the material of others and listing himself as editor, Cable was indeed, as Turner says, engaging in "a shaky type of business transaction that invited misunderstanding and ill feeling."[18] But it was Cable's theory that true stories, only slightly edited, were often as effective as fiction, and those in *Strange True Stories of Louisiana* were designed to demonstrate this. Unfortunately for his theory, the one story in that volume which does hold up well as narrative, "Attalie Brouillard," is the one which Cable most completely rewrote and redesigned, so that it comes close to being pure fiction. Based on a court case, it is the account of a quadroon actuary who attempts to secure for a quadroon woman the inheritance that her white lover had meant her to have, but which was jeopardized when he died intestate. The quadroon climbs into the dead man's bed, has the woman summon witnesses, and dictates a "deathbed" testament, in which he also cuts himself in for a sizeable share of the proceedings. But friends of the dead man, grasping what has happened, force the actuary to be executor and to discharge the debts and expenses out of his share, so that the woman receives her due legacy. Cable tells the story with much wit and dramatic suspense. Of all the stories in the collection, it is the only one that is of much more than historical interest.

Thus Cable's entire literary production, from the time of *Dr. Sevier* in 1885 until the publication of the novel *John March, Southerner* in 1895, consisted of a set of three connected stories about the Acadians and the edited tales of *Strange True Stories of Louisiana.* None of these is among his best work, and it is obvious that as a writer of fiction Cable had arrived at a considerable hiatus. His removal from New Orleans had apparently not helped his literary productivity at all.

The slackening of writing impetus is not surprising, because for the ten years following his move to New England, Cable was chiefly interested not in imaginative literature but in arguing the case for civil rights. His removal to the North did not represent for him any backing away from the race problem in the South; it only intensified his efforts to awake the Southern conscience to the inequities of its treatment of the Negro. For a while he carried on personal correspondence with certain Southerners who had questioned his views, and in some cases succeeded in forcing an admission that he was correct in his statements. When Scribner's collected several of his essays on the Negro issue in a volume entitled *The Silent South,* published in 1885, two correspondents wrote to question his ideas. Cable published their letters and his replies to them in the *Century* and in a second edition of *The Silent South* in 1889. For the most part, however, he refrained from personal exchanges, realizing the enormity of the problem and the futility of piecemeal response. Instead, in a number of public addresses, most of which were also published in essay form, he fought his battle.

Through the auspices of Professor William Malone Baskervill, who had read and admired Cable's stories and novels and taught them to his students, Cable was invited to make the literary commencement address at Vanderbilt University on June 14,

1887. Baskervill had in correspondence with Cable expressed his sympathy with much of Cable's argument about the South, and assured him that he could speak in Nashville without fear of reprisal.[19] Major Pond wanted to arrange for a series of readings throughout the South as part of the trip, and sent out telegrams of inquiry, but only four acceptances were received, and three of these were soon afterward withdrawn. Nevertheless, Cable decided to make an extensive tour throughout the South to talk with people there, study conditions, and do whatever he could to stimulate progressive thought. He wrote back to his wife that "the light is breaking"; he felt encouraged and confirmed in his belief that behind the articulate public expression of pro-segregation dogma in the South was a vast body of right-thinking white Southerners who wished to give justice to the Negro, but were afraid to speak out. The only unpleasant part of Cable's trip came in New Orleans, where once more he found that save for such old friends as Marion Baker, James B. Guthrie and a few others, he was greeted with embarrassment and coldness.[20]

While waiting for the train in Washington that would carry him south to Richmond, Cable met another *Century* author, Thomas Nelson Page. Though Page had not at this time published his novels of the post-Civil War South, he had already achieved considerable renown for his stories, in particular that entitled "Marse Chan" which had appeared in the *Century* for April, 1884. Like Cable, Page was interested in the Negro, but their views and their fictional depictions of the Negro were diametrically opposed. Page's Negroes were designed to defend and to extoll the golden days of slavery; in picturesque dialect, they recounted tales of the blissful time before the Civil War when kind masters and beautiful mistresses reigned benevolently over lovely plantations and cared for legions of happy, contented, carefree slaves. An aristocrat himself, Page had little use for post-Civil War America or for civil rights; he constituted himself a defender of the old regime. What he represented can be glimpsed from the way that the New Orleans novelist Grace King, a Creole herself and an arch foe of Cable's, wrote of him many years later. "It is hard to explain in simple terms what Thomas Nelson Page meant to us in the South at that time. . . ," she said. "Charming and personally unaffected in his manner and conversation, and unconscious of the effect he produced, never-theless Mr. Page made an impression upon the North such as no other Southern writer had been able to do. Wherever he went, he made friends, not only for himself but for his people, and he portrayed the Negro character, humorous, shrewd, and loyal to his master and his family as it has been stereotyped in fiction. . . . "[21]

In a letter to Louise, Cable told her that Page "recognized me in the Washington depot & introduced himself. I traveled with him, his wife & one or two other Richmond people."[22] Apparently Cable liked Page; years later he wrote a sketch describing the meeting and praising Page as a writer and a man. Page, however, did not respond as warmly to Cable, though he disguised his feelings well. On several occasions in later years he spoke and wrote unfavorably of Cable; on this occasion, however, he was all cordiality. He wrote to Gilder:

> I fell in with Mr. Cable on the platform in Wash[n] yesterday; made his acquaintance by boldly asking if it wasn't himself. We had a pleasant ride together. . . . I do not agree with all of his views, but I had made arrangements to have him meet some of our Editors who I believed on meeting him would come to understand him better than they do generally in the South. I introduced him to a friend of mine, the red-hottest, old, Bourbon democrat, who sent him a card to the Westmoreland Club.[23]

How much of this was due to Page's desire to be kind to his fellow Southern writer, as Herbert Franklin Smith notes, and how much to his desire to impress Gilder with his broadmindedness and tolerance, it is difficult to say. In any event, Cable enjoyed the privileges of the Westmoreland Club, though, as he reported to his wife, "the gentle negatives are very obvious" in that "the house is about empty of members and no attempt has been made to have me well met here. It is not I but their own courtesy they are trying to take care of. . . . "[24]

In Nashville he was received with cordiality and even enthu-siasm. The *Daily American* published a biographical sketch which compared him to Hawthorne. An interviewer quoted him on his views of the South. He delivered his speech before a full house, which the *American* said "was a most complimentary recognition of one of the greatest men of letters who lives in this country today." [25] Cable's address, "The Faith of Our Fathers," was later revised into a magazine essay entitled "The Negro Question." In the final version he pointed out how, by the tacit acquiescence of the North as well as the instigation of the South, seven million American Negroes were being denied the civil rights that were supposedly the just due of all American citizens. He detailed some of the indignities and injustices meted out to the Negro in the South, and stressed that at the base of the white South's attitude toward the Negro was the conviction that the white race must keep the Negro race in an inferior position. Two irreconcilable positions were involved, he declared, both of them part of the American heritage. One was the belief that "the only permanent safety of public society, and its highest development [was] to require the constant elevation of the lower, and thus of the whole mass, by the free self-government of all under one common code of equal civil rights." The other was that "public safety and highest development . . . require the subjugation of the lower mass under the arbitrary protective supremacy of an untitled but hereditarily privileged class, a social caste."

The North's philosophy was based on the former attitude and the South's on the latter. Thus "it was inevitable that the most conspicuous feature of one civilization should become the public schoolhouse, and of the other the slave yard." The Civil War had been fought to settle the question; yet it had not been settled. Many people of the North now believed that the experiment of freedom for the Negroes had been tried during Reconstruction and had failed, but the truth was that the South had never permitted it to be tried fairly. The only solution to the problem was to remove the white South's fear that if the Negro were enfranchised and given his full civil rights, he would "usurp the arbitrary dominion now held over him and plunder and destroy society." That fear, Cable said, rested in turn on the fear that civil equality would result in social equality. All evidence showed that this was unrealistic. Racial integrity did not depend on the impersonal and unselective relations of public society, but on private society, which had nothing to do with laws and civil rights. If the white South would only recognize this obvious truth, it would be willing to grant the Negro his civil rights, and a debasing and corrupting situation would be ended.

Cable praised the remarkable material progress being made in some sections of the South. "May the South grow rich!" he declared. But unless the wealth of the South were founded upon genuine liberty, it could never be permanent. The prosperity of what was "loosely called the New South" was not so based, he said; "it is only the Old South readapting the old plantation idea to a peasant labor and mineral products." Lasting prosperity for the South depended upon broadly based wealth and full educational opportunities for all. Wealth and intelligence followed from education and liberty, not vice versa. Those who believed that greater liberty and education would follow prosperity in the South were wrong: "the community whose intelligent few do not make the mass's elevation by public education and equal public liberty the cornerstone of a projected wealth is not more likely to provide it after wealth is achieved and mostly in their own hands."

The best and only hope for the South and for the nation, Cable concluded, lay in granting to all Americans full equality and full educational opportunities. All the South needed to do was "more completely Americanize" her upper class so that it could take the lead in providing for equal opportunity and education. What was needed was a return to the philosophy of the Southerners, who had in former times led the nation in the striving for democratic society; a return to "the faith of their fathers." If this could take place, "there will be a peace and a union between the nation's two greatest historic sections such as they have not seen since Virginia's Washington laid down his sword, and her Jefferson his pen." [26]

In the version of the speech delivered in Nashville, Cable apparently made the Negro question only a part of his remarks; he stressed the signs of progress throughout the South, and emphasized that the Negro problem was only one aspect of the larger problem of democracy and the education of the masses. The Nashville *American,* editorializing on "Mr. George W. Cable's Great Error," endorsed most of his points, and protested primarily his impracticality in seeking to attain at once what the South was working toward slowly. But, the editorial continued, Cable should leave the South alone, report the progress already made, and not ask for greater haste. [27]

Convinced by his reception in Nashville and elsewhere that

there was indeed an important body of Southern opinion that favored greater rights and opportunities for Negroes as well as whites and that opposed the racial intransigence of most Southern politicians and editors, Cable felt that the urgent necessity was to encourage others with his views to speak up. It was with this in mind that he conceived the idea, in correspondence with Baskervill, of an Open Letter Club, in which leading Southerners would set forth their views, criticize each other's ideas, and publish the results in the form of symposia. Thus with Baskervill as secretary, a distinguished group of Southerners was formed: they included college presidents, professors, physicians, lawyers, judges, ministers, educators, and editors.[28] Cable's friend the Negro writer Charles W. Chesnutt, whose work Cable tried unsuccessfully to help get published, was among the number; Cable wanted him to serve as his personal secretary, but plans did not work out. Adelene Moffat handled most of the clerical duties, and soon became devoted to the undertaking.

The first symposium of comment appeared in the *Independent* for February 21, 1889. Entitled "Shall the Negro Be Educated or Suppressed?", it consisted of a group of commentaries on the Methodist minister Atticus Greene Haygood's reply, in the *Independent* of November 8, 1888, to an article on racial antagonism in the South by Senator J. B. Eustis of Louisiana. There were eight contributors, including Cable and Baskervill, and three more were included in a pamphlet republication. Soon another symposium was under way, with six men taking part. Cable was delighted; he believed that genuine headway was being made in getting enlightened Southern opinion expressed.[29]

Appearances, however, were deceptive; the growing conservative trend both in the South and throughout the nation was not favorable to calm debate, and the Open Letter Club soon came to grief. The immediate occasion was another visit that Cable made to Nashville in late November, 1889, to talk with Baskervill and to address the students of Fisk University. On December 6 the Nashville *American*, which on his previous visit had been so conciliatory, published an editorial in which it announced that before leaving Nashville, Cable had spent a social evening in the company of "our colored elite," entertained by J. C. Napier, colored. Cable had often urged social equality of the races, and "we are glad to see him following his own advice on the subject. In the South, however, a man must choose the race with which he associates and Mr. Cable having signified his preference for the negro race over his own should be left undisturbed to his choice." The newspaper did not mean to imply, the editorial continued, that in accepting the hospitality of a Negro, Cable had lowered himself; "on the contrary we think he found his proper level." And it concluded with the familiar accusation that Cable had turned renegade to the South in order to gain Yankee money.[30]

Letters defending Cable and further editorials attacking him swiftly followed. Cable wrote in his own defense to give his version of what had happened. He had made an appointment with Napier to discuss problems of the Open Letter Club with him and other Negroes. Knowing that they would not be permitted to sit down in any public room, he met the group in Napier's parlor and granted their request to have some of their wives and daughters join them. "When all were gone," he wrote, "I, seeing that my host and hostess were in a dilemma between asking a white man to sit at their board and sending him away supperless, said bluntly I had not eaten. We broke bread together. Was I wrong in that? To anyone who answers yes, I can only reply, Shame on you! Shame on you!"[31]

The Open Letter Club was already in difficulties, both from want of funds to distribute its pamphlets and because of the growing differences of viewpoint between some of its members. The Napier incident, which was promptly taken up in newspapers throughout the South, had the effect of discrediting Cable anew on the very issue that he knew was the stumbling block for those who advocated Negro civil rights: social equality. His support began dropping away, the various contributors to the Open Letter Club became reluctant to take part in further ventures, and the group soon disintegrated. Baskervill, as Cable's Nashville sponsor, came in for severe attack, and the upshot was that he resigned as secretary. He wrote Cable on January 6 that "as a question of expediency I think you made a mistake in 'breaking bread' with the Napiers. The bugbear used to frighten the southerner is social equality and this act came near enough to suit the purposes of our young editors and all who think like them. If you had not eaten with the Napiers, you could have come here & filled a house. Now your coming would be the signal for a personal attack on you in every newspaper of the city. . . ." Though he knew Cable did not favor social equality, he said, "still your enemies can claim, as they now do," that he favored it. Thus the solution to the problem had been made more difficult by Cable's action.[32]

Cable's reply was that though he regretted the inconvenience caused to Baskervill, he was glad that his own enemies knew where he stood. "I tell you, this soothing and pacifying and conciliating these people intoxicated with prejudice and political bigotry, is helping neither them nor any worthy interest. I am glad my record is made and that I stand before them as unclothed with any reservation as a swimmer." [33]

Baskervill, like many another Southern liberal who had spoken out on civil rights and then been subjected to continuing hostility and misrepresentation, had been weakening in his zeal, and the Napier incident was a key point in a retreat from the high ground he had earlier assumed. By the time he published his volume of essays on Southern writers in 1897, he had so changed his views that he included a severe attack on Cable for his failure to understand the South's treatment of the Negro. Cable's inability to grasp the realities of Southern conditions, Baskervill wrote then, "has so affected the sensitive nature of an extremely artistic temperament as to make this writer give a prejudiced, incorrect, unjust picture of Southern life, character, and situation. This domination of one idea has vitiated the most exquisite literary and artistic gifts that any American writer of fiction, with possibly one exception, has been endowed with since Hawthorne. . . ." [34]

The Open Letter Club was Cable's last active venture in the cause of civil rights, but he was far from done with his speaking and writing on the subject. Throughout the late 1880's and into the 1890's, he continued to use every opportunity that presented itself for keeping the issue before the public. In an essay for the *Forum* for December, 1888, he replied to several authors who had written articles for that magazine either apologizing for or denying the existence of the disfranchisement of the Negro voter in the South. Entitled "A Simpler Southern Question," Cable's essay attacked the contention that extending the franchise to the Negro constituted any threat to the white South. Again he scorned the notion that a fair trial had been given to Negro suffrage during the Reconstruction, or that the intent of Reconstruction measures that gave Negroes the vote had been, as several writers claimed, an attempt to Africanize the South. The key question, he said, was this: "Must the average mental and moral character of the whole Negro race in America equal that of the white race, before *any* Negro in a Southern state is entitled to the civil and political standing decreed to all citizens of the United States except the criminal and insane?" On that crucial point, whether the Negro was to be treated as an individual citizen or as a class, the issue rested. The question was whether the American government should or should not be a government " 'of the people, by the people, and for the people,' according to the Constitution's definition of who the people are." A true American loyalty could give but one answer.[35]

In a short article for the Chicago *America*, June 13, 1889, Cable took up the problem of "What Makes the Color Line?" Here he castigated the idea that there was any natural, instinctive antagonism between white and Negro races, and contended that the so-called Negro block vote was not the product of an inborn instinct but a direct result of white attitudes and behavior. If the Negro voted Republican rather than Democratic, it was because the Republican Party had given him "freedom and citizenship, and *promises,* at least," while the Democratic Party "still says to him not only that he belongs to a degraded and inferior race, but that in all his public relations he must be judged and treated according to his *race's* merits and demerits, while his white fellow citizen monopolizes the ennobling liberty of being judged and treated according to what he is himself." The only way to expect the Negro voter to divide his vote was thus for both parties to cease treating him as a member of a class and begin treating him as an individual. The color line was drawn in the South not by the Negro but by the white man.[36]

In 1889 Cable also spoke out on a public question which was closely related to the cause of Negro rights in the South, and which for some years had caused considerable debate throughout the nation. Senator Henry W. Blair of New Hampshire had introduced a bill in 1883 calling for ten annual appropriations—

beginning at \$15 million and diminishing by \$1 million each year—to be distributed among the states in proportion to the amount of illiteracy in each. In order not to run afoul of the race question, the bill would have permitted expenditures to segregated school systems; and because of the widespread illiteracy in the South, principally among the Negroes, the Southern states would have received the largest share of the appropriations. From 1883 through 1890 it was hotly argued. Party politics was involved, because the bill had been introduced by the Republicans in order to relieve the treasury of a large surplus due mainly to revenue from the protective tariff. Thus support of the bill could be construed as tacit support of the tariff.[37] The Blair Bill was opposed, therefore, both on political lines and on the grounds of constitutionality. Many Southern industrial leaders favored the measure in part because of its relation to the tariff issue, while other Southerners who were in general favorable to increased educational expenditures opposed it for the same reason. At the same time, the race issue was involved; the money would have to be spent for Negroes as well as whites, and there was fear that more and better education for Negro children would make them less easily manipulable in elections and less malleable in general.

Cable favored the bill, and published an essay to say so in the *Independent* for August 29, 1889: "The Nation and the Illiteracy of the South." After making a specific plea for the Blair Bill, he took up the matter of whether the Federal government should make appropriations for public schools. The nation, he declared, owed a national debt to the South, because educational destitution there was the direct result of defects in the social order caused by the longtime existence of Negro slavery. The costly and bloody sacrifice of the Civil War, he claimed, may have been an expiation for slavery, but an expiation was not a restitution. The loosening of the bonds of the Negro's ignorance as well as of illiterate whites would permanently safeguard civil freedom.[38]

Even while Cable continued his active and increasingly lonely campaign for Negro civil rights, the plight of the Negro in the South continually worsened. What Cable said and what he thought was not what majority sentiment in the white South said or thought; he was an annoyance, a lone crusader uttering annoying statements in the national press, and his remarks had absolutely no effect whatever on Southern opinion. The late 1880's and the 1890's were a period of darkening despair for the Southern Negro. The crop lien system was fixing him into a seemingly permanent inferior economic status. State after Southern state was enacting disfranchisement laws; the upsurge of agrarian resentment against the Bourbon governments was accompanied by an irresistible pressure for disfranchisement of the Negro; the fact that the Negro vote in the "black counties," in which the population was largely Negro, was often shamelessly manipulated by white conservatives in opposition to Farmers Alliances and Populists only increased the Southern rural white's resolve to bar the Negro from all political office. What Negro political power still remained after the end of Reconstruction was gerrymandered, legislated, and intimidated out of existence. Jim Crow laws were enacted in every Southern state, and made more thoroughgoing and uniform where they already existed. The share of educational appropriations going to Negro schools was steadily reduced, so that per capita expenditures for Negro education declined both relative to white expenditures and absolutely.

Paradoxically, much of the public rationale for Negro political disfranchisement took the line that it was a step toward pure government and against political corruption. The Negro could not vote intelligently, so he must be disqualified, the argument went; only when he was removed from the political picture would pure government be possible, and bribery and corruption eliminated. The argument was received not unsympathetically in much of the North, where political corruption was likewise a burning issue in the cities, and where bloc voting by immigrants seemed to imperil good government. Faced with the human results of the rise of industrialism and the Civil War, political opinion throughout the nation turned increasingly conservative; businessmen and property owners recoiled in horror as the implications of unrestricted democracy seemingly began manifesting themselves. Serious attention was being given to the idea of an educational qualification for voting, so that the ballot would be withheld from unqualified Negroes and unqualified whites.

To Cable the notion was menacing; it struck at the very roots of public education and of American freedom. In speeches in New Haven, Chicago, and Cleveland he attacked the idea, and in

Boston on Washington's Birthday, 1890, he incorporated these talks into an address, "The Southern Struggle for Pure Government."[39] The only kind of pure government possible, he maintained, was self-government; "No man is good enough to govern another without his consent," he quoted. Pure government can only follow after free government, because anything less than free government will keep classes and parties preoccupied with one another's actual or possible aggressions. A government not free must be corrupt, and a free government cannot remain corrupt and continue free.

In the South, "conditions are seemingly so peculiar and exceptional" that "no theorizings on the relations and necessities of pure and free government can be made to appear practically applicable." It has been contended that a whole class of Southerners was inferior, and neither knew nor cared anything about good government; to give them free government, therefore, would result not in pure but in corrupt government. This premise Cable denied. What happened during Reconstruction, when the Negro could vote, only showed that "there can be no effective effort for pure government, while an insecurity of free government keeps classes or parties occupied with one another's actual or possible aggressions." The white South had almost unanimously opposed and refused to cooperate with the Reconstruction governments.

The great majority of Negroes in the South remained illiterate, improvident, reckless, and degraded, said Cable, but "so is the Irish peasant. So is the Russian serf." The same arguments now advanced against giving the Negro the right to vote were applied barely a century before against millions of white men. They were based "on the same specious assumption, that the ignorant, unintelligent, and unmoneyed man is virtually in all cases dangerous to society and government, and most dangerous when invested with civil and political liberty."

In the twelve years that had followed the end of Reconstruction, Cable continued, the political power of the Negroes had been nullified, and "the white, intelligent, wealth-holding class" had been in control. Yet the South had not known pure government, for "even the present ruling class [in the South] is not strong enough or pure enough to establish and maintain pure government without the aid and consent of the governed." The struggle to keep the Negro out of power "keeps the colored vote solid, prevents its white antagonists from dividing where they differ as to other measures, and holds them under a fatal one-party idea that rules them with a rod of iron."

Cable then took up the matter of the New South. Barely three months before, the late Henry W. Grady of the Atlanta *Constitution* had made an impassioned speech in Boston on the race problem in the South. Speaking in opposition to the threat of civil rights legislation pending in Congress, and defending the disfranchisement of the Negro on the grounds of the need for pure government, Grady had linked his case for the South's being trusted with its own handling of the Negro with the promise of everything that the industrializing New South held for the future. Cable praised the growing wealth of Southern industrial cities and towns, but warned that "a sagacious and enterprising few may get rich in any country blessed with natural resources, but no *country* ever won or can win a large and permanent prosperity save by the prosperity of its poor." The notion that the New South policy of material development could ever solve the Southern problem was absurd, he said; "it is simply fantastical to expect a mere aggregation of private movements for the building of private fortunes to unravel the snarled thread of civil and political entanglements in a commonwealth." There were prosperous Negroes in the South, and they worked in peace. "But what a peace! A peace bought by silent endurance of a legalized system of arrogant incivilities that make them, in almost every public place, conspicuous objects of a public disdain which is not always even silent." What opportunities had the New South given to its Negro citizens? he asked. "Where has this New South movement opened to colored people, paying taxes or not, professionally educated or not, the privileges of a single public library?"

For twelve years the South had asked the nation to let it be responsible for preparing the Negro for citizenship and had even refused to accept Federal funds to help with the burden of public education. Yet it had not yet made the slightest provision for allowing any Negro to achieve full civic or political rights by virtue of having earned them. In order to allow the white South to attain "pure government" through white supremacy, the nation "has endured more deadly outrages against its citizens within its own borders than it would have tamely submitted to from all the great powers of the earth combined."

What, then, should be done? Cable was speaking in 1890, with the knowledge that the plight of the Negro in the South had steadily worsened, and that the white South had now made it clear that it was not going to give the Negro his civil and political rights. He made a proposal to the South, therefore, and a suggestion to the North and the West, that was different from anything he had ever before said or written.

Let the South, he said, go on with its material development, and let it continue to strive for pure government. A complete about-face, he conceded for the first time, was impracticable; "we do not demand a sudden and complete revolution of Southern sentiment and policy. All the nation is really impatient for is to see the South once turn and *start* in the right direction." If the South cannot reconcile itself to declaring full equality, let it try a few steps at a time. Let it end segregation in railroad transportation and admit Negroes to public libraries. This at least would be a beginning.

Thus for the first time Cable asked for less than full civil rights for the Negro. Significantly, he spoke not as a Southerner to Southerners any longer, but as an American to a section of the country of which he was no longer a part. "These concessions—or such as these—will we make for you," he declared, "if you will join with us politically for pure men and purifying measures." But if the white South refused to make such concessions, and remained adamant in the denial of civil rights to its Negro citizens, then, Cable said, only two alternatives remained to the rest of the United States. One was direct Federal intervention—a last resort, but necessary if no other solution were forthcoming. The other was for the Democratic Party of the North and West to dissociate itself from the Southern policy again, as it had done in 1860. Just what the result of such dissociation would be, Cable did not say; presumably it would mean not merely a separate political identity for the Northern Democratic Party, but support in Congress of measures designed to protect Negro civil rights in the South, which would doubtless mean the passage of laws and their subsequent enforcement.

Thus did this onetime Confederate cavalryman come, after

more than a decade of pleading with the South to give the full privileges of citizenship to the Negro, to speak out in support of a policy of direct Federal intervention in the South once again, twelve years after the last troops of Reconstruction had been withdrawn. No doubt he spoke with the knowledge that Massachusetts Senator Henry Cabot Lodge had introduced in the Senate a bill whereby Federal supervisory officials were to be appointed in any election district where 500 voters petitioned Federal authorities, and that these officials would have power to pass on the qualifications of challenged voters in all Federal elections and to receive ballots refused by local officials. He was thus, in effect, lending his support to the so-called "Force Bill" if the South continued to refuse civil rights to Negroes.[40]

This was Cable's last major polemic on civil rights. Eight thousand copies in pamphlet form were distributed throughout the South by the Massachusetts Club, and the speech was included in a second book of his writings on civil rights, *The Negro Question*, which Scribner's published late in 1890. He must have known that there was little hope of what he asked coming to pass. Lodge's election bill, though passed by the House, was permanently blocked in the Senate. A deal between Southern Democrats and Western Republican senators for support on a silver coinage bill ensured that it would not have the necessary Republican votes to win Senate approval.[41]

The truth was that the vast majority of Americans both North and South did not want the "Force Bill" passed; they were tired of the race issue, and did not wish further agitation. The revulsion against Reconstruction had not worn off. The South was to be allowed to handle the Negro in its own way; the plight of the freedman was not the nation's concern any longer. Not race, but economics would be the principal factor in the election of 1892. Widespread agricultural discontent, bitter industrial strife, and a business recession combined to put the race issue out of the public mind. The Democrats, threatened by the farmers' revolt, could not afford to antagonize the South; the Republicans were burdened by resentment against their high tariff policy and their unpopular alliance with big business. A Democrat, Grover Cleveland, was swept into office, and Southern electoral votes were instrumental in his victory. The Negro would have to shift for himself. It would be another sixty-seven years after Cable's Boston speech before a United States President would use Federal force to guarantee Negroes their civil rights in the South.

Cable wrote two more essays on the Negro in the South, "Does the Negro Pay for His Education?" in the July, 1892, *Forum,* and "Education for the Common People in the South" in the November, 1892, *Cosmopolitan.* In both he opposed the poll tax, criticized the South's failure to provide adequate schooling for the Negroes, and emphasized that not merely Negroes but poor whites as well suffered from the South's failure to provide rural schooling. With these articles, and the pure government address, he ceased his public agitation of the Negro question. It had brought him ostracism in New Orleans, and had failed utterly in its effort to arouse the conscience of the South. In the North, among the leaders of literary and cultural opinion in the genteel establishment, he was coming increasingly to be regarded as a crank. Gilder, who had once been sympathetic, had long since ceased to accept his essays on civil rights for the *Century,* and was urging him to leave off his pamphleteering and return to fiction. In the South, the leading spokesman for the Negro, Booker T. Washington of Tuskegee, was advising his fellow Negroes to learn trades, become useful members of their communities, and cease striving for civil and political rights for the present. "Keep your vote alive; better nine free men than ten half free," Cable had told a Negro club;[42] the policy that Washington was advocating represented to Cable a tragic mistake. Washington was a political realist; better than Cable he knew what was taking place in the South and the nation. But it was Cable, and not Washington, whose writings on the role and plight of the Negro in the South would seem to ring with the clarity of prophecy three quarters of a century later. What Cable was saying and thinking in the 1880's and 1890's, almost entirely alone among white Americans, would one day be what millions of Americans, many of them Southerners, would say and think. The South might build monuments to Henry W. Grady, but it would be the social ideas and the moral convictions of George W. Cable that eventually became the conscience of the nation.

Though Cable himself withdrew now from the hustings, he was not finished with the South. In his late forties, with the intention once and for all of saying what he thought and felt about his native region, he set to work in earnest on a new novel.

XIII

John March, Southerner

John March, Southerner was begun in 1889. Written in the summers, and on trains and in hotels during Cable's lecturing tours, it was revised several times before publication. After serialization in *Scribner's Magazine* in 1894, it was published in book form in February, 1895. It is not Cable's best novel; *The Grandissimes* is probably that. But in terms of its author's life and career, it is his most interesting work, and certainly his most ambitious. He wrote it during the years when his heroic and futile campaign for Negro rights was drawing to an end, when he was forced to recognize that the South had no intention of permitting the freedman to retain the rights of citizenship granted him during the Reconstruction period, and that "enlightened" opinion in the North was willing to acquiesce in allowing the South to do what it would with its Negro citizens. Almost single-handedly he had fought against Southern recalcitrance and Northern indifference as best he could, gone into exile from his native New Orleans rather than remain silent, and on the lecture platform and in the columns of magazines had denounced what was going on with devastating logic. But the South was not willing to listen, and his unwillingness to give up the fight had begun to weary and even to embarrass his Northern friends.

When Richard Watson Gilder had published "The Silent South" in the *Century* in 1885, he and his fellow *Century* editors not only had been proud of the consternation it had caused among orthodox Southerners, but had even doubled the customary rate of payment to express their approbation in tangible form. But by now Gilder had in effect gone over to the other side, and was no longer eager to use the columns of the *Century* to attack Southern racial injustice; one after another the essays that Cable wrote in the late 1880's were rejected. Gilder made no secret of the fact that he wanted Cable to leave off agitating the racial situation and return to the writing of fiction, by which he meant local color fiction. This, he felt, was Cable's appointed task; his campaign for Negro rights Gilder thought an aberration, a misuse and waste of his God-given talent.

Cable, however, was not willing to surrender. The cause of racial and political justice represented to him a challenge second to none; the distance between his new place of residence in Northampton and the South he had left seemed only to intensify, for a time at least, his sense of obligation to his native region. For awhile he had accepted Gilder's attitude, to the extent of keeping such matter out of his fiction and confining it to the lecture platform and to magazine essays. But now that he began to realize that his crusade for civil rights in the South was failing, he apparently changed his mind, and determined that his next novel would not be devoid of political and social content. If it was as a novelist that he was best heard, then he would use his fiction in order to say what he thought about the South and the Negro. Not another *Bonaventure*, but a novel on the order of *The Grandissimes*, would be his aim. Only his new book would be different from anything he had ever before attempted.

He set out to produce a novel which would allow him to describe what was going on in the South. He wanted to comment on the region's problems, to show the limitations of the New South ideology of industrialism and development as a solution for the region's troubles, to demonstrate why the Negro must be fitted into Southern plans instead of being disfranchised and set off by himself. More than that, he wanted to describe the South as he knew it, to show how narrow evangelical religion was failing to bring out the best in Southerners, to depict the character of some of the men who were claiming the role of leadership, to strike out at lethargy and complacence, to show how good people with good intentions were acquiescing in injustice and in materialistic schemings. He wanted to show that the outworn shibboleths and conventional responses of the past were inadequate to the needs of the present. This was to be his book about the South—as it was and as it could be—and he did not intend to leave out anything important.

For his locale, New Orleans and the rest of French-speaking Louisiana would not be appropriate this time. The presence of the quaint, bantering Creoles would militate against his objectives, both because the Creoles were not typical or representative of the largely Protestant South and because the specific problems of urban, settled New Orleans were not typical of those of the rural, undeveloped South. So his new novel was not set in Louisiana. Tentatively he selected the area around Monteagle, in southeast Tennessee and northern Georgia, near the mountains but not in them. Not only was the population of that portion of the South more representative of the region; the mineral resources of the area would also give him the opportunity to deal directly with Southern problems of industrialization and expansion.

He would not, this time, preach; he was aware of the dangers inherent in the direct use of literature for propaganda, and he knew that if his novel were to succeed in accomplishing what he intended, it would have to do so as fiction, and by fictional means. He was dissatisfied with the shallowness of the local color fiction that was the order of the day, and dissatisfied with books which oversimplified or romanticized the reality of Southern experience. He knew that the Southern question was not easy, and he was aware of the tremendous burden of habit, prejudice, custom, and lethargy that Southerners must bear in their attempt to do what was right. So instead of ignoring all this, he would face it squarely; he would choose for his protagonist a young Southerner of good will, but equipped with a great deal of the excess baggage of custom and attitude that would hamper him in his objectives until finally he learned what had to be done, and what must be discarded in order to do it.

Cable's original title for his novel was *Johnny Rebb*. The protagonist, however, would not be a Confederate veteran. The novel would open as the war ended. It would show a youth, with the troubled heritage of the South for his birthright, growing to maturity and attempting to exercise leadership. Though he would have to contend with Confederate veterans, and live in a time when the Lost Cause was fresh in everyone's mind and heart, he must not be a former rebel himself, for that would have meant that he had been born and raised amid an inheritance of slavery. Cable wanted his protagonist to represent the new, nonslaveholding, post-1865 South, and to be thoroughly and squarely of it; it would be part of his task to realize the demands and the opportunities inherent in the South he inhabited, and to learn that he and his region need not labor under the yoke of the Confederate, slaveholding past if only there were sufficient courage and determination to throw it off.

At some point close to the heart of his story of the South must necessarily be the fact, and the problem, of the Negro. Cable had been accused, even by Southern moderates, of romanticizing and idealizing the freedman, of making him out to be completely ready for full citizenship and full participation in government, when any Southerner knew that the mass of former slaves was incapable of undertaking the duties and privileges of citizenship, and needed to be governed, for its own benefit, by the whites. Cable of course was well aware of the limitations of the freedman; he had lived in the South for the first four decades of his life, and did not labor under any illusions as to the general level of attainment of a race only recently freed from bondage. His contention all along had been that the white South's proper attitude toward the Negro should be one of doing all that it could to help him prepare himself for citizenship, and to deny him no rights lawfully his; if the Negro were treated fairly, he would lend his political support to those whose good will and interest he trusted, and would in no sense constitute a threat to good government.

The South's duty, Cable felt, was to assist the freedman to become a useful citizen, and the way to do this was emphatically not to deny him his civil rights, segregate him from all contact with the whites, and force him into the status of a permanent peasant class. He wanted, therefore, in this novel to show that the Negro, even at his worst, could and should be trusted, and that civil rights for the Negro did not threaten the best elements of Southern life. So he chose, for his leading Negro character, a man embodying many of the least attractive aspects of the freedman's personality, determined to show that even *this* Negro (whom none could accuse him of romanticizing or idealizing) knew that his best interests lay with those who would increase Southern educational opportunities and seek economic development for the benefit of all the people, not merely the wealthy few.*

Finally, Cable wanted to show how the Confederate tradition was being misused by so many Southern politicians and economic entrepreneurs for purposes of profit and power, and how the cloak of genteel respectability was masking, throughout the South, economic and political rapacity of the most unbridled sort. He wanted to show how old prejudices and outworn attitudes were being allowed to get in the way of the South's realizing and acting in its true interests. He would therefore seek to demonstrate how difficult it was for his protagonist, a man of the best intentions and the most patriotic attitudes, to ascertain what were really his true interests, and how to further them.

This was a large order for a novel, and it would all have to be done without overt preaching and lecturing; the story and the characterization must be made to carry the whole burden of the argument. And since it was to be George W. Cable's novel, written for George W. Cable's audience and, hopefully, for serialization in Richard Watson Gilder's magazine, it would have to contain a great deal of material that was pleasing and ennobling, which meant that a love story must play a prominent part.

Cable had his new story under way by May of 1889; on May

*Such have been the changes in American racial attitudes since the decades following the Civil War that it is sometimes difficult to read the work of even the best intentioned writers of the period without being brought up sharply by the presence of attitudes and beliefs that seemingly are in contradiction to what they say they believe. Specifically, in Cable's instance we sometimes encounter unmistakable evidence of racism in the writings of this man who dedicated much of his career to seeking justice for the Negro. In *John March, Southerner,* for example, he resorts to some of the traditional racial stereotyping that we ordinarily associate with nineteenth century local color fiction. Some modern critics have denounced Cable for just this, and have pointed to his repeated insistence that he favored political but not social equality as evidence of bigotry and even of intellectual dishonesty. Such objections seem to me misplaced. The point surely is not that this ardent crusader for civil rights privately held some of the views that the vast majority of white Americans of his day also held, but that, even though holding these views, he nevertheless felt impelled to battle so valiantly against the denial of civil rights to Negroes. To demand that this nineteenth century author be free of the pervasive influences of his time and place is to demand a virtual impossibility. What is important is that Cable was able to transcend them, in a way that few other Americans of his time and place did.

3, he reported to Louise that he had written on it all day long on the train while returning from a reading in Omaha, and all the next day while waiting for an evening reading in Oberlin, Ohio. "I'm making some real progress with my pen," he reported.[1] Two days later he wrote from Utica, New York, to say that the new work "is very sermony and pamphlety as yet, but I shall kick it into shape by and by. I almost believe I have begun my novel!"[2] As we have seen, his original idea was to locate the story in the Tennessee country near Monteagle. Immediately before the furore of the visit to Nashville which resulted in the end of the Open Letter Club, he had gone to Monteagle and toured the area with a guide, "he answering my questions & making innumerable suggestions concerning the scenery, life, geology, botany, &c &c of the country, & I writing as fast as possible on a pad these valuable notes." He then left with Adelene Moffat's sister, Mrs. Jennie Moffat Weir, "a long series of questions such as I made out & got the answers to when I studied the Acadians & the Opelousas-Atchafalaya regions in the 1880–81, so effectively and profitably."[3] In between his lectures, the furore over the Open Letter Club, and the preparation of the essay on "The Southern Struggle for Pure Government," he continued his work. By April 1 he wrote Louise that he had completed about 5,000 words.[4] "The plot is so fully in my mind," he went on a few days later, "that I do not find myself delayed by it. I mean of course the pivotal facts—it isn't good to have the details of plot worked out in advance."[5]

Perhaps because of the unpleasantness of the Nashville incident and the embarrassment he had caused Baskervill, he decided about this time to shift the locale from southeast Tennessee to northwestern Georgia; "I find I can get to Marietta Ga. by midnight tonight," he wrote Louise on May 17 on board a train, "& it is almost central to my imaginary state of Dixie—central as to convenience of movement, and on the direct route back northward."[6]

The following two days he spent in Marietta; he walked about the town, attended church, visited the National Cemetery where the Union dead from Sherman's 1864 campaign lay buried, and walked all the way up Kennesaw Mountain, feeling very lonesome and even dejected. "I suppose this dejection is only fatigue," he wrote Louise. Perhaps it was, but one suspects that mixed in with the fatigue was Cable's awareness of the difficulty of the fictional task confronting him, and also the enormousness of the whole Southern problem, and the pathetic inadequacy of one man to make inroads against it. For there he was, quite alone in a northern Georgia mountain town, in a region which, although part of the South he had once fought for and with whose fortunes he had concerned himself so deeply and thanklessly, was alien to his native New Orleans; nearby was a battlefield where Southerners and Northerners had fought. Now, a quarter century later, the issue that had divided them was still far from being resolved. During that quarter century he had grown to middle age and become a "famous" writer, yet apparently he was as far from financial security as ever for all his books, and so estranged from the good folk of that little Georgia town that his anonymity was a welcome protection, save only with the keeper of the Union cemetery "to whom I can speak my name & be sure of giving no offense." [7] Ahead of him were more and seemingly endless train trips, more speaking and writing; before long he would have enough of the manuscript ready for Gilder to see. Perhaps he already guessed all too well what Gilder's response was likely to be.

The dejection passed, and he continued on his journey. "I have been very fortunate in finding just the region I was looking for," he wrote Louise two days later from Cartersville, Georgia, where he had visited Dr. and Mrs. W. H. Felton, "& just the people in it I wanted to show it to me." [8] By mid-July he was ready for Gilder to examine the manuscript; he proposed that he come and read him "the 1st and 2d installments, complete, of a 12 months serial, which, after all, you may not want to print, although I am trying to get my very best into it. . . ." [9] Gilder preferred to read the manuscript himself rather than hear it read aloud, however, so Cable had Adelene Moffat copy it, and on August 16 forwarded 115 typewritten and 5 penciled pages of manuscript. [10]

Gilder's response was what Cable had feared. "I could weep for disappointment." he declared. "Here are gleams of the delightful old art—but . . . a tract, not a story,—to my mind. Instead of a return *to* literature; an attempt to fetch everything into literature save & except literature itself. . . ." Apparently "everything save & accept literature itself" for Gilder included violence, for he continued: "'John Rebb' opens with a corpse, then goes into a brutal thrashing, & continues with a series of political conversations between which scarce an incident is interjected—though here & there comes in a piece of natural description; or some human or humorous touch inimitable;—but not enough to make the story readable; or to make the story a story." "Shades of Tourgee!—" he continued. "My dear Cable, forgive me for being so damnably blunt; but I am fearfully chagrined." Cable's sin was that he was using his reform material in fiction: "If it needs must be that all this *must* go into an (allegory) story—a pill with the sugar on the inside & the quinine on the outside—so must it be. I fear you have hoped to put much of your most serious thought on public, political & humanitarian questions into just this form; and that it must be worked off this way & not merely in essays & addresses." He promised to let his *Century* associates see the manuscript without telling them what he thought, and closed with a postscript: "I can't tell whether the story could, with your conscientious consent, ever be what I hoped for. *Beware of the fate of Tolstoi.* A greater use of language—and a more conscientious man never lived." [11]

Gilder's complete failure to perceive any value in the novel, however much Cable had suspected it might happen, obviously shocked Cable profoundly. For what he had shown Gilder, whatever its shortcomings, was *not* a tract. It must have become obvious to Cable that what Gilder considered nonliterary, didactic material was the presence within a story of anything of political and social relevance, regardless of how it was used or in what form it appeared. It was *unpleasantness* that Gilder objected to; he wanted Cable to deal with no material that would offend the sensibilities of his readers. His objection to the "brutal thrashing" was to a scene in which a returning Confederate officer whips an ex-slave for daring to suggest that the outcome of the war had made them equal—it is a powerful scene, and, in later versions at least, not handled polemically. Gilder simply did not want ex-Confederates whipping uppity Negroes in his magazine. This was no way to begin a novel that was to be serialized in the *Century*.

It was quite clear what Gilder desired of Cable. He said as much in the postscript to a letter written two months later; Cable had not replied to his comments on the novel, so Gilder added, in a letter introducing a British journalist, this remark: "My letter about the book must have disappointed you—I trust it did not hurt you. I wrote in great disappointment myself, for I had great hopes of the next book to follow Bonaventure the Beautiful!" [12] He wanted another bland pastoral idyl; in his eyes Cable was squandering his talent by writing fiction about ex-Confederates beating former slaves, and Southern Bourbons struggling to win back control of the South during the Reconstruction, when he could be producing more local color stories.

Cable's failure to acknowledge Gilder's harsh critique is not surprising; throughout his career Gilder had been his editor and mentor, and surely it must have been shocking to have to realize that such a man was now completely uninterested in and unsympathetic to his desire to deal in his fiction with the most passionate and deeply felt concerns of his life. His loyal New Orleans friend Marion Baker recognized what was involved; he knew what Cable wanted to do, and he understood its importance. The Bakers visited Cable in Northampton in late August, and were apparently there when Gilder's letter arrived, for on September 6 Baker wrote to Cable: "I trust Gilder's letter did not discourage you. Too bad the state doesn't pension literary people so that they can write as they please—especially needed for you. Give me news of John Reb Gentleman." [13] Baker reiterated his support several months later. "I [hope] you will not be bull-dozed into eliminating all the strength out of [your novel]," he declared, and added that "if Cleveland is elected, perhaps Gilder will get a mission abroad and you can write as you please for the Century." [14]

But Gilder's ideas of what was proper in fiction were also those of his associates. When in May of 1891 Cable sent three revised chapters to the *Century,* the verdict, this time from Clarence C. Buel, was the same. Cable was informed that on the basis of these chapters the story would not do. Cable was some $4,000 overdrawn on his account, but even so he was assured that he was at liberty to place his manuscript elsewhere. As Arlin Turner notes, there was considerable pique on both sides. The longtime relationship between the *Century* and its most famous literary discovery was coming to an end, even though Cable tried still another revision on the magazine two years later. [15]

Since the first draft of the novel does not exist, it is impossible to know exactly what the story was like before Cable began revising it to meet Gilder's complaint that it contained too much violence and didacticism. The earliest manuscript available, apparently that written in late 1890 and 1891 and rejected in part by Buel, does not open "with a corpse," as Gilder had complained of the original. Since both versions apparently began with Major Garnet and his adjutant Jeff-Jack Ravenel pausing on the site of a recent battlefield near the town of Suez on their way back home from the war in 1865 (one surmises that Cable had in mind Marietta, Georgia, and the nearby Kennesaw Mountain battlefield), it is difficult to see why the sight of a corpse would have been so inappropriate. In any event, what happens instead is that the two ex-Confederates merely pick blackberries, gaze on the sight of Rosemont College in the distance, pledge themselves to the future of the college, of which Garnet is president, and ride off toward it.

In June of 1893 Cable was ready to try the *Century* again. He sent Gilder an extensively revised manuscript. Gilder read it at once, and was not impressed. It would not serialize properly, and had "less 'charm' than any of yours I have read." What he disliked about it was quite clear: "There is an innate disagreeableness that seems to pertain largely to the conditions described. The mind is irritated continually & can never rest in any pleasantness—the spirit is not free—the happiness or the unhappiness of the characters—everything seems to be spoiled—both the mirth and the misery seem to lack dignity and completeness[?] . . . sociological or economical [sic] discussions are not seriously sugar-coated by being put into dialect.—To tell truth I'm dreadfully blue over the book. . . ." [16] Three days later Gilder wrote again; he had sent the manuscript on to the New York office (he was vacationing in Massachusetts), and would not tell Johnson or Buel what he thought until they had been able to read it. But he felt that the "fundamental trouble with the story perhaps is that it does not seem to have its origin in a deep sense of art." He did not find the story offensive, with slight exceptions, in its criticism of the South, "although of course I dare say it might not please them. The trouble is a sort of unpleasantness, and in the writing there is a staccato quality that makes it somewhat difficult to follow.—To me it is entirely outside of your beautiful old art work. There is an apparent effort to conceal salutary purpose in the book—but it is there, all the same,—running along in a sort of irritating way. . . . After it is off your hands—we'll go to work in the old spirit of Beauty and of Art and add to the number of your long & short exquisite artistic masterpieces." [17]

In vain Cable tried to reassure Gilder that he could make it into what the *Century* wanted: "If there is any preaching, cavilling, arguing or drivelling in it, it can come out and it shall. If this is not the best book I ever wrote, it shall be before it is printed, and you shan't be blue about it, my true and good friend. . . ." [18] "My goodness, Gilder," he pleaded in response to Gilder's second letter, "this is a better story every way than Dr. Sevier dared to be. The movement is stronger, deeper, and infinitely more varied. Dr. Sevier may have more youth in it, but this has more virile energy." He added in a postscript that two other leading editors had expressed interest in the book, "but their ways are neither yours nor mine and what I want is to pass the thing through your crucible." [19]

Gilder was unmoved, and when his associates had confirmed his verdict, he wrote Cable briefly and finally that it would not do for the *Century*. "The objections are so fundamental that I think it would be a waste of time to try to adapt it to our use," he said. "I have said all I could before, but I will only say again that I am more sorry than I *can* say." [20] With this exchange, Cable's close relationship with Gilder and the *Century* was at an end. The novel was accepted by Edward L. Burlingame for *Scribner's Magazine,* serialized throughout 1894, and published by Scribner's as a book on February 11, 1895 (though the first edition is dated 1894). The original title, *Johnny Rebb,* was changed first to *Wildwood* and finally to *John March, Southerner.* [21] During the remainder of his life Cable published only three short pieces in the *Century.* One of them was a eulogy of Gilder after his old editor's death in 1909.

What editing and revision was done on the successive drafts of *John March, Southerner* after the first revision of 1891 would appear to have been not so much in the effort to remove controversial material as to make it more pleasant for the reading public. Early in the novel, for example, after young Barbara Garnet has been greatly upset by her father's whipping of the ex-slave on the very first evening of his return from the war, she is told by her mother that she must ask God's blessing for her father in her prayers. "Well, I'll ask him, but I don't think he'll do it," the child replies. Apparently this kind of irreverence would not do, for in the published version the comment has been eliminated. On another occasion the two former Confederate officers, Garnet and Ravenel, encounter a sociable Union officer who offers them a drink of whiskey. In both extant manuscript versions the two ex-Confederates disdain the proffered offering, and a violent political argument results, in which the Union officer denounces them for their aloofness and their opposition to the Reconstruction government. Garnet soon afterward arranges with a Union major-general to have the offending Bluecoat transferred to the West. In the novel as published, however, the encounter is brief, the drink is declined politely but curtly, and the episode ends. Here the artistic gain in the revision is clear, even though an instance of the subverting of Reconstruction efforts by the former Confederates has been eliminated.

What we do not know, however, is not only what Cable took out of the first, unrevised version of 1890 after Gilder had criticized its violence and its political passages, but also what he put *into* the story in order to make it more pleasant and less overtly political. Gilder's reiterated insistence upon "sugar-coating" the pill, his demand that what Cable wrote must have "charm" and must be pleasant, must have had its impact. It should be noted that Gilder at no time proposed making the political and social material into acceptable fiction as such, or even considered that the possibility existed for doing so. His assumption was that what Cable was doing was trying to make unusable material usable by adding "pleasant" material.

No doubt this was precisely what Cable thought had to be done. There was no room in Gilder's aesthetic for "unpleasant" novels, and nothing in all the extant Gilder-Cable correspondence from the mid-1870's onward indicates that Gilder ever sought to show Cable how to *use* his most urgent concerns to better fictional advantage. One can only agree with Edmund Wilson's statement that "the influence of the Northern editors was to prove in the long run as lethal to Cable's career as the South's hostility to his views on race," and that "the slow strangulation of Cable as an artist and a serious writer is surely one of the most gruesome episodes in American literary history." [22] Gilder, however unintentionally, was being very revealing when he told Cable that he did not think "the story could, with your conscientious consent, ever be what I hoped for"; as an editor he did not for a moment doubt that his editorial ideas of what Cable's fiction should be, and not the author's, came first. Nor did it occur to him that a novelist of Cable's stature and reputation ought to be permitted to have his say more or less on the terms he wished. Such was the attitude of the distinguished editor of the leading American magazine of the day on the proper literary roles of editor and author.

Did the first draft of *John March, Southerner* depict a Negro politician—Cornelius Leggett—as not merely an unscrupulous knave but the comic blackface character he is in the first revision? Or did Cable "sweeten" Leggett in order to make him ridiculous, hoping thus to dilute the unpleasantness? We do not know; but the fact that Gilder made no mention of Leggett in his correspondence of 1890, while in 1893 he praised the characterization, calling him the "best & most original character" and admitting that "the reader does get some fun out of him!" [23] might seem to indicate that Gilder was seeing him in a comic role for the first time in the 1893 version. And was the lengthy and syrupy love affair between John March and Barbara Garnet, which so spoils the latter half of the novel, developed to such interminable length by Cable in a desperate effort to please his editor?

We do not know, and in a sense the question is irrelevant, for however much one may deplore the role of Richard Watson Gilder, the final responsibility is Cable's; he wrote the love scenes, and there is no evidence to suggest that he did not think them appropriate. The John March-Barbara Garnet relationship is in the novel not merely because of Gilder, but because of the whole Genteel Tradition; it is typical magazine material, no better and no worse than most of the fictional romances of the period, written by a man who wrote willingly and eagerly for a magazine audience. What makes it so noticeable is its continual presence in a novel that is otherwise as realistic a depiction of a time and place, and as honest an attempt to grapple with the most urgent issues and problems of that time and place, as exists in pre-twentieth-century Southern and American fiction.

As it finally appeared, *John March, Southerner* opens not with Major Garnet and Jeff-Jack Ravenel approaching Rosemont, but with Judge Powhatan March purchasing a gift for his seven-year-old son John in a general store in the town of Suez, located "in the State of Dixie, County of Clearwater, and therefore in the very heart of what was once the 'Southern Confederacy'. . . . " The year is 1865, the season late spring, and the war has just ended. In the second chapter the Judge and his son come home to Wildwood, their estate. Mrs. March, considerably younger than her husband, is revealed at once as being selfish, self-pitying, and demanding, while the Judge is gentle, fond, forbearing. Daphne Dalrymple March is a comic character, a consummate satire on Southern Womanhood, United Daughters of the Confederacy-style, who is renowned locally as a poetess and adored by her husband. She uses her "frailty" to make her adoring husband wait on her hand and foot. The Judge's sweetness, his devotion to his son, and his essential impracticality are revealed in the gift he has selected for John, a copy of Chesterfield's *Letters*.

It turns out that the Marches are impecunious, despite their vast holdings of land. They are "land poor"; the Judge will not sell any of "ow hund'ed thousand an' sixty acres" because of a longtime pledge to his own father to hold onto the family estate and to "fill these lan's with a great population, p'osp'ous an' happy." It is this legacy and this trust that Judge March passes on to his son, and John's efforts to develop the land during the post-Reconstruction South constitute the chief narrative development of the novel.

There are two other leading families, the Garnets and the Hallidays. The Reverend John Wesley Garnet, A.M., until recently major in the Confederate Army, is a onetime preacher who has founded and serves as president and proprietor of Rosemont College. Ambitious, thoroughly secular despite his religious training, Garnet is anxious not only to develop Rosemont College but to enrich himself as well. Throughout the novel, he is busy with real estate and stock transactions, often of a highly unscrupulous nature, in order to further his aims. His wife, who does not figure importantly in the novel, is gentle, sickly, and quite unaware of her husband's shady practices. Their daughter Barbara, who is several years younger than John March, is the romantic heroine of the novel. Quite early in her life Barbara learns to suspect and distrust her father's machinations, and when John March, grown to manhood, begins to try to develop his landholdings, she does all that she can to foil her father's plan to gain control of the March lands. Garnet is eager to dupe the unsuspecting young man and secure the property, not only for its unexploited commercial and mineral wealth but because—as we learn at the end of the novel, after many devious hints by Cable—through a mixup in titles made many years before, the land on which Rosemont College is located is actually the property of the Marches.

The other important family of the novel is made up of General Halliday, a politician who makes the mistake of accepting the verdict of the war and being elected to office as part of the Reconstruction government, and his daughter Fannie. The daughter is older than John March and Barbara Garnet by some ten years, and although Barbara is the novel's heroine, Fannie Halliday is a much more interesting and fully realized character. John March worships her, despite the disparity in age, and is grievously disappointed when she marries Jeff-Jack Ravenel, Major Garnet's onetime adjutant, now his business associate and editor of the Suez *Courier*.

Ravenel is another very realistically drawn character—so, for that matter, are almost all the major characters in the novel, with the exception of Barbara Garnet and, in his role as romantic lover, John March himself. What is most remarkable in Cable's novel is the roundness and thoroughness of his characterizations. Where we might, in the typical Southern fiction of the period, expect local color stereotypes, Cable gives us characters such as rarely appear in Southern novels before William Faulkner.

Ravenel is a fine example. Handsome, a war hero, he is highly intelligent; he sees what is going on in Suez and the South, recognizes the hypocrisy and double-dealing in the politics of the day, is quite aware of his partner Garnet's lack of scruples—and yet willingly goes along with the whole business. He is narrowly honest, in that he will not do anything that is patently crooked financially; but in a larger sense he is quite corrupt. He is entirely willing to use his newspaper to support "worthy" causes that will also promote his and Garnet's financial welfare; he is ready to provide lofty editorial rationalization for political maneuvers that will defraud the Negro population of its rightful share of public educational expenditures, even though he knows exactly what he is doing; and he is highly skillful at political and legislative sleight of hand designed to divert public funds for private benefit. Arlin Turner comments accurately that Ravenel "assumes no clearly consistent character, perhaps reflecting the author's view of Southern journalists as at best sincere men wanting the good of the region but led to defeat their own purposes through lack of understanding."[24] Ravenel is more than that. He is Cable's example of the dubious integrity of even the leading Southerners of the period, honest by narrow standards, by no means intentionally dishonest, but willing as a matter of habit to take part in transactions and activities that by any absolute standard are flagrantly self-serving and morally wrong. Ravenel is very convincing; no allegorical figure, he is thoroughly believable and human. In his amiability and his weaknesses—he gets drunk on his wedding day, and is locked out of the compartment on the train by his bride—he is one of Cable's most memorable people.

His bride, Miss Fannie Halliday, is no stereotype either. Beautiful, accomplished, intelligent, very much the Southern belle in full flower, she is a thorough realist; she marries a man of whose weaknesses she is thoroughly aware, knowing full well that in their romance it is she, and not he, who is the seeker, and that, as she tells Barbara Garnet, "after the wedding I've got to do all the courting. I don't doubt he loves me, but Barb, love isn't his master. That's what keeps me scared." She marries Jeff-Jack not only because she realizes his less than complete moral rectitude, but because she also knows her own shortcomings along that line. The characterization of Fannie Halliday at times seems Jamesian in its subtlety.

Major Garnet, Cable's villain, is also a character whose full lineaments very much transcend the usual stereotypes of Southern local color fiction—so much so, in fact, that they quite enraged Cable's onetime admirer William Malone Baskervill. Baskervill (as we have seen) by 1897 had retreated far back from his earlier advanced position on the Southern question, so it is not surprising that he found *John March, Southerner* "one of the most dismal failures ever made by a man of genius," with "hardly a true note in it." His prime example of its falsity is that "an old Confederate,

plucky enough to fight to the end and brave enough to save the
life of a comrade at the risk of his own, is chosen for the villain."
Garnet, Baskervill says indignantly, "beats a negro unmercifully,
slaps his grown daughter in the face, kills his wife with cruelty,
swindles John March out of his estate, seduces his friend's wife,
and then shoots the friend down on the street."[25]

In nineteenth-century fiction, ex-Confederate heroes did not do
such things, of course; nor did they connive in real estate deals
and mineral exploitation, use public funds for private advantage,
talk religion and seek emolument, or work to disfranchise the
Negro and deprive him of his share of public expenditures whether
by fair means or foul. The reader whose ideas of the post-
Reconstruction South have been formed from reading its local
color fiction will not recognize Garnet—but the reader of C. Vann
Woodward's *Origins of the New South, 1877–1913* and other good
historical accounts of the period will. Garnet is not drawn from
literary romance; he is drawn from post-Reconstruction public
life. The same is true of General Halliday; more than one authentic Confederate hero held public office under a Reconstruction
government, and then after the white South gained full control
once again, managed to hold onto his gains and even win reelec-
tion. To suggest that Halliday's public career is not typical is to
fly in the face of the indisputable evidence of, for example, the
careers of at least a half-dozen prominent politicians in the very
state of Georgia in which *John March, Southerner* is supposedly set.

General Halliday, however, is no villain; indeed, he has greater
principle than most of the other public figures. The fact that he
could advocate Negro rights during the Reconstruction period,
and then afterward help to oust the Negro leader Cornelius
Leggett from office, is no more inconsistent than the actions of
numerous other human beings. Cable's characters are rarely
one-sided; all of them—again, except for the romantic leads—
contain a mixture of good and evil in their makeup. Even Major
Garnet is by no means entirely despicable. And in the characterization of Cornelius Leggett, the Negro leader, Cable makes the
paradox of good-in-evil a central theme of his novel.

Leggett *is,* in important ways, a stereotyped local color Negro:
there is no denying that. Whether Cable originally intended him
to be the comic he eventually becomes as the novel unfolds, or

whether he intensified Leggett's blackface role in order to answer Gilder's demands for "charm," one cannot say; in any event, Philip Butcher's comment is true: Cable "descended to minstrelry and stereotyping in presenting Negro character."[26] Cable plays for laughs by having Leggett misuse the English language for purposes of pomposity, in the manner later made famous by such blackface characters as Amos and Andy: "'Mr. Mahch, I'm impudize to espress to you in behalfs o' a vas' colo'ed constituency— but speakin' th'oo a small ban' o' they magnates with me as they sawt o' janizary chairman—that Gen'l Halliday seem to be ti-ud o' us an' done pass his bes' dotage, an' likewise the groun's an' debasements on an' faw which we be proud to help you depopulate yo' lan's, yass, seh, with all conceivable ligislation thereunto.'" Leggett is lustful, inconstant—he has a succession of wives, and he is quite corrupt and crooked. He takes bribes, uses blackmail, lines his own pocket with public funds, in the style of the Negro Reconstruction politician as traditionally limned in all Southern white accounts of Carpetbagger rule. If, as has been suggested, Cable determined in *John March, Southerner* to lean over backward in order to show that he was not idealizing the Negro, he succeeded. (Though it should be pointed out that, just as with his ex-Confederates, Cable had solid historical precedent for depicting a post-Civil War Negro politician along such lines; possibly Cable had in mind William Hooper Councill, of Huntsville, Alabama, though there were numerous examples available to him in the course of Reconstruction government in Louisiana.)

But Leggett is not merely a rogue and a scoundrel, not merely a comic character. He is also, and this is important, a skilled and devoted advocate of Negro advancement and a strong supporter of education. For all his personal corruption, Cornelius Leggett politically represents the side of the right; whereas for all Jeff-Jack Ravenel's personal integrity, he is politically on the side of wrong. Leggett will go along with various schemes to exploit resources and utilize public funds for private advantage, but he has his price: and his price is money for Negro schools. "'Yass, sah, faw of co'se ev'y man got his axe to grime,'" he tells John March. "'I got mine. You got yo's, ain't you?—Well, o' co'se. I respec' you faw it! Yass, seh; but right there the question arise, is it a public axe? An' if so, is it a good one? aw is it a private axe?

aw is it both? Of co'se, ef a man got a good public axe to grime, he espec'—and you espec' him—to bring his private axe along an' git hit grime at the same junction. Thass natchul. Thass all right an' pufficly corrosive. On'y we must take tu'ns tunnin' the grime-stone. You grime my axe, I grime yo's. How does that strack you, Mr. March?' " As he tells John a few minutes later,

> "Ef you wants to make a rich country, you ain't got to make it
> a white man's country, naw a black man's country, naw yet mix
> the races an' make it a yaller man's country, much less a yaller
> woman's; no, seh! But the whole effulgence is jess this: you got
> to make it a po' man's country! Now, you accentuate yo' reflections
> on that, seh!—Seh?"

The point about Cornelius Leggett—he makes it himself—is that while he commits little thefts here and there, and is publicly branded a thief and a charlatan, the Garnets and their like connive at making big deals, enriching their private coffers to an extent quite impossible to Leggett, and are termed developers of the state's natural resources and public benefactors. Leggett commits no crime or sin which is not also committed by white men, and usually on a much larger scale.

What Cable wanted Leggett to symbolize was the fact that the natural interests of the Negroes of the South lay with those whites who supported measures genuinely aimed at the public good, and that anyone who would deal not favorably but simply fairly with them could command their support. Granted for the purpose of argument, Cable was saying, that the Negro is ignorant, vain, not above chicanery at times—that, in short, everything that Southern whites said of him is true; *even so,* his true interests necessarily lie with the cause of popular government and public education, and he will support anyone, white or colored, who will genuinely work for that cause.

All of this is in the characterization of Cornelius Leggett, not merely implied, but dramatized and embodied; so that for all the blackface stereotyping and low comedy involved, he is an effective and genuinely realized creation, who comes across to the reader with considerable force and meaning. Underneath the surface cliché there is genuine depth. There is not another figure like him in all nineteenth-century Southern literature, and he is far larger than the local color stereotype in which he is cast. Butcher's conclusion, that Leggett "is an ineffectual spokesman for the author, since Cable never ratifies his pronouncements," [27] seems to me mistaken; Cable makes his point with Leggett very effectively.

It is chiefly with John March, however, that the fortunes of Cable's novel about the New South rise or fall. John is a character of mixed success and failure—and what is right and wrong about him is in effect what is successful and unsuccessful about the novel. I have already said that insofar as John is the male romantic lead, he is a figure of conventional magazine romance and, to modern tastes at any rate, neither very interesting nor very believable. Unfortunately, Cable gives us a great deal of John in this role; the courtship of Barbara Garnet throughout the second half of the novel is interminably long-winded and sentimental, with tediously coy conversations about true love and the like. The worst of it is that this has little or nothing to do with the basic problems of the novel; as lover, John March could be a high-minded but bashful young man from anywhere in the world of romance, and his characterization in this respect carries no significance for Wildwood, the town of Suez, or the post-Reconstruction South. Indeed, not only does the love plot neither grow organically out of nor contribute to the novel's main problems, but it even serves as a positive hindrance to such matters. The demands of romance, and romance alone, dictate that John March must fall in love with Barbara Garnet, the daughter of the villain; and because as heroine Barbara must be completely good, she is obliged to act against her father's interests, and seek to foil his nefarious designs against the March estate.

This produces some exceedingly contrived and unconvincing moments, which but for the requirements of the love story need not have been included. The most deadly touch of all is the business about the mixed-up property titles. There was no reason why Cable's story needed to depend for its meaning or resolution on so contrived a trick as that, with all the laborious hints and melodramatic foreshadowings. The land title episode exists (and apparently existed from the first draft onward) as a stock device of second-rate melodrama, to give a romantic (and terribly contrived) twist to the love story.

Yet having said all this, I would nevertheless insist that the essential characterization of John March is not a failure, and that John's role as romantic hero may flaw, but does not spoil, Cable's novel. For when not occupied with Barbara Garnet, John March is not a stock figure, and is neither unconvincing or oversimplified. Instead, in his pride, his innocence, and his capacity for painful learning, he successfully embodies the meaning of Cable's novel. He is indeed John March, *Southerner*. Born of good but impoverished gentlefolk, heir to vast tracts of land, anxious to develop them, imbibing the attitudes of the nineteenth-century South as part of his birthright, John March must learn to think and act for himself, and to do so he must understand what is going on in the society around him. Tradition, prejudice, loyalty, piety, all conspire to make it exceedingly difficult for him to attain that understanding; and the long, painful struggle whereby he comes to such knowledge is very much the structural development of the novel.

It is to Cable's credit that he does not make the achievement too easy, and does not invest John with any sort of easy moral superiority over his less high-minded fellow Southerners. John learns everything the hard way, and all his instincts are arrayed against his being able to learn what he needs to know. In the instance of Cornelius Leggett, for example, there is every reason why John should *not* learn to see him for what he really is, instead of as merely a dangerous Negro demagogue to be suppressed at all costs, which is the way that most white temperates automatically regard him. Leggett's corruption, his airs of familiarity, his ignorance and vanity all go against the young white Southerner's grain. In addition, Cable gives John a personal reason for despising Leggett, for while John is still a child, Leggett, smarting from the beating given to him by the outraged Major Garnet, takes out his anger on John by giving him a cruel beating in turn. It is therefore hardly to be marveled at that John has no use for Cornelius Leggett, and that while a youth in college, he takes part in an episode in which the concupiscent Negro politician is satisfyingly duped and embarrassed.

But what John comes to learn is that for all Leggett's obnoxious qualities, he is not a really important threat to Suez society, while some of those who in the name of virtue would strike Leggett down are guilty of much greater crimes against the community. John comes to realize that Leggett, boastful and personally dishonest though he is, is *right* in his insistence on equal educational opportunities for the Negroes, and *right* in his opposition to Major Garnet's schemings, and that Garnet himself is a far more dangerous threat to the public welfare. Garnet is no petty thief or small operator. He is out to steal on a grand scale and, using his respectability as a badge to cloak his corrupt manipulations, will engineer legislation and manipulate public opinion so as to commit his depredations. Garnet, and people like him, pose as public benefactors, and make skillful use of resentment against Leggett and Negroes in general, in order to gain private ends. The Garnets, not the Leggetts, are the real threat to the South.

John March comes to realize this, despite all his training and instincts, and not until he is able to see it can he act to protect his own interests and the general welfare of the community. To Cable's considerable credit, this is not handled didactically or pontifically; it is not achieved through abstract declamation and ponderous ideological discussion. It is part of John March's experience, and embodied concretely and convincingly within his experience.

Cable gives John some of the customary attributes and attitudes of young Southern youth; he is headstrong, proud, sentimental, with a quick temper and a readiness to resent insult. There is a key incident in which John and his mother are passengers aboard an excursion train making the initial trip along a newly completed railroad that links Suez with the trunk lines. An Englishman is along, come to consider investing money, arrogant and insufferable. He makes some offensive remarks about Suez, the South, and Jeff-Jack Ravenel, and John bridles; only some cooler, more investment-minded fellow townsfolk prevent him from giving the visiting Englishman the slap that he merits. But however insufferable the Englishman, and however rude and smug his way of saying what he thinks, his criticism of the dishonest trick played by the whites upon the Negroes is deserved, and it is only John March's Southern pride and loyalty that prevent him from recognizing it. When John's temper cools down, he realizes as much.

A great deal of *John March, Southerner* is concerned with developmental schemes, holding companies, industrial ventures, and the like. As such, it is very much a New South novel, in that it assumes as its starting point the value and the necessity of developing land and mineral resources, just as the New South did. We have already seen how in his essays on the Negro question Cable expressed serious reservations both about the materialism of the New South ideology and the assumption that the South could ever be industrialized and made commercially prosperous while retaining traditional racial attitudes and keeping the Negro in a situation of fixed inferiority. *John March, Southerner* represents an extensive critique of the whole notion. Cable does not oppose commercial development; he accepts it as inevitable. But he is trying to show that too often what goes on in the name of Progress and Development is no more than rapacious exploitation, not motivated by progressive ideals but using those ideals to mask a vicious materialism. The difference between what John March wants to do with Wildwood, and what Major Garnet wants to do, is the difference between true progress—which involves democratic government, equality of opportunity, and sound use of resources for the benefit of everyone—and ruthless exploitation of land and people for selfish private advantage.

Taught to believe in the virtues of gentility and the trustworthiness of the best people, and to mouth the customary clichés and slogans of the New South of progress and development, John March is too quick to accept at face value the professions of noble intentions by the Garnets of his time and place. In his innocence and naïveté he is so thoroughly duped that he almost loses all his land, although given ample warning by Cornelius Leggett and by the young Northern investor Henry Fair. He must, to repeat, learn the hard way; he must become able to think and see for himself, when all his training and instincts work against that knowledge. And again, Cable does this not through preaching or abstract discussion, but through plot and dramatization; John March does not learn about an abstraction called the South, he learns about *his own* immediate and particular situation. The result is not a tract, but a convincing work of fiction.

There is, to be sure, some rhetoric. Fair invites John March to come North to live, and to work for and with him. It is a tempting possibility, but John refuses:

"... Fair—I spent a year in Europe coaxing men to leave their mother-country for better wages in this. Of course, that was all right. But it brought one thing to my notice: that when our value is not mere wages, it isn't every man who's got the unqualified right to pick up and put out just whenever he gets ready. Look out that window. There's the college where for five years I got my education—at half price!—and with money borrowed here in Suez! Look out this one. Mr. Fair, right down there in those streets truth and justice are lying wounded and half-dead, and the public conscience is being drugged! We Southerners, Fair, don't believe one man's as good as another; we think one man in his right place is worth a thousand who can't fill it. My place is here!— . . ."

But however empty such rhetoric, it is not made a substitute for dramatic realization; it exists alongside it, a verbal excess that is ineffective in that it involves a too self-conscious striking of attitude, but not because it represents an effort to pronounce a meaning that the action and characterization themselves do not embody. For the most part we believe in John March, because what he is appears convincing and appropriate. The novel might well have been called *The Education of a Southerner,* for that is what it is all about.

It has been suggested that in having John March declare emphatically that he must stay in the South, just as many years later Cable has Philip Castleton in *Lovers of Louisiana* reach the same decision, Cable was saying in effect that he too should have stayed in the South. But if March represents Cable on that level, it might be pointed out that the reasons John March gives for staying in the South—"right down there in those streets truth and justice are lying wounded and half-dead, and the public conscience is being drugged"—are the reasons why for ten years George W. Cable had fought a passionate and increasingly lonely battle against racial discrimination, a battle in which, when every inducement was offered for him not to do so, he stayed "in the South" in the sense of continuing to concern himself with the South's most pressing social problems. Cable's real Southern involvement was that of his art, his essay writing, and speechmaking, and no one can contend that he gave in to expediency or took the easy and profitable way out. So that March's decision to remain on the Suez scene and work for its improvement can hardly be said to represent what Cable himself did not do. Nor is it likely that Cable felt that he had in any way surrendered;

he would have needed to have a very low estimate of himself to feel so.

John March does indeed stand for George W. Cable—a less articulate, less logical Cable, a "man of action" rather than of contemplation, concerned with developing his lands rather than speaking forth on the issues involved. Cable himself had learned a bit more readily than John, but he too underwent a long apprenticeship before he was able to recognize what he considered the true condition of Southern society in his time. And unlike Cable's previous "autobiographical" protagonists, such as Frowenfeld or John Richling, there is sufficient distance between author and spokesman so that believable characterization is possible; Cable was able to show March slowly and painfully learning to recognize the errors of his way of thinking. Perhaps it is fortunate in this respect that Cable chose to set his novel far away from New Orleans; it enabled him to dissociate the people and the situation from his immediate personal experience.

Edmund Wilson has repeated the general verdict on the novel when he says that it is polemical, didactic, a "notebook product" without believable people.[28] Here I can only say that, in this instance at least, Wilson is simply mistaken. The novel is not argued polemically, and it does not preach self-consciously. In the sense that it is not set in Cable's own New Orleans environment, it is, to be sure, a "notebook product," but not at the expense of credibility of scene or characterization. Its faults lie, as we have seen, in its romantic love formula. Perhaps this is especially evident because, not having set the novel in New Orleans, Cable has not peopled his narrative with a host of minor local color characters or lightened his major characters with the quaintness and oddities of the Creole scene. There is nothing in this novel reminiscent of the Bras Coupé episode in *The Grandissimes,* with its Faulknerian overtones of Gothic exaggeration and the supernatural; what takes place happens in plain daylight. Unfortunately for Cable, such a choice of fictional milieu matched ill with his romantic love plot; had he set the story in New Orleans, or had he written historical romance pure and simple, as so many writers of the Genteel Tradition were doing at the time, his love story and his lovers might have been more acceptable, because the criteria of realism would not be used at all in judging them. But in *John March,*

Southerner, Cable tried to mix an essential realism of time and place, a technique and subject matter based squarely on the problems of the here and now, with a badly stylized and unconvincing love plot.

It is a flawed but notable novel, representing the attempt of a writer of insight and skill to describe and define a situation of considerable human importance. The authenticity of the situation, growing as it does out of Cable's foremost concerns, provides an embodiment for the problems presented that results in convincing and moving fiction.

True, *John March, Southerner* is probably not as appealing a novel, to most readers, as *The Grandissimes,* and it lacks the unified tone of the stories of *Old Creole Days.* In both instances this is largely because the Creoles—with their rich texture of characterization and incident in an exotic and colorful time and place—are missing. To tell his story more accurately and undividedly, Cable abandoned the Creoles in *John March, Southerner,* and the result is that the shortcomings of his plot technique are exposed much more glaringly. But with the sacrifice of the advantages of local color came the compensating advantage of being able to deal directly and boldly with a subject Cable cared deeply about, and which he knew and understood as few others did. It is an impressive, sometimes even stunning examination of a region filled with torment and passion, stung by defeat, emboldened by opportunity, grappling with the problems of commerce, race, class, and belief, facing the challenge and hope of change. Before Faulkner, before Ellen Glasgow, before any other important Southern writer, Cable was working in this novel with the specific problems of human definition that have enabled the best Southern writers to produce literature of stirring dimensions.

"Any deliberately sectional portrayal," Randolph Bourne wrote in 1918,

> comes to seem desperately near an exploitation. The novelist is exploiting his material, digging out his marketable ore instead of making his human landscape reveal some significant veracity. This is the difference between *John March, Southerner* and *The Grandissimes.* In the latter one feels the exploiting touch. But fundamentally to Mr. Cable's honor, it must be said that he does not deserve that stigma. He has felt deeply enough about his land to be its sound and bravely passionate counselor. And he has been

artist enough not to let either this idealism or his own very strict personal moralism impede his portrayal of all the sweetness and gaiety of that life which his youth loved.[29]

Bourne's assessment, written twenty-four years after the novel appeared, was one of the few evaluations of the book written during the author's lifetime that adequately recognized its importance and its attainment. *John March, Southerner* was ignored, or else treated indifferently, upon its publication, and forgotten thereafter. The country was weary of the South, the Negro, and the attendant problems; it had no desire to read a depiction, no matter how searching, of subject matter that almost no one wanted explored. For the most part there were perfunctory reviews, which said little.

As for Cable, he too had had enough. Though he never lost interest in the South and the Negro's role in it, he ceased largely to speak out. He became, for the next dozen years, almost exclusively a writer of costume romances. Only late in his life would he once again feel impelled to say something important about his native region, and by then he had lost the artistic skill to do so with much cogency. For now, his best efforts had been rejected.

XIV
Historical Romancer

With the publication of *John March, Southerner* in 1895, the literary career of George W. Cable, so far as its principal achievement goes, all but comes to an end. He was fifty years old, and was to live for three decades longer. During that time he was to publish nine more books, including five novels. Yet with the exception of several short stories also written in the 1890's, little that he produced after *John March* is of any literary significance or adds to his artistic reputation. He became a writer of romances devoid of social importance, designed to entertain and, vaguely, to provide some sort of moral uplift, in that the characters were supposedly ennobling and worthy of emulation. It is as if the failure of *John March* had so convinced Cable that he could neither support his family nor accomplish social good by writing fiction, that he ceased to take it seriously.

Yet ironically, Cable in the 1890's was at the height of his powers as a writer. Not only *John March, Southerner* but the several short stories he wrote during those years are evidence of that. He collected three of these stories in a volume entitled *Strong Hearts,* published in 1899. One of them, first published in *Scribner's Magazine* for August, 1896, under the title "Gregory's Island" and retitled "The Solitary" in the book, is among the most powerful things he ever wrote. This curiously neglected tale of a drunkard, Gregory, who cures himself by spending a month of enforced isolation on a coastal sand island in the Gulf of Mexico is a compelling narrative. Much of its force derives from its gripping account of the protagonist's fight to survive when a hurricane sweeps across the low island just as he is about to give up his struggle to remain there and is ready to return to the mainland and renewed drinking. The epic contest with the hurricane restores him; in winning out against it, he has also won out against "the prisoner within himself."

The story is prefaced with an account by the narrator, Richard Thorndyke Smith, of a meeting with Gregory during the war; at that time Gregory had told of how he allowed a prisoner to escape without shooting him because the prisoner *"looked so much like me.* All the time I had him something kept saying to me, 'You're your own prisoner—you're your own prisoner.'" After the war, rejected by the girl he loves, Gregory turns to drink, squanders his fortune, and is at a point of lowest self-respect when he resolves to go to a remote coastal island, burn his boat so that he cannot leave, and spend a month without whiskey. Though marred somewhat by Richard Thorndyke Smith's philosophizing, the narrative itself is astoundingly skillful; it draws masterfully on the Louisiana setting, and the depiction of the storm is magnificently done. Philip Butcher does not exaggerate when he declares the story comparable to Crane's "The Open Boat." [1]

Another, longer tale, "The Entomologist"—also published in *Strong Hearts*—is, if not the very best Cable, at least worthy of a place along with his best work. Cable's model for his entomologist, a German collector who is so preoccupied with his work that he fails to appreciate his good wife and her devotion, was his friend the Baron Reizenstein, who in 1881 had named a moth after Cable. The likeness is hardly a flattering one. This story, of novella length, involves three couples: the Fontenettes, the husband a Creole and his wife a Northerner; the entomologist and his German-born wife; and the Thorndyke Smiths—the narrator is again Richard Thorndyke Smith, Cable's persona throughout the three stories in *Strong Hearts*. Mostly out of boredom, the Northern-born wife of the Creole sets out to attract the entomologist, who is singularly devoid of interest in anything save his collecting. Eventually she succeeds, but an epidemic of yellow fever strikes the city, and through a long ordeal of illness and suffering in all three families, both the Creole's wife and, to a lesser extent, the entomologist repent of their selfishness. Both die of fever, along with Thorndyke Smith's son, while all the others except Thorndyke Smith and the entomologist's wife are ill with the disease. The story is a portrayal of jealousy, and though Thorndyke Smith is a bit too quick to point out the moral, it is mainly successful fiction; the description of the yellow fever epidemic, drawn closely as it was from Cable's own experience, is vividly done. The story is somewhat spoiled by the intrusion of the inevitable happy ending—the Creole widower and the entomologist's widow, who has become a countess, eventually marry—but it is authentic in its details and its portrayal of people, and the characterization of the entomologist is extremely well done.

The third story in *Strong Hearts*, "The Taxidermist," is slighter than the other two. It involves a Creole, P. T. B. Manouvrier, who calls himself "Pas Trop Bon" and who is enthralled with his work, which involves not simply stuffing and mounting but also restoring or suggesting the souls of the animals or birds on which he works. Thorndyke Smith is much taken with the perfectionist Creole. When the taxidermist wins $75,000 in a lottery, he and his wife build a magnificent house, but prefer not to live in it; finally they donate it to replace an orphanage destroyed by fire. For the taxidermist, his work is everything, he is not interested in money. The taxidermist's work is portrayed as almost a fine art, and it is possible, I believe, to read the story as an allegory of the artist who works at making his material seem to possess and embody the life upon which it is patterned. But if the taxidermist is meant to suggest Cable himself, then it must be said that the temptation of great wealth that confronts him is hardly drawn out of Cable's own experience up to that time.

In general, the stories that make up *Strong Hearts* are extremely well done, and the volume is among Cable's best. All three stories represent the skillful and effective use of the New Orleans scene in fiction, without yielding to quaintness or sentimentality. If the thick texture of the early work is missing, so that there is less exoticism and quaintness, the fictional line is firm and the characterization quite effective. Yet *Strong Hearts*, like *John March, Southerner*, earned for its author very little money, only slight critical notice, and no encouragement from his editors. His financial situation was still unsatisfactory, and he continued to depend on his lecturing to bring him the revenue needed to support his large family.

For a time Cable turned to magazine editing, in the hope that it would provide the income he required. In 1896, he converted the little monthly publication of the Home Culture Clubs into a full-fledged magazine which he called *The Symposium*. It contained essays, stories, and reviews, including pieces by Cable himself, and he had high hopes for it. But it lasted only three months; after the third issue came off the press, he called the staff together and tearfully told them, one by one, that it was to be the last.[2] Several months later Cable became the editor of *Current Literature* and moved to New York on a six-month contract. His salary was very low, but there was the promise that permanent arrangements could be made. As editor he secured numerous original contributions, added more critical and biographical pieces, and conducted a series called the "Editor's Symposium," in which he published his own comments alongside short articles and letters from others. He also wrote editorials on literary matters. For a time the venture appeared to be prospering, but his hopes failed to materialize, his financial problems remained acute, and after six months he gave up the editorship and returned home to Northampton.

During the mid-1890's, both as part of his editorial work and as lectures for various occasions, Cable wrote a series of essays and shorter pieces about literature and art. They are for the most part quite undistinguished, and seldom rise above triteness. They are written, too, with a kind of affected coyness that interferes with what little they do have to say. They are largely concerned with the contemporary dispute over realism and romance: Cable proposed to heal the schism by insisting on the romance of truth and the truth of romance. They deal plentifully with abstractions, and in general present their author, usually through his surrogate Richard Thorndyke Smith, as a benevolent, gentlemanly philosopher, pausing amid the contemplation of Nature in and about Tarryawhile to chat with friends about Truth and Beauty. Absolutely none of the fire and bite of Cable's reformist writings is in evidence. One would never guess, from reading these literary meditations, that he could possibly have written the Bras Coupé episode, or the description of John March losing his temper at the Englishman aboard the excursion train.

Philip Butcher, in both his books on Cable, sees the middle

and late 1890's as a time when Cable had lost all his urge to do good and wanted only comfort and renown. His "personal integrity was on the decline," Butcher says,[3] and maintains that "the change is not astonishing. Many a zealous young reformer has turned staunch conservative by middle age; more than one social critic has become a social climber."[4] There is no doubt that the Cable of the years after *John March, Southerner* was doing his best to adapt himself to what he considered the role of genial romancer in a genteel time. But Butcher is too harsh. We misunderstand Cable's seeming apostasy if we see in it any loss of personal conviction. Surely the fifteen-year battle that he had waged for Negro rights, at great personal sacrifice, in which he had been willing to leave the place of his birth and the scene of his art rather than remain silent, should suffice to safeguard him from any charges of being prone to sacrifice integrity for personal advantage.

What is involved, rather, is *defeat*. Here was a brave and passionate man who had wanted to do two things: to awaken his native region to the injustice and error of its treatment of its Negro citizens, and to write the very best fiction of which he was capable. On both accounts he had reached the point of despair. We must remember that Cable's effort on behalf of Negro rights was not merely an expression of righteous indignation; he had genuinely believed he could do something to change the South's racial attitudes. Cable really thought that there was a "Silent South," which did not agree with the bigots and the demagogues and which was not being represented by racist politicians. If only this hitherto-silent majority of well-intentioned Southerners could be made to speak out, then the racial injustice of the post-Reconstruction years would be brought to an end, and the South would give its Negro citizens the rights and the opportunities needed to enable them to become full-fledged American citizens.

He thought that by speaking out, he was giving a tongue to this "Silent South," and that others would then follow his lead, and justice and good would triumph. Surely the Open Letter Club was not the project of a man who wanted merely to enjoy the personal satisfaction of having advocated a righteous cause; it was a highly realistic venture, entered into because Cable believed that through it he could marshal Southern public opinion on the side of Negro rights. But he had met defeat on every side; his friends dropped away, his voice fell upon deaf ears, and instead of conditions for the Negro improving, they grew steadily worse. There *was no* "Silent South," he found; the vast majority of white Southerners fully believed the Negro race to be inferior, and thought that racial segregation and the denial of civil rights to Negroes were justified. Not only that; enlightened Northern opinion did not really care, one way or the other. The Gilders and Johnsons and others were tired of having the matter agitated. Cable had lost his battle; his defeat was total and conclusive.

In literature, the result had scarcely been more satisfactory. So long as he had written pleasant local color stories about indolent Creole men and lovely Creole ladies, his literary status had prospered; Gilder and his colleagues on the old *Scribner's* and later the *Century* had begged him for ever more material. But as he had begun to work more and more of what he considered the major problems of his environment into his fiction, so had his popularity suffered. His editors, and the magazine readers they represented, did not want the stresses and strains of post-Reconstruction Southern political and social life set forth and argued out realistically in fiction; they wanted quaint Creoles, exotic quadroons, and picturesque darkies. More than that, the vogue of local color itself was now passing. The historical romance was the new stock in trade of the magazines. Yet when he had thrown aside local color, and put everything of which he was capable into a work of realism about the South in which he sought to show, with a minimum of didacticism, what was taking place there, he had met with a vast disinterest and discouragement. Again, thoroughgoing defeat: as an artist, he had labored as best he knew how, and had been rejected.

How keenly Cable felt his failures we can only conjecture. Only occasionally do we get a glimpse of what he must have been undergoing, as in the letter he wrote to Gilder in which he had sought desperately to make his editor see what he was doing with *John March:* "My goodness, Gilder, this is a better story every way than Dr. Sevier dared to be. The movement is stronger, deeper, and infinitely more varied. Dr. Sevier may have more truth in it, but this has more virile energy." Or in a letter he wrote to Louise from New York in 1897, when the magazine venture was coming to an end: "On one point I am determined; not to go back to a life of imaginative writing alone; it wears me out and keeps me worn out. I shall try my best to find something . . . which will keep me in the current of affairs."[5] Surely one as dedicated as Cable was to the causes he believed in, and to the art for which he had sacrificed all and on which he had risked everything, must have suffered deeply as he met nothing but defeat, rejection, incomprehension wherever he turned.

Thus Cable's reaction in the years that followed the end of the civil rights campaign and the failure of *John March, Southerner* might better be viewed not as a sign of his having reached a point at which, in Philip Butcher's words, "he was unwilling to make consequential sacrifices for worthy causes and was uninterested in working to improve the lot of the underprivileged,"[6] so much as a kind of numbed acquiescence in the face of defeat, an expression of emotional exhaustion. He seems to have turned from public agitation and from literary realism because, in truth, given his talents and his capabilities, he realized that there was little else he could do along either line. And like many another good man who had done his best and lost, he now drew back into himself, and did not want to hear or think further about it. His silence was not an indication of his not caring any more so much as of caring so deeply that he could not bear to think about it. Or so I interpret those years after 1895, when Cable became a romancer pure and simple.

For all the defeat on civil rights and the failure of *John March,* however, Cable had become a literary figure of international reputation. And in early 1898 he had the opportunity to go abroad and enjoy his fame. When James M. Barrie had come to the United States in late 1896 together with his friend Dr. W. Robertson Nicoll of the *British Weekly,* they had straightway gone to visit Cable. The visitors spent three days at Tarryawhile, and a fast friendship developed, so much so that Barrie canceled his previous itinerary and decided instead to see New Orleans. Before Barrie and Nicoll went back to England, they had secured Cable's promise to return their visit. A group of lectures was arranged to cover his expenses, and on April 20, 1898, Cable sailed for England aboard the White Star Line's *Majestic.*[7]

His trip was a decided success. Not only Barrie, but Arthur Conan Doyle, Rudyard Kipling, and Henry James were his hosts. He met and for the most part charmed numerous other English notables, including Sir Henry Irving, "Ian Maclaren," Sir Frederick Pollock, George Meredith, George Gissing, Walter Besant, Leslie Stephen, Andrew Lang, and Mrs. Humphrey Ward, and his visit culminated with a stay at Andrew Carnegie's Skibo Castle, in Scotland, where he went trout fishing with Carnegie, read from his work, and enjoyed the spectacle of the kilted Carnegie dancing merrily while the castle bagpiper played "All the Blue Bonnets Over the Border." His visit with James at De Vere Gardens for tea was most amusing. He found several young Americans there, including Gellett Burgess, who did not impress him. James, however, "was attractive beyond all my expectations and beyond all account I have ever had of him. To me he was positively affectionate." He set down his impressions at length in his diary:

> One thing happened which made me gasp for the desolation of the Downs wherein I might run and whoop my laughter—for I dared not even smile at it where I was: we were talking of the underground railway system of London, which James said he liked; when [Henry] Harlands [sic] was so unlucky as to speak of our host's "passion" for the "underground." James winced as if a whip had been cracked at him and in his worst stammer mildly repudiated the word. It was too howling funny, to see his polite distress at the idea of his having a passion for anything under the heavens or elsewhere. His manner of speech is very amusing and strongly indicative of the studious finish of his writings. He will say—'Hm-m—I walked eh—I walked to the—hm-m—the eh—hm-m-m—the—what shall I say?—the corner! and took a—hm-m-m—a—I suppose I may call it—hm-m—a hansom—a hansom cab!" But all the time the man himself impresses you as bringing honor to the name of gentleman; a clean, true man who always feels more than he says. . . .[8]

Cable sailed for home on the *Friedrich der Grosse;* the day of his departure he received an affectionate goodbye letter from James. "I wanted to see you more—to talk with you *most;* to talk with you endlessly . . . & your room will always be ready," James told him.[9]

Throughout the 1890's, Cable retained his directorship of the Home Culture Clubs. By 1897 there were eighty-six clubs, fifty of them in Northampton and the majority of the others in Massachusetts, but with thirteen other states represented on the roll. In 1897, there was something of a financial crisis. Adelene Moffat, who had been serving as general secretary of the clubs, felt it necessary to resign because of the inadequacy of her salary and the burden of the work, which made it extremely difficult for her to pursue an artistic career. Cable ultimately persuaded her to stay on, after a patron, E. H. R. Lyman, had agreed to guarantee payment of one half her salary. At the same time the decision was made to continue only with the Northampton activities. From this time onward, the Home Culture Clubs became increasingly an enterprise in adult education, with formal classes and less emphasis on home reading circles.[10]

Before leaving for England, Cable had begun work on another novel. In 1899, he visited the Mississippi-North Louisiana country in which he had done his soldiering during the Civil War, to refresh his memory of the terrain. He began negotiations with the *Century* for serialization of the new book, but was unable to sell serial rights to the *Century* or any other magazine. However, the absence, this time, of Gilder's and Johnson's close direction as he worked on the manuscript seems to have enabled him to enjoy the writing more than usual.[11]

The Cavalier was a best seller when it appeared in 1901. It is noteworthy primarily because it represents the abandonment by Cable of almost everything for which his fiction had previously stood, and for which his work today remains important. The new novel was a historical romance, squarely within the popular vogue, without a serious thought or a notable characterization in all its 311 pages. Written by a former Confederate cavalryman who had served in some of the war's most arduous and bitter campaigning, *The Cavalier* is a novel of storybook soldiers and impossible heroines, with almost none of the sweat, dirt, and pain of military combat depicted. It is devoted to a far-fetched romantic situation involving intrigue and hidden identities, with much devious plotting, absolutely devoid of social or political content. The heroine, Charlotte Oliver, part-time journalist and spy, is quite unbelievable. Cable's skill at description and at delineating a scene is present as always, but this time to no purpose beyond that of popular entertainment.

Incredibly, Cable wrote to his wife, after finishing the first draft, that "I think I have done a beautiful thing. Certainly it is far better than John March." [12] One marvels that he could be so insensitive to what he was leaving out of his fiction this time. Was he now so fully and completely a figure of the genteel establishment that he could mistake vague, romantic inspirational characterization for anything involving real moral significance? Or was he so involved in the problems of pure literary craft when he made the remark that he was, for the moment, oblivious of all except questions of narrative technique? In any event, *The Cavalier* contains nothing to interest the contemporary reader except some few details of war experience that offer clues to Cable's own military service.

Ironically, this least serious of all his efforts so far enjoyed the greatest popular success; published in October, by Christmas it had sold 100,000 copies.[13] Several of the reviews, however, noted the absence of serious statement in the new book; the author, the *Nation*'s reviewer declared, "appears to have yielded to the pressure of a fashion, and not to the urgency of an inward voice bidding him write." [14] But the continued sale must have seemed to Cable almost a confirmation of what Gilder, Johnson, and others had been telling him for years: that he should seek to fill up his books with pleasantness. To Charles Scribner, Cable wrote: "One of my most pointed pleasures in the large sale of 'The Cavalier' is that my patient publisher has at last something to show for his belief in me." [15]

The Cavalier also proved to be the first of Cable's works to be successfully dramatized. The actress Julia Marlowe read advance proofs and liked the story, had it dramatized, and rehearsals of the dramatized version began in November, 1901. The play opened in New Haven in December, and then was produced at the Criterion Theater in New York. The reviews were mixed, but the play drew well for a time, though Jeanette L. Gilder told Cable late in the season that "it is generally known in the profession that it has not been a success, I mean not a success from the Marlowe point of view." [16] Before its career was over, however, it received road production twice.

While *The Cavalier* was in production, Cable wrote a novelette, *Bylow Hill*, which was serialized in the *Atlantic Monthly* in early 1902 and published in book form by Scribner's in May the same year. *Bylow Hill* has the dubious distinction of being Cable's worst novel. A story of jealousy in marriage, it is set in New England; the protagonist, Arthur Winslow, a clergyman, is depicted as being so consumed with unwarranted suspicion of his bride's relationship with a former fiancé that he comes close to murder until, grown entirely demented, he dies from a fall downstairs. Cable got the idea for the plot from the novelist S. Weir Mitchell, who had no interest in using it himself. It was no novel for Cable to have attempted; his talent was utterly unsuited to the task of portraying the psychological abnormality involved. The characters are wooden, the situations unconvincing, and the story possesses no redeeming literary qualities. (One feature *Bylow Hill* does share with *The Cavalier* and *John March, Southerner* is an attack on religious hypocrisy; in each of these novels a clergyman is portrayed as being less than worthy of the cloth.) As Arlin Turner says, Cable's decision to strip his narrative of all materials involving setting and period resulted in the elimination of the elements of his greatest literary strength.[17]

On February 27, 1904, Louise Bartlett Cable died. During the thirty-five years of their marriage, Louise was never robust and had often been ill. But to her husband she had been a constant source of moral strength. Unflinchingly, she had backed him in his highly unpopular fight against race prejudice during the New Orleans years and afterward, and though it must have cost her severely to leave the city of her birth and the place where she had spent her entire life until then, she loyally supported the decision to move to New England in 1884. She had borne eight children, of whom one had died during the yellow fever epidemic of 1878. In the years that followed Cable's resignation from his clerkship at the Cotton Exchange, she had kept the household in order and tended to business affairs during her husband's extensive lecture trips away from home. At no time during their long marriage had the family ever known financial security; the checks that Cable was able to send home from the proceeds of his lecture tours were often barely enough to keep food in the house, while pressing debts went unpaid. Yet she had loyally managed. The union between Louise and George Cable was intense and passionate; the many hundreds of letters Cable wrote to her while away from home testify to a deep and uncomplicated relationship. In a letter to Henry Van Dyke, Cable wrote of the immense comfort that the knowledge of his wife's absolute affection for him had been to him throughout his adult life: "It is glorious to see—it is glorious to remember—how in the days of her last illness, when she began to see her mortal peril, her love to her friends, her children, and, most of all to me—who know as no one else ever may know how poorly merited it was—set in like a great storm and raged through all her being. . . . She never breathed of happiness, of any gladness, while believing that I was unhappy. . . ." [18]

As so often happens when so thoroughly domestic a man loses a wife, within less than two years Cable married again. On November 24, 1906, at the age of sixty-two, he took as his bride Eva Colegate Stevenson, a native of Versailles, Kentucky. His new wife was "a woman of forty-eight," he wrote Andrew Carnegie, "of charming social accomplishments, a beautiful musician, large in mind and heart, of a mirthful temper and ardent affections. My children seem as glad as I over my good fortune and I trust my dear friends may find cause to rejoice with me as well." Cable took care to inform Carnegie that contrary to newspaper reports, the new Mrs. Cable was not wealthy; "she has merely enough income to assure her that our marriage adds nothing to my burdens." [19]

Within a few months after his marriage, whether as cause and effect one cannot say for sure, Cable came to a parting of the ways with his longtime secretary and assistant, Adelene Moffat. On March 8, 1907, he wrote her that a reduction in expenditures for the Home Culture Clubs made it necessary that a single male secretary be hired in her stead. On March 18, the board of directors of the club accepted her resignation. There followed a considerable contretemps in which charges and countercharges were made; Frank Lyman, who had become a close friend of Miss Moffat's and whose family's benefactions had made up a considerable portion of the Home Culture Clubs budget, resigned from the board of directors, with several other resignations following. [20]

Philip Butcher, who describes the episode in considerable detail, places the blame for the rupture of relationships squarely on Cable, citing letters Cable wrote to his son-in-law and other correspondence as showing that Cable chose to think that Miss Moffat had been making highly derogatory remarks about his first wife and others in the family. Butcher, who talked at length with Miss Moffat herself from 1949 through 1955 (she was then in her nineties), clearly believes that there was absolutely no basis to the stories about Miss Moffat's gossiping. He depicts the episode as an example of Cable's egotism and pettiness, and of his lack of gratitude toward a longtime friend and admirer.[21] The letters that Cable himself wrote to various people in the course of the affair do show that the incident disturbed him as few other things did throughout his life; it is almost the only instance in his extensive correspondence in which he expressed himself about anyone with such bitterness and resentment.

From a letter written by Cable to his son-in-law, Harold Brewster, and from Brewster's reply, however, it would appear that some basis did exist for the accusation against Miss Moffat. Brewster reported that some years before his marriage to Cable's daughter Margaret, Adelene Moffat "told my sister Gertrude that Mrs. C. scolded you & the children like a vulgar Irish woman. . . . Most people have by now learned to discount what Miss Moffat says, & so no great damage was done by this remark."[22] On the other hand, Harry Taplin, former secretary of the men's activities of the Home Culture Clubs, indignantly denied that Miss Moffat had ever made such remarks to him as Cable had reported.[23]

With all deference to Professor Butcher's research, my own surmise is that the separation of Miss Moffat from the Home Culture Clubs is not unrelated to his second marriage. One has the feeling that Miss Moffat, who had served Cable so loyally for two decades, probably thought of herself as next in line, and that when Cable married Miss Stevenson, the situation became so tense that it was impossible for Cable and Adelene Moffat to work together any longer. As for Miss Moffat, she secured a position with a Boston philanthropist, Mrs. Quincy A. Shaw, and remained active in social work and her painting almost until her death in 1956. She was also an early supporter of the National Association for the Advancement of Colored People.[24]

The withdrawal of the Lymans from the affairs of the Home Culture Clubs caused a financial crisis within the organization. Cable now wrote to his friend Andrew Carnegie, describing what had happened and asking him for help.[25] Carnegie, whose $50,000 gift to the Home Culture Clubs in 1903 had enabled Cable to build new quarters for the club, came forward with a gift of $1,500 a year to meet current expenditures. Cable then launched a campaign to raise a permanent endowment for the clubs to guard against another emergency. He himself contributed $1,000, and later added an additional $250. The goal of $30,000 was reached ten years later. The club was renamed the People's Institute in 1909, and thereafter remained on solid financial ground.[26]

On June 2, 1908, Cable's only surviving son, William, died. He had long been invalided by a faulty heart; between father and son there had been a close relationship, and the loss was a hard one for Cable to bear.[27] Gradually, one by one, his daughters grew up and left his home. Louise had married James Alfred Chard in 1894, Mary married the historian Alfred L. P. Dennis in 1899. Lucy, who went with her father on a second visit to England and Scotland in 1905, moved to New York to work on the staff of the *Ladies' Home Journal.* Margaret married Harold Brewster. In 1906 Isabel married, and the youngest daughter, Dorothea, went to live with the Alfred Dennises at the University of Wisconsin. Only William Cable had remained with his father; until Cable's second marriage they lived in the small study-house next to Tarryawhile, taking their meals with Cable's sister Mary Louise.[28] "My boy was my bosom friend and as perfect a gentleman and irreproachable as ever I knew," Cable wrote to Charles Scribner in July, 1908.[29]

Cable's next novel, *Kincaid's Battery,* was published in November 1909. "I believe I am blameless in this story of trying to prove anything or preach anything," he declared in an article about the new book in the New York *Herald-Tribune* for October 25, 1908. ". . . I hope it may preach as character and conduct always will and must whenever they are, as the critics say, convincing."[30] Constructed very much on the order of *The Cavalier,* which is to say, pure historical romance with no social content and no attempt to present wartime experience realistically, *Kincaid's Battery* is somewhat more readable than the earlier Confederate novel. This is primarily because there is nothing to offend one's sense of plausibility and credibility comparable to the business of the female journalist and spy Charlotte Oliver in *The Cavalier.* It is set in upper-class New Orleans just before and during the war, and both Creoles and non-Creoles are involved. The villainess is a Creole girl, the hero and heroine non-Creoles, so that Cable may be said to have reverted somewhat to his earlier habits. There is nothing, however, in *Kincaid's Battery* that could have offended anyone; no attempt at representative social portrayal is involved. The characters, in all they do and say, are creatures of the purest romance, and the novel's chief points of interest today are some descriptions of the coming of the Union fleet to New Orleans, an exciting description of the battle of Mobile Bay, and the occasional appearance, as very minor characters, of earlier Cable heroes and heroines. Unfortunately for Cable, *Kincaid's Battery* was not much of a financial success, which is all that might otherwise have been said for it.

The following year, Scribner's published a volume made up of the early story "Posson Jone'" and a sequel, "Père Raphaël," which Cable had written almost a decade earlier and published in the *Century* in 1901. To make *Posson Jone' and Père Raphaël* a plausible unit, Cable wrote a short introduction. The second story continued the adventures of Jules St.-Ange, but the vigor and the ironic wit of the earlier story were lacking almost entirely.

Since *John March, Southerner* in 1895, Cable had produced almost nothing of literary worth. To those who admired his earlier fiction, his art must have indeed seemed played out as the first decade of the twentieth century came to an end. Though *The Cavalier* had sold well, the historical romances he was writing added nothing to his reputation, and the attempt in "Père Raphaël" to go back to the milieu of his early local color fiction indicated that the once fascinating and charming milieu of the Creoles had dried up for him too.

Meanwhile the ranks of Cable's old friends were thinning. In 1908 Marion Baker, who had so loyally supported him and encouraged him when he had taken on the entire South in the argument over Negro rights, died. So, too, Richard Watson Gilder. In 1910 Marion Baker's brother Page, who had led the onslaught against Cable, died. On November 30, 1910, Cable spoke at a memorial service for Mark Twain, who had died the previous April. "It seems to me evident to all of us, if not to all the critical world," Cable declared, "that that great human kindness of his was one of the foundations, the fundamental element, of his humor, and by it he gained the heart of the world." He told proudly of how he had called Twain's attention, while on their joint reading tour, to Malory's *Morte d'Arthur,* and how when Twain later told him that he was at work on *A Connecticut Yankee in King Arthur's Court,* he had claimed godfathership of the novel, and Twain had answered, "Yes; you are its godfather." [31]

A quarter of a century had gone by since that tour. For as long a time again Cable had lived far away from New Orleans, the scene of his earliest and best work. To his friends, and to himself as well, it must have seemed highly unlikely that he would ever recover the spirit and the zeal which had so motivated his art long ago. In early 1909, however, Cable and his new wife journeyed down to New Orleans for a visit, Cable's first in some years. He had already begun planning out a new novel, to be based on life on the Mississippi River in the heyday of steamboating, before the Civil War. It too was to be a historical romance, just like its immediate predecessors. But apparently his reception in his old home city, and the memories that the return stirred up within him, had the effect of rekindling within him something like the old vigor and resolve, with consequences that would be interesting for his remaining books.

XV

An Engagement Renewed

The Cables reached New Orleans on January 4, 1909, having sailed down aboard the steamer *Antilles* from New York. It was a rough sea voyage, and Eva Cable arrived in her husband's native city in a state of exhaustion.[1] Their reception in the city where Cable had once been so controversial and disliked was gratifyingly warm. The newspapers carried interviews, he was invited to read before the girls of the New Orleans Institute, and seemingly all delighted to do him honor.[2] Cable had come in part to do research on his next novel, and he set to work at once. "I am at work daily," he wrote to Charles Scribner, "and I find the greatest eagerness on every hand to aid me in gathering my material. It is a very comforting and compensating experience."[3]

He was a celebrity now in New Orleans, and only the old-timers remembered how unpleasant things once had been. Gayarré, Page Baker, Marion Baker, James Guthrie, Warren Brickell—they were all dead. Now Canal Street, which had once marked the boundary between Creole and Anglo-American New Orleans, was a broad and busy thoroughfare, with streetcars operating down its center. The French Quarter seemed even more run-down than ever, in part almost a slum area, but already restoration was being talked of, and the tourist values of the area were beginning to be exploited. As for the Creoles, they had long since made their peace with the Anglo-Americans, the Germans, the Irish, the Italians, and the other elements of the city's heterogeneous population, and only the old people still conversed in French patois. In the Negro districts, especially the red light area known as Storyville, Negro musicians were playing a new kind of music which would eventually bring the city worldwide fame surpassing that which Cable himself had given it. Along the river, where once the twin-stacked stern-wheelers had lined up by the dozens in their rococo glory to take on passengers for the 5 P.M. departure upstream, there were only a few drab vessels; the railroads had usurped the once prosperous river trade. But lower downstream, numerous great oceangoing freighters were tied up, not along the levee as in earlier days but at modern covered piers. Nearby the swamps were being drained and ground reclaimed; the open canals and cesspools which had once been so grave a menace to health were all but gone; the yellow fever that had periodically ravaged the city, and in 1878 had claimed the life of Cable's son, was a thing of the past, now that the mosquito had been identified and recognized as its source. New Orleans had changed, no doubt of that.

But as Cable walked about the old city where he had lived, he saw much that must have dismayed him. All that he had once feared would come to pass for the city's Negro population had happened. New Orleans was more rigidly segregated now than ever it had been during his residence there. The bloody three-day race war of 1900 had left the city divided and the Negro population disfranchised and beleaguered.[4] What had once given promise of becoming a flourishing Negro middle class was now but a tiny segment of the city's vast poverty-stricken Negro population. Steadily the Negro had been pushed out of the various trades: where there had been numerous Negro carpenters, cigar makers, painters, clerks, shoemakers, coopers, tailors, bakers, blacksmiths, and foundry hands, the Negro was now doomed to the lowest, most menial occupations.[5] Negro schools were poorly staffed, wretchedly housed; there was no longer even a Negro public high school in the city. Teach the freedman, encourage him, let him participate in government, give him the civil rights necessary to human dignity, Cable had once urged not only his own city but the entire South; the plea had not been heeded. The onetime slave was gripped in a peonage, whether urban or rural, that pervaded every aspect of his life.

Exactly what went through Cable's mind as he revisited the scenes of his youth and young manhood we cannot say. But this much is clear: the novel which he had begun to plan out that winter, and which now progressed steadily, took on overtones that had been absent from his fiction for many years. When *Gideon's Band* finally appeared in 1914, readers found within it a meaning that went beyond historical romance and individual drama. Though set back in the 1850's, it contained what had been missing from his work since 1895: genuine social criticism.

Like *The Cavalier* and *Kincaid's Battery,* there is a great deal of atmosphere in *Gideon's Band.* To modern readers at least, the detailed and careful depiction of steamboating along the Mississippi in the 1850's is interesting in its own right in a way that Civil War romance (if only because of constant fictional repetition) has ceased to be. Cable not only drew on his own extensive memories of the steamboat days and the lore that all New Orleans boys of the 1850's and 1860's must have accumulated; he also did extensive research. Indeed, the technical descriptions of steamboating and river piloting provide considerably more factual information than may be found in Mark Twain's *Life On The Mississippi*—which is not to say that it approaches that work in literary merit, for indeed it does not. But unlike *The Cavalier* and *Kincaid's Battery, Gideon's Band* contains a great deal of comment on the social and moral questions involved in the setting, and specifically on the problems of race and democracy. The novel is at times almost an indictment of the antebellum Southern aristocracy—and the objects this time were not the Creoles, but the Anglo-Americans who composed the power structure, for the sole person of Creole blood, Madame Hayle, is a compassionate, admirable woman who risks her life to nurse victims of the cholera.

Most of the story takes place aboard a steamboat, the *Votaress,* during the course of a voyage from New Orleans to Louisville. The *Votaress* is a Courteney boat, and as such she is a rival to the competing fleet of Hayle boats. Aboard her as she moves northward are Madame Hayle, her daughter Ramsey, and her three sons, along with a senator, a general, a Methodist bishop, a backwoods evangelist, an actor and actress, a planter, and various other travelers. The hero is young Hugh Courteney, also on board, whose father is captain of the *Votaress* and whose grandfather is commodore of the Courteney fleet. Shortly after leaving its berth on the levee at New Orleans, the *Votaress* stops to take on a contingent of German immigrants bound for the Northwest, who take up their quarters in steerage. Cholera breaks out among the immigrants as the steamboat moves northward on her journey; the vessel becomes an arena in which various elemental human and social attitudes and traits are exposed and tested.

The villains of the novel are the two Hayle twins, Julian and Lucian. These two young men are designed to represent, as is remarked by a gentleman aboard the *Votaress,* "the faults, madam, of all our young Southern gentlemen . . . faults of which we may almost say, sir, that we may almost be proud!" To which the gentleman's wife objects: "Oh, well . . . please almost don't say it! They-re the faults of our 'peculiar institution' and I wish our 'peculiar institution' were—" The Hayle twins are characterized by "their unqualified straightforwardness, their transparent simplicity of mind and heart, their fearlessness, their complacent rusticity, their childish notions of the uses of wealth, their personal modesty and communal vanity, their happy oblivion to world standards, their extravagance of speech, their political bigotry, their magisterial downrightness, their inflammability, and their fine self-reliance." They are arrogant, boastful, bigoted, vain, selfish.

Arriving drunk just as the *Votaress* has left the dock, they are enraged at having to drive two miles to board the ship at the next landing, and throughout the voyage seek to make trouble for the hated Courteneys. They thus fall in readily with the plans of the senator, the general, and others, who want to have the boat pull ashore and discharge the German immigrants, with their cholera, at some unpopulated place along the river to fend for themselves as best they can. Eventually a deputation, led by the senator, the judge, and the bishop, goes to the captain to make this demand, but the Courteneys refuse to comply. The attitude of the whole group of upper-class Southerners is one of contempt for the lives and welfare of mere immigrants. Young Julian Hayle expresses the matter quite succinctly:

> "One thing to be stopped at all cost . . . is this deluge of immigration. Every alien who comes to New Orleans, and especially every alien who passes up on this river into the West, strengthens the North and weakens the South commercially, industrially, and politically, and corrupts the national type, the national speech—"
> "The national religion,"—prompted the bishop.

"The national love of law and order,"—said the judge.

"And of justice and liberty,"—put in the general.

"And the national health," said the youth. "New Orleans should refuse every immigrant entrance to the country, and every steam boat on the Mississippi ought to decline to carry him to his destination!"

In *Gideon's Band,* too, the Negro question comes back into Cable's fiction. As in the Bras Coupé episode of *The Grandissimes,* there is within this novel a story of the past that casts shadows over the present. It involves a glamorous octoroon, Phyllis, who had been the mistress of one of the Hayles, and who had caused the burning, some years ago, of a Courteney boat, the *Quakeress,* during which both she and her lover had supposedly drowned. It was the story of Phyllis and her violated humanity that caused Madame Hayle to become an Abolitionist, and that was the source of the enmity between the Hayles and the Courteneys. Thus, throughout this novel of the antebellum South and its feuding families, the treatment of the Negro and the heritage of miscegenation play their part.

It turns out that Phyllis is not dead; she had been rescued and befriended by the actor and his wife, and is with them aboard the *Votaress.* When a Kentuckian named "California," free of the prejudices and notions of caste of the South, offers to take her West with him and make her his wife, Hugh Courteney is dubious. The solution of the race problem, he says, is not to mix the races; there is something that his grandfather calls race conscience. To which Madame Hayle retorts: "Of w'at race has Phyllis the conscien'? An' you would know Phylliz' race—ad sight—by the color?" But Hugh (who is not himself quite convinced of his own arguments) and his grandfather both declare that "race conscience is a wonderful, unaccountable thing which men will give their life-blood [for] by thousands." If it is a matter of pleasing a hypothetical "Mrs. Grundy," then "poor, blundering old Mrs. Grundy . . . is really fighting hard for a better human race," and "we who presume to fight the blunders of that battle must fight them unselfishly and to help her win." At this point Joy, the Hayles's old Negro servant, declares that "Phyllis ain' gwine [to go west with "California"]. She know' you cayn't make her white by takin' her to whah it make' no odds ef she ain't white. Phyllis love' folks. She love' de quality, she love' de crowd. . . ."

It is an interesting passage. Cable seems to have written a polemic against racism and caste, and joined to it the statement that purity of race in itself is not an evil ideal. Presumably, the fighting of the battle of race "unselfishly" meant the recognition of the importance of racial separateness without the use of that separateness as an excuse for one race demanding privilege and superiority. Now, there is no indication that even in his most active days as a crusader for civil rights Cable had ever denied the existence of racial differences. Yet the Cable of the 1880's would have directed his rhetoric to a different goal; he would have closed with Mrs. Hayle's devastating refutation of the idea of "race conscience," not merely inserted it in passing. That he felt impelled in *Gideon's Band* to couple his renewed attack on racial injustice with a clear statement that he believed in racial purity probably indicates not so much a change in attitude on the civil rights issue (which by 1910 and on was a very dormant issue indeed) as a wish not to allow his novel to be read as social protest. He was apparently hesitant to surrender his status as genteel romancer; the Mrs. Grundy passage is obviously designed to limit the meaning of Phyllis's story, and various other anti-racist remarks, to the status of a historical condemnation of slavery in the antebellum South, without also constituting an attack on racism in the twentieth century.

If so, however, it fails in its intent, for the whole bent of the novel, insofar as it involves race and racism, is clearly anti-racist, and the Mrs. Grundy passage seems a forced, unconvincing intrusion into the story. Cable the novelist wins out over Cable the theorist; and the novelist—just as in *The Grandissimes, Old Creole Days,* and *John March, Southerner*—is so bound up in the struggle for human justice and freedom that the basic sweep of his narrative constitutes an attack on Southern racism. At the age of seventy, George W. Cable had reasserted himself.

Which is not to say that *Gideon's Band* is as successful a work of fiction as his earlier books. In important ways the book remains a costume romance, with most of the defects of that genre as practiced by Cable. Much of the potential drama of the situation is diluted by the inclusion of too much scenic material about river travel, and by the awkward device, in the best tradition of romance, of having the passengers aboard ship stage a play to keep their spirits up and their minds distracted from the threat of disease. Such episodes, done well enough to be sure, nevertheless undercut the developing tension of the basic situation. Cable did not need to use such stagy material in order to hold the reader's interest. But so involved was he in the genre of the historical romance that he did not hesitate to crowd his novel with "atmosphere" at the expense of weakening his main plot. There is too much use of river songs and spirituals; entire texts are included, sometimes with musical notation. It is unfortunate, too, that instead of concluding his novel with the end of the journey upstream, Cable chose to add an additional eight chapters (some 15,000 words in all), set eight years later. There we are treated to a melodramatic deathbed scene in which the two Hayle twins die of poison, and Hugh Courteney and Ramsey Hayle plight their troth at last.

Even so, *Gideon's Band* stands far above Cable's other historical romances. It holds the attention, and it draws importantly on its author's greatest strength, still very clear at the age of seventy: his deep social conscience, his compassion for the victims of caste and discrimination, his burning detestation of injustice and prejudice. But if Cable thought that the reading public of the early twentieth century was any more ready for the discussion of matters of race and caste than it had been in the 1880's and 1890's, he must have been sadly disappointed in the reviews of *Gideon's Band*. The novel was praised for its depiction of steamboating days along the Mississippi, while what it had to say about Southern society was hardly noticed at all.

In the same year that *Gideon's Band* appeared, Cable also published a book called *The Amateur Garden*, in which he included a group of the essays and articles he had been publishing in periodicals over a number of years. When he had visited Andrew Carnegie in Scotland in 1898, Cable, himself an avid gardener, had been impressed by the garden competition that Carnegie sponsored at Dunfermline, his birthplace. On returning home, Cable had instituted a similar competition in Northampton, with Carnegie providing the prize money. By 1913 some 1,000 gardens, almost a fourth of those in the town, were entered in the contest. At first Cable did all the work of enrolling, visiting, and judging himself, but soon the women's council of the People's Institute took over the work. The 150 gardens judged best were selected by the women's council, whereupon Cable picked those to receive the lesser prizes and in company with a professional gardener and another amateur judged the four finalists. The garden, Cable felt, should be democratic: only the competitor should work in it, without hired help, and without professional advice. Improvement from year to year was taken into consideration in the judging. Prizes went to gardens in all sections of town, thus ensuring that the poorer areas would be represented. Judging was based on four points: layout, harmony, condition, and duration.[6] As Cable went about his own gardening and encouraging gardening generally, he wrote about it; articles of his appeared on "Neighborly Gardens," "The American Garden," "The Midwinter Gardens of New Orleans," "The Cottage Gardens of Northampton," and "My Own Acre," and most of this material was collected in *The Amateur Garden.*

Cable's revenue from his writings was not enough to live on, however, and attempts to have his stories made into plays and movies were unsuccessful. Thus in 1911 when Andrew Carnegie told him that if ever he needed a pension, it would be forthcoming, Cable soon wrote to ask for a loan of $5,000. Carnegie preferred instead to send $1,000 a year until Cable could finish *Gideon's Band.*[7] It was a fortunate windfall, for Cable also faced the need for an operation to remove a cataract that for three years had left him blind in one eye. His friend S. Weir Mitchell in Philadelphia recommended a surgeon and looked after arrangements, and on November 19, 1913, the operation was performed. To Carnegie he wrote in January: "Your goodness has been more to me than I can tell you without a longer letter than I feel free to impose on you. Without it I do not see how we could have saved our home."[8] During his convalescence he began to use a dictating machine, which he adopted enthusiastically.[9]

Cable now went down to New Orleans almost every winter. By the time *Gideon's Band* was published, he was at work on another novel. "I am living in an extremely pleasant Creole family whose head is Mme. J. Numa Augustin," he wrote to his daughter Margaret in March, 1915, "and shall be there thru this month. My new story is of Creoles of to-day."[10] And to Charles Scribner he wrote proudly: "I am most happily disappointed in my experiences with the Creole people themselves. It would be but little exaggeration for me to say that they are receiving me with open arms. Also I am living in a Creole household of the highest social standing."[11]

On March 17, Cable read before the Louisiana Historical Society in the Supreme Court Room of the Cabildo. He was received with enthusiastic applause, and afterward New Orleans citizens by the score came up to shake his hand. He had been publicly forgiven. The novelist Grace King—who as a friend of Gayarré had once spoken so fiercely about Cable to Gilder, and whose own stories of Creole life had been first undertaken to counteract the picture of the Creoles in Cable's work—told of this reading some years later to a Boston *Evening Transcript* interviewer:

> I understand him now. I would say he wrote too well about the Creoles. . . . He captured the audience. Everyone rushed up and shook hands with him. Many of us never dreamed the day would come when we would shake hands with Cable. . . . The hall was packed. When he finished everybody stood up, and I never heard such applause. I am so glad that at last he got this compliment from New Orleans. He deserved it, not only as a tribute to his genius, but as compensation for the way we treated him. I am glad. He is an old man, very picturesque, very sad, with beautiful manners.[12]

But in 1932, when Miss King's *Memories of a Southern Woman of Letters* appeared, she had changed her mind. Cable, she said then, "was a native of New Orleans and had been well treated by its people, and yet he stabbed the city in the back, as we felt, in a dastardly way to please the Northern press."[13] Joseph Pennell went back to New Orleans in 1921, forty years after *Scribner's Monthly* had sent him down to illustrate *The Creoles of Louisiana* for serial publication, and wrote Cable: "I realized yesterday how fine and true your work was—and how well remembered—and that you were remembered from the old days and not forgotten—or forgiven. . . ."[14]

The "new story of Creoles of today" on which Cable was at work may have been either the novel *Lovers of Louisiana* or the book of interwoven short stories entitled *The Flower of the Chapdelaines,* both of which are set in New Orleans during World

War I, and involve Creole families. It was not until 1918 that either appeared. *The Flower of the Chapdelaines,* which is the slighter of Cable's two final books, appeared in March of that year; it contained, as separate narratives within a larger story, "The Clock in the Sky," originally published in *Scribner's Magazine* in 1901, "A West Indian Slave Insurrection," published in *Scribner's Magazine* in 1892, and "The Angel of the Lord," published anonymously in a volume entitled *A House Party* by Small, Maynard and Company of Boston in 1901.[15] Cable put the volume together in 1917 because he was especially hard up for money, having exhausted the $5,000 that Scribner's had advanced for a new novel. To make his southward journey that year, he wired Scribner's to ask for an additional $400; again an advance was forthcoming, though Charles Scribner wrote Cable that the $10,000 in advance royalties that Cable had received for the two books was more than the firm could ever hope to recover.[16]

While based on the three earlier stories, *The Flower of the Chapdelaines* is actually more tidily woven together than either *Bonaventure* or *Strong Hearts,* Cable's two earlier volumes constructed in similar fashion. The frame which Cable wrote for the narrative is actually longer than the three stories and, except toward the end when it becomes over complicated and contrived, makes for an appealing story in its own right. The narrative concerns a young attorney who takes up residence in New Orleans and is consulted by a Creole about a manuscript that he wishes to sell on behalf of three Creole ladies. The attorney becomes very much involved in the life of a group of Creole families, finds (improbably) that a manuscript in his own family is a direct link with that owned by the Creoles, and ultimately weds one of the Creole ladies. The manuscripts—the three stories Cable had published earlier—all have to do with slavery, and are among Cable's most effective narratives of that type. In putting together the book Cable drew on his own experiences in Reconstruction Louisiana, and on some other autobiographical material. His portrait of the modern-day Creoles is affectionate, with a great deal of gentle humor involved, much in the manner of his portrait of the Mesdames Nancanou in *The Grandissimes.* Most of the social criticism has to do with the recital, by Aline Chapdelaine, of her grandfather's and father's experiences during the Reconstruction, in which they were aligned with the hated Reconstruction government. There is also, however, another character, Ovide Landry, a Negro, once a slave, who deals in old books and maps. Ovide Landry is one of Cable's best characters, and his situation *vis-à-vis* white New Orleans, mostly implied and never too strongly stressed, does involve interesting ramifications. But most of the potentially controversial material involves events that took place long ago, and neither the Reconstruction episodes nor the slave narratives are given much direct contemporary relevance. The fact was that in the four decades that had transpired since Cable had written his first Creole stories, what had been a dangerously bold presentation of vital issues had become historical fiction, and was largely taken as such by the readers of 1918.

The Flower of the Chapdelaines was not the last word that George W. Cable was to address to New Orleans and to the South about the questions that had so preoccupied him for the better part of his long life. For late in 1918 appeared the novel *Lovers of Louisiana*. In this, his last published work of fiction, he spoke out in terms of unequivocal clearness about contemporary Southern racism. Set in New Orleans in 1914 and 1915, it involved Creoles and Americans, and at its center lay the question of whether the South was to continue with its racial policies or move toward justice and equality for all its citizens.

The hero of the book is Philip Castleton, a young Southerner educated at Princeton and now teaching at Tulane University. As Philip Butcher notes, Castleton's career is very much like Cable's.[17] He speaks out on the racial question in defiance of popular sentiment. When he makes a speech to a Negro group, and opens by remarking: "I can hope for no whole-hearted acceptance of what I have to say unless while I bear in mind that you are colored you kindly forget that I am white," he is denounced throughout the city, ostracized by its society, shunned by most of his onetime friends, and threatened with bodily violence. Like Cable, too, he serves on a grand jury, and his eyes are thereupon opened to corruption within the city. He also writes essays on Southern problems which are published in Northern magazines and win him a national reputation, even while his fellow Southerners ridicule him.

Unlike Cable, however, but like John March, Philip Castleton declines to move to the North when offered a lucrative and attractive position there. His love for New Orleans makes him determined "to see her faults—I'd rather call them ailments—and to want to help cure them—as I couldn't help from a distance." It is as if Cable were indeed saying now that he had made a mistake in leaving New Orleans in 1884. But we are also informed that Philip Castleton's father, who would have been close to Cable's own age, *had* remained in New Orleans, condemned lynching, the Ku Klux Klan, and racial segregation, and died a martyr to his beliefs—so that, as Butcher says, Castleton's father represents what Cable felt would have happened to him had he not moved away, while Castleton himself may be what Cable would have wanted his son to be had he grown to maturity. In Castleton's devotion to ideas, his zeal for airing his views on every possible occasion, he resembles Cable himself when young—and also Joseph Frowenfeld of *The Grandissimes.* Like Joseph, too, Philip Castleton ultimately marries his Creole lady, Rosalie Durel.

Many of the familiar elements of Cable's fiction are present in *Lovers of Louisiana.* Philip Castleton's grandfather marries his own sweetheart's grandmother; Cable was fond of introducing these multiple marriages among several generations into his fiction. Once again there is an octoroon who is the helpless prey of a lustful Creole. The villain of the story, Zéphire Durel, is very much like certain earlier male Creoles portrayed by Cable; he is racially bigoted, a ladies' man, conceited, vain, and sexually promiscuous. Thus Castleton's triumph over Zéphire is, once again, a triumph of the Anglo-American over the Creole, resulting in his marriage into a distinguished Creole family. This time, however, the Castletons are made to be of equally distinguished lineage, so that the social mobility that characterizes the career of Joseph Frowenfeld in *The Grandissimes* is not as marked in *Lovers of Louisiana.*

Ovide Landry, the Negro bookdealer who appeared in *The Flower of the Chapdelaines,* figures even more importantly in *Lovers of Louisiana.* He represents, much more clearly, the evidence that the Negro is quite capable of full participation in society, and can be trusted with the same responsibility as the white man. When a shortage is discovered in the Durel family bank, and it is desired to have the books audited without the news getting to the public in any way, Ovide is pressed into service, and by cover of night examines the books and produces the evidence to show that Zéphire Durel has been embezzling funds. It is Ovide who then lends Alphonse Durel the money to make good his nephew's defalcations—though what the elder Durel does not know is that the Castletons have provided Ovide with the funds to do so!

The romance between Philip Castleton and Rosalie Durel ends happily only after a long series of hindrances, not the least of which are Philip Castleton's political and social views. Throughout the novel, Castleton stands firm on his belief that the South must turn away from its narrow ways and embrace democracy whole-heartedly. And, just as in *John March, Southerner,* there is the same insistence that the kind of materialistic commercial and industrial progress glorified in New South ideology is no solution. In a typical utterance, Philip at one point says:

> a true lover of his city, to deserve her smiles, her arms, must do his finest to help fit her for a high place in the world—oh, better—for a high place in the world's service! And he can't do that, sir, by following political fashions. Nor can he do it by echoing the provincial flatteries of her office-seekers and her press. It can't be done, you know, by keeping her the mother city of an antiquated Dixie out of step with the nation and the world; and much less by Americanizing those fine old Creole ways—in manners, in architecture, in social and domestic life—which are just what ought, instead, to Creolize her American crassness.

Philip's disapproval of New Orleans's commercialism even extends to the city's beloved Mardi Gras week. He tells Mr. Durel that "when a great modern city, capital of a civilization, makes that organized old puerility—which is neither reality nor good dream-stuff, celebrates no achievement, initiates no enterprise, presents no contest of strength or skill, and offers no illustration worth saving overnight of any art, literature, or other refinement—makes that, I say, its greatest event of the year, the sooner she cuts it out the better—the happier for her—and Dixie!" And when Durel objects that "they'll tell you how thad pay' prettie well, that Carnival," Philip replies: ". . . it pays only in the dollar of the moment. It reaps the dollars and loses what they're for; loses in civilization—for New Orleans—for all Dixie. Why, sir, imagine half that yearly flood of outlay being put into the things that truly refine and glorify a city; that make it a splendid instrument for a modern civilization to strike its chords on."

A great deal of the sharpest social criticism in *Lovers of Louisiana*, however, is made not by Philip Castleton but by a Scotsman, Mr. Murray, who is visiting the United States for the first time. Early in the novel, Murray replies to Philip's assertion that the race question is "a strictly Southern question, which we will take care of if the rest of the country will only let us alone." "But it isn't and ye don't," the Scot says. "Doctor Castleton, it's a British question and a world question and it's getting bigger every day." Perhaps Cable had Andrew Carnegie or his friend James M. Barrie in mind when he created Murray; in his kindness, his good nature, and his generosity, he is very different from the officious Briton who expressed similar heretical opinions to John on the excursion trip in *John March, Southerner*.

Thus did George W. Cable, at the age of seventy-four, publish a novel in which he updated, for another day and another generation, the same criticism of New Orleans and of the South that he had first offered to a city and a region just emerging from the shock of Civil War and the ordeal of Reconstruction. Coming back from exile, as it were, he had been received with honors and praise by his native city, and had repaid her with what coin he had always had to offer: fiction in which, as best he could, he gave an image to the life, the problems, and the aspirations of New Orleans. After all those years of separation, he had not compromised with his ideals or his attitudes; as a citizen of New Orleans, he had done his best to speak the truth.

Lovers of Louisiana, alas, is a very poor novel. Its shortcomings derive not from any desire to avoid controversial material, as had been true of his historical romances of the early 1900's, but from a failure to impart life to his characters and to dramatize, rather than merely set down, his ideas. The conflict between individual Creoles and *Américains* which made *The Grandissimes* so effective an embodiment of conditions of race and caste is almost entirely missing in *Lovers of Louisiana*. In the 1918 work, the themes of the story remain undramatized ideas and are no more than rhetoric. The characterization of Philip Castleton is wooden and artificial; he appears on the scene with certain set ideas, and throughout the novel he does little more than restate them. There is no internal struggle between what he has been taught to believe and what he learns for himself, such as makes John March so interesting a person except when playing the role of romantic lover. Coming back to the New Orleans milieu, and seeking to create fiction out of it once again, Cable was unable to give his ideas the imaginative grounding in people and events that had been possible when the experience of living in New Orleans was a reality embodying actual people and events from which ideas grew. It had become an abstract problem now, and he could deal with it only in abstractions. The Cable of the 1870's and 1880's, had he wished to criticize the Mardi Gras, would have presented his characters involved in the events of the carnival, and his ideas would have come through what they said and did. Philip Castleton merely delivers a speech on the subject. So it is with almost every issue argued in the novel.

Even the New Orleans scene itself is largely absent from *Lovers of Louisiana.* The writer who had once been able to invest his fiction with so rich a tapestry of people and places now produced a story consisting mostly of dialogue. Save for occasional set pieces, there is little description of the city itself. Early in the novel there is an incident in which the Castletons attend a performance at the French Opera House. In Cable's earlier work his protagonist would never have done such a thing, because at that time in Cable's life the Calvinistic proscription of the theater as sinful had barred him from such experiences himself. Cable had long since thrown off the prohibition against the theater, and doubtless he had attended performances at the opera house before writing *Lovers of Louisiana;* but his imagination was powerless now to convey the setting through having real characters live in it. There is more effective and memorable composition of place in almost any given story of *Old Creole Days* than in the whole narrative of *Lovers of Louisiana.*

Cable's last published novel, then, is interesting not so much as fiction as because Cable wrote it. Returning to the scene of his most memorable work, viewing again the life of a community of which he had once been part and in which he had evolved the ideas and attitudes that had given so compelling a direction to the whole course of his life, he had sought in his old age to continue the same struggle for human justice that had once caused him so much grief and pain, and seemingly had dealt him so devastating a defeat. The novel he now produced was an artistic failure, little read during his lifetime, and afterward almost entirely forgotten.

All the same, there are moments in *Lovers of Louisiana* in which the words and sentences, though written in the 1910's, seem now to leap out from the printed page with the immediacy of current events and the burning clarity of prophecy. Thus at one juncture, the Scotsman Murray brings up the race issue, whereupon the Creole banker Alphonse Durel responds that "tha'z the deadest queztion in Ammerica!" The Scot disagrees.

> "No, Mr. Durel, it isn't dead, it's merely 'possuming. I say it wi' no vaunting, but wi' drread. Ye may crrack its bones and never get a whimper, yet 'tis but 'possuming. Lorrd! Ye can't *neglect* it to death; the neglect of all America can't kill it. It's in the womb o' the future and bigger than Asia, Africa, and America combined. Ye'll do well to be friendly wi' its friends and trreat it kindly while it's young and tractable."
>
> "My dear sir—"
>
> "Hold on, this is my last word. 'Tisn't dead, I say. It's but lost its place in the line and been sent back to the wurruld's tail-end. Wi' war and a swarrm o' lesser things on yon side, and preparedness and a swarrm o' lesser things on this, it's pitifully out o' fashion; but fashions have an uncanny trrick o' comin' back, and there's a day ahead, whether far or near God only knows, when that question—and they that are out o' fashion wi' it—will come round again, as big an' ugly as hoop-skirrts."

XVI
The Final Days

He had settled in, now, to a pattern. Each winter he went south, to New Orleans, Bermuda, or Atlantic City. The remainder of the year he passed at Tarryawhile, writing every morning in the same slow, painstaking way he had always composed. In the afternoon he wrote letters, read proof, worked in his garden.[1] His children were all gone from home. In 1915 his brother James died, in 1918 his sister Mary Louise.

Finances were even yet a problem. He collected an advance from Scribner's on a new novel, begun while *Lovers of Louisiana* was in production. It was set in New Orleans, during World War I. It was never finished; some 300 pages of manuscript had been completed at his death. He had also begun collecting material for a story about a haunted house in New Orleans, but he did not write it.[2] In 1919 he signed a contract for a series of movies to be made from his novels, but none was ever begun.[3] But for Andrew Carnegie's annual benefaction he would have been close to destitution. Then in 1919 Carnegie died, leaving Cable an annual bequest of $5,000 for the rest of his life, to be continued for his wife if she outlived him.[4] Thus at the age of seventy-five, for the first time in his life he was free of money problems.

He took an interest in the American Academy of Arts and Letters, of which his friend and onetime *Century* editor Robert Underwood Johnson was permanent secretary. When the United States entered the war he did what he could for the war effort, writing and making a few speeches. In the autumn of 1918 his oldest grandson, George Cable Chard, was killed in France. In November, 1920, his daughter Margaret, long ill, died in California. Then in 1923, after four months of confinement to her bed, his wife Eva died.[5] They had been married for seventeen years. His daughter Dorothea—Mrs. Charles Boardman Hawes—with her husband and two children came to Tarryawhile to live with him, but scarcely a few weeks passed before Hawes died tragically at the age of thirty-four.[6]

Almost all Cable's old friends, the men who had once composed so formidable a literary phalanx in the heyday of the Genteel Tradition, were gone. The names that one read about now—Dreiser, Cabell, Lewis, Mencken, O'Neill, Sandburg, Eliot, Pound, Anderson—were new to him. They did not write his kind of books. His eyes had grown too weak for much reading anyway. Even to write a letter to Henry Van Dyke, to Johnson, to his sister Nettie, his children and grandchildren, now became an ordeal.

He missed the company of Eva very much—just as he had so missed Louise. In December, 1923, at the age of seventy-nine, he married Mrs. Hanna Cowing, a Northampton neighbor.[7] From Atlanta he wrote to Charles Scribner: "You will be surprised to have me tell you that instead of dying I have married for the third time—Dec. 16th and am now on my way to Florida, leaving immediately after the ceremony. This hurried union only six months after my bereavement calls for an explanation. Mrs. Cable has been an intimate friend & neighbor of all my family for 35 years & has enjoyed their confidence and have grown into each others [sic] lives, completely. I cannot write any more at this time—please wish us a happy New Year as we wish yours."[8]

He returned to Northampton when summer came to enjoy his garden at Tarryawhile once again. In the fall he journeyed down to St. Petersburg. There, on January 31, 1925, he died.

For two days his body lay in state in Carnegie Hall at the People's Institute in Northampton. After the funeral, he was buried in Bridge Street Cemetery, beside Louise.[9]

His passing was commented upon in a few of the magazines of the day. "In Cable's pictures of plantation life, in his story of the French civilization absorbed in our South, there were a charm and an importance that are perhaps not fully appreciated now," *The Bookman* declared.[10] "George W. Cable . . . was a distinguished American novelist not because he exploited Louisiana life in the ordinary local colorist's fashion but because, transcending that fashion, he anticipated the critical spirit which in the present generation is inspiring something better than a narrowly national literature," the *Nation* said.[11] Though he wrote so well about New Orleans, he was not even born there, *The Outlook* mistakenly declared; in his tales of local color he "struck a new vein and new people, and he won his reward in universal approval." Although it was said that he was less appreciated in the South than in the North, his love for the South and the Southern people always endured.[12]

In 1928 Cable's daughter, Lucy Leffingwell Biklé, published his biography. In no way critical, with scarcely any discussion of the controversies that his writings had once occasioned, it consisted in large part of excerpts from his letters. By then there were few who realized what his life had consisted of or what his works had meant. The vogue of local color had long since passed, and it was only as an early local colorist, a writer of romantic stories about quaint Creoles, that he was remembered. But one young critic knew differently. Edmund Wilson, reviewing the Biklé biography in the *New Republic,* pointed out that "the whole American problem of diversity and unity" was present in the New Orleans of Cable's youth, and declared that "no writer ever studied it more thoroughly or thought about it more intelligently than George Washington Cable did." Cable, he continued, "was essentially a sociologist. He was not in the least a fancier of lavender and old lace. He was a good deal closer to Upton Sinclair than to Myrtle Reed." Cable "was one of the clearest-minded Americans of his time, and in the South after the Civil War, so detached and realistic an intelligence was uncommon and unwelcome. It was not common or welcome anywhere."[13]

When the early stories and novels of George W. Cable were first being published, it was customary for their author to be compared, and not unfavorably, with Nathaniel Hawthorne. Few people today would think to accord such status even to Cable's best work. Yet it is not difficult to see why, to the readers of the 1870's and 1880's, the fiction that Cable was producing would have seemed to merit such high praise. In presenting interesting people living in an interesting place, he was not only opening up new fictional territory and exploring new areas of American experience, but was doing so with a literary artistry that infused his stories with a convincingly original atmosphere and tone. Much as Hawthorne had done, he seemed to be creating a unique and recognizable fictional universe of his own, with a rich density of social texture given structure and meaning by an austere and unflinching moral scrupulosity. Like Hawthorne's, Cable's art drew its life and its importance from the demands of clashing loyalties and impulses within the writer's own complex personality. With Hawthorne it was the contention between the recalcitrant heritage of his New England Puritanism and his allegiance to the liberating values and attitudes of nineteenth-century America. For Cable there were the opposing energies of his Calvinistic moral compulsions and the allurement of the sensuous ways of Creole New Orleans. For both writers, the creative tension that resulted imbued their art with profoundly human qualities.

Yet how different, and how disparate, the outcomes. Hawthorne wrote several novels and a host of stories that not only have outlasted their times but have even broadened their appeal and their relevance for succeeding generations of readers, while Cable's fiction has for the most part receded into literary history. Only a small portion of all that Cable wrote continues to be read today, and even the one novel on which his ultimate reputation probably rests is a flawed work, with a deficiency of development lying at the heart of its accomplishment. Not even its density of social portrayal, or the host of fascinating characterizations, or even the boldness of its political and social meaning, can quite make up for the artistic vacuum that exists in the self-awareness of its most important character, Joseph Frowenfeld.

Cable has been underrated. Impressive novels and stories, important in the development of Southern and American fiction and full of unique insight into Southern and American experience, well worth reading in their own right as fiction, have gone unread and unappreciated. Of this there can be no doubt. Yet on the remorseless and absolute scale by which works of literature are tested and weighed, it must be said that Cable was a failure. He was and is a minor writer, important more for what he sought to do than for how well he did it. He wrote about the South and its people, white and black, as no one before him had ever done; he opened up areas of experience that had hitherto been ignored, exposed problems and attitudes that no one before him had been willing or able to delineate, including several that remain of compelling urgency in our own time. Some of the things he sought to reveal have yet to be better shown. Yet his artistry was inferior to his intentions, and his fiction, as fiction, never fulfilled the promise that it seemed to hold.

Appearing out of the war-ravaged South on a literary scene that badly lacked the honesty and insight of a major literary imagination to give it the direction and clarification it needed, Cable quickly disappeared into the Genteel Tradition. A greater artist than Hamlin Garland, like Garland he never fulfilled the hopes that his earliest published work aroused. The cutting edge of his acute social conscience, his keen sympathy for oppressed human beings laboring under a difficult and barren circumstance, was soon blunted by the timidity and compromises of a literary milieu that sought to escape from whatever was harsh or unpleasant by pretending that it did not exist. And as in the case of Garland, however mitigating the circumstances and however understandable the capitulation, the responsibility must at the last be laid to him.

It was a failure, finally, of artistic intelligence. What is wrong with Cable's fiction, what prevents it from attaining major stature, is the failure of the writer to look within himself long enough and hard enough. Thus the characters whose consciousness might have given the scenes he sought to portray the human complexity and urgency that would elevate them into enduring art, remain at key points in their development unexamined and unrevealed. What they are deficient in finally is, to use Hawthorne's phrase, the "truth of the human heart"; so that, to continue Hawthorne's metaphor, they have insufficiently to do with the clouds overhead, however graphically they describe portions of the actual soil of the state of Louisiana.

And this must be said, too, of the life and work of George W. Cable: the failure was not only artistic, but—and therefore—political and social as well. For Cable did not succeed as reformer, either. I do not mean by this that he devoted years of his life and vast reserves of his energy in eloquent and fervent advocacy of a cause that, for his own time at least, was foredoomed to failure, posited as it was on the existence of a "Silent South" that did not in fact exist at all. I mean, rather, that the stories and novels that he wrote toward this end did not succeed as social protest. However less militant and less personally courageous his friend Mark Twain may have been in speaking up as a man against racism and against civil rights and the denial of human dignity to the Negro, *The Adventures of Huckleberry Finn* is surely a document in human liberty, and a weapon in the arousing of the American conscience to bring an end to racial injustice, more formidable and more potent than anything Cable wrote or said or did. Ironically, *because* it is a more profound work of art, it has also been a more effective vehicle of political and social protest. For the sad truth is that in a writer, the artistic and the polemical impulses cannot really be viewed separately; the failure to look within himself deeply enough is inextricably connected on Cable's part with the failure to understand the people of the South in their time and place. He knew what they *should* do; that they would and could not do it baffled him all of his life. Such a judgment, I think, though harsh is inescapable. No amount of admiration for Cable's high courage and moral integrity can get around it. The failure is there.

Yet however posterity may evaluate the success or the failure of what a writer or a reformer seeks to do, such success or failure surely has nothing to do with one's estimate of the quality of the man himself. Whatever his artistic shortcomings, whatever his failure may have been in changing the course of his times, one can find little to fault, and much to praise, in the life and behavior of George W. Cable. Against incredible odds, at tremendous cost to his reputation and his career, he battled for what he believed in with every ounce of strength in his slight body and his large heart. Exile, obloquy, personal want were, finally, not as important to him as the right to speak out against injustice and bigotry. Nor can his intentions as an artist be faulted. He wanted to write in a certain way, about certain things important to him, and he did so to the best of his ability throughout most of his career. Not only that, but he did it well, so well in fact that for a great many years he went unpraised and unread.

Not until the 1950's did many people begin to read George W. Cable's work again. It was then, when the centennial of the Civil War in which Cable had fought as a Confederate cavalryman was drawing near, and the long-dormant conscience of the nation had at last awakened to the unfinished business of that war, that a Louisiana writer's remarks many decades ago about the Negro and what was being done to deprive him of the civil rights supposedly guaranteed him by the Constitution of the United States began to be remembered. Just as he had predicted in his last novel, the race issue had come round again, and with it a writer long out of fashion had come back into notice. Those who read his essays on the Negro question discovered that there was scarcely a single argument now being advanced against racial injustice that had not been made by Cable sixty years earlier. And with the scrutiny of his novels and stories that resulted, critics began to realize that long ago, in the heyday of the Genteel Tradition, there had been a Southern writer who alone in his time had broken through the trappings of local color and costume romance and sought to depict his native region in the rich daylight of reality. What William Faulkner, Thomas Wolfe, Robert Penn Warren, and the other writers of the twentieth-century South made into literary art of national and even international importance, George Washington Cable had, however imperfectly, first sketched.

Notes

I: Mardi Gras

[1] Oliver Evans, *New Orleans* (New York, 1959), p. 149.

[2] Arlin Turner, *George W. Cable, A Biography* (Durham, N.C., 1956), p. 51.

[3] Robert Underwood Johnson, *Remembered Yesterdays* (Boston, 1923), pp. 96–97.

[4] Turner, *Cable,* pp. 51–52.

[5] *Ibid.,* pp. 46–47.

[6] *Ibid.,* pp. 53–54.

[7] Lucy Leffingwell Cable Biklé, *George W. Cable: His Life and Letters* (New York, 1928), pp. 46–47.

[8] GWC to Fred Lewis Pattee, July 21, 1914, quoted in Biklé, *Cable: His Life and Letters,* p. 47.

[9] Turner, *Cable,* p. 53.

[10] Edward King, *The Great South* (New York, 1875), p. 34.

[11] *Ibid.,* p. 93.

[12] *Ibid.,* pp. 17 ff.

[13] *Ibid.,* p. 28.

[14] *Ibid.,* p. 29.

[15] *Ibid.,* p. 40.

[16] Evans, *New Orleans,* p. 149.

[17] Paul S. Buck, *The Road to Reunion, 1865–1900* (Boston, 1938), pp. 130–132.

[18] Quoted in *ibid.,* pp. 131–132.

[19] *Ibid.,* p. 131.

[20] King, *The Great South,* pp. 18, 28.

[21] GWC to Pattee, July 21, 1914, quoted in Biklé, *Cable: His Life and Letters,* p. 48.

[22] Edmund Wilson, *Patriotic Gore: Studies in the Literature of the American Civil War* (New York, 1962), p. 579.

II: Youth

[1] Turner, *Cable,* p. 3.

278

[2] Kjell Ekström, *George Washington Cable: A Study of His Early Life and Work*, Essays and Studies on American Language and Literature, No. 10 (Uppsala and Cambridge, Mass., 1950), pp. 3-4.

[3] Biklé, *Cable: His Life and Letters*, pp. 2-3.

[4] *Ibid.*, p. 3.

[5] Evans, *New Orleans*, p. 50.

[6] *Ibid.*, pp. 50-51.

[7] *Ibid.*, pp. 52-53.

[8] Turner, *Cable*, p. 7.

[9] King, *The Great South*, p. 36.

[10] Biklé, *Cable: His Life and Letters*, p. 2.

[11] Turner, *Cable*, pp. 8-9, 14.

[12] George W. Cable, "New Orleans," *St. Nicholas*, XXI (November, 1893), 40-49.

[13] George W. Cable, "Some of My Pets," *Youth's Companion*, LXXV (Sept. 5, 1901), 472.

[14] George W. Cable, "New Orleans," *St. Nicholas*, XXI (December, 1893), 150-154.

[15] *Ibid.*

[16] Turner, *Cable*, pp. 10-13.

[17] *Ibid.*, pp. 16-19.

[18] Quoted in Biklé, *Cable: His Life and Letters*, p. 4.

[19] Jay B. Hubbell, *The South in American Literature, 1607-1900* (Durham, N.C., 1954), p. 817.

[20] Turner, *Cable*, p. 21.

[21] *Ibid.*, p. 22.

[22] George W. Cable, "New Orleans Before the Capture," *Century Illustrated Monthly Magazine*, XXIX (April, 1885), 918-22.

[23] *Ibid.*

[24] Turner, *Cable*, pp. 24-26.

[25] *Ibid.*, pp. 26-30.

[26] GWC to Louise Bartlett Cable, Jan. 12, 1885.

[27] Turner, *Cable*, p. 30.

[28] C. M. Clay, "George W. Cable," *The Critic*, I (Oct. 8, 1881), 270-271, quoted in Turner, *Cable*, p. 28.

[29] Turner, *Cable*, pp. 28-29.

[30] *Ibid.*, p. 32.

[31] Arlin Turner (ed.), "George W. Cable's Recollections of General Forrest," *Journal of Southern History*, XXI (May, 1955), 22-28.

[32] GWC to James Boardman Cable, Nov. 26, 1864.

[33] GWC to James Boardman Cable, Nov. 29, 1864.

[34] GWC to Rebecca Boardman Cable, March 20, 1865.

[35] GWC to Rebecca Boardman Cable, April 16, 1865.

[36] Turner, *Cable*, 27.

[37] Quoted in Biklé, *Cable: His Life and Letters*, p. 20.

[38] George W. Cable, "My Politics," in Arlin Turner (ed.), *The Negro Question: A Selection of Writings on Civil Rights in the South,* by George W. Cable (Garden City, N.Y., 1958), p. 4.

III: New Orleans Days

[1] Biklé, *Cable: His Life and Letters,* p. 24.

[2] GWC to Rebecca Boardman Cable, Jan. 10, 1866.

[3] Turner, *Cable,* p. 36.

[4] GWC to Rebecca Boardman Cable, Jan. 26, 1866.

[5] Turner, *Cable,* p. 37.

[6] Biklé, *Cable: His Life and Letters,* p. 36.

[7] Turner, *Cable,* p. 38.

[8] *Ibid.*

[9] Arlin Turner, "George W. Cable's Literary Apprenticeship," *Louisiana Historical Quarterly,* XXIV (January, 1941), 168.

[10] *Ibid.,* 181.

[11] New Orleans *Picayune,* Feb. 25, 1872, quoted in *ibid.,* p. 18.

[12] Turner, *Cable,* pp. 39–41.

[13] Cable, "Drop Shot," New Orleans *Picayune,* June 28, 1870.

[14] Turner, *Cable,* p. 45.

[15] Cable, "My Politics," in Turner (ed.), *The Negro Question,* p. 8.

[16] *Ibid.*

[17] *Ibid.,* pp. 9–10.

[18] *Ibid.,* p. 10.

[19] Turner, *Cable,* pp. 46–50.

[20] GWC to Charles Scribner's and Company, Oct. 17, 1871.

[21] GWC to Charles Scribner's and Company, Oct. 31, 1871.

[22] GWC to Charles Scribner's and Company, Dec. 25, 1871, Jan. 14, 1872.

[23] Cable, "My Politics," in Turner (ed.), *The Negro Question,* p. 11.

[24] Turner, *Cable,* p. 54.

[25] Biklé, *Cable: His Life and Letters,* p. 48.

[26] Edward King to GWC, April 13, 1873.

[27] Edward King to GWC, March 25, 1873.

[28] Edward King to GWC, April 24, 1873.

[29] Edward King to GWC, May 9, 1873.

[30] Edward King to GWC, July 22, 1873.

IV: Local Color: *Old Creole Days*

[1] Claude M. Simpson (ed.), Introduction to *The Local Colorists: American Short Stories, 1857–1900* (New York, 1960), p. 8.

[2] *Ibid.,* p. 4.

[3] [John W. De Forest,] "The Great American Novel," *The Nation,* VI (Jan. 9, 1868), 27–29.

[4] Turner, *Cable,* p. 63.

[5] Herbert Franklin Smith, *The Editorial Influence of Richard Watson Gilder, 1870–1909,* Rutgers University, 1961 (University Microfilms, Ann Arbor, Mich., 1967), p. 92.

[6] William Malone Baskervill, *Southern Writers: Biographical and Critical Sketches,* Vol. I (Nashville, Tenn., 1897), p. 313.

[7] Quoted in Biklé, *Cable: His Life and Letters,* p. 49.

[8] Johnson, *Remembered Yesterdays,* p. 122.

[9] Philip Butcher, *George W. Cable* (New York, 1962), p. 40.

[10] *Ibid.,* p. 64.

[11] Richard Watson Gilder to GWC, March 31, 1875.

V: A Published Author

[1] Turner, *Cable,* p. 65.

[2] GWC to Rebecca Boardman Cable, July 11, 1875.

[3] Smith, *The Editorial Influence of Richard Watson Gilder,* p. 88.

[4] William Allen White, "Fiction of the Eighties and Nineties," in John Macy (ed.), *American Writers on American Literature* (New York, 1934); quoted in Louis D. Rubin, Jr., and John Rees Moore (eds.), *The Idea of an American Novel* (New York, 1961), p. 94.

[5] See Robert Berkleman, "Mrs. Grundy and Richard Watson Gilder," *American Quarterly,* IV (Spring, 1952), 66–72, and Smith, *The Editorial Influence of Richard Watson Gilder, passim.*

[6] Larzer Ziff, *The American 1890s: Life and Times of a Lost Generation* (New York, 1966), pp. 128–29.

[7] Smith, *The Editorial Influence of Richard Watson Gilder,* p. 384.

[8] Richard Watson Gilder to GWC, Aug. 29, 1873.

[9] Richard Watson Gilder to GWC, Jan. 4, 1874.

[10] Quoted in Turner, *Cable,* p. 67.

[11] Quoted in Biklé, *Cable: His Life and Letters,* pp. 48–49.

[12] Turner, *Cable,* p. 66.

[13] GWC to Louise Bartlett Cable, July 19, 1875.

[14] Turner, *Cable,* p. 71.

[15] *Ibid.,* p. 72.

[16] Mary E. Burt and Lucy L. Cable (eds.), *The Cable Story Book: Selections for School Reading* (New York, 1899), p. 167.

[17] GWC to Rebecca Boardman Cable, Sept. 9, 1875.

[18] Turner, *Cable,* p. 71.

[19] GWC "Journal," entry for Dec. 7, 1888.

[20] Cable, "My Politics," in Turner (ed.), *The Negro Question,* p. 11.

[21] *Ibid.,* pp. 12–13.

[22] *Ibid.,* p. 13.

[23] Cable, "After-thoughts of a Story Teller," *North American Review,* CLVIII (January, 1894), 17–18.

[24] H. H. Boyesen to GWC, Feb. 18, 1877, quoted in Arlin Turner, "A Novelist Discovers a Novelist: The Correspondence of H. H. Boyesen and George W. Cable," *Western Humanities Review,* V (Autumn, 1951), 345–346.

[25] H. H. Boyesen to GWC, March 17, 1877, quoted in *ibid.,* pp. 346–347.

[26] H. H. Boyesen to GWC, Nov. 24, 1877, quoted in *ibid.,* pp. 348–349.

[27] GWC to H. H. Boyesen, quoted in *ibid.,* pp. 349–351.

[28] H. H. Boyesen to GWC, Jan. 8, 1878, quoted in *ibid.,* p. 351.

[29] Turner, *Cable,* p. 81.

[30] GWC to H. H. Boyesen, Jan. 14, 1878, quoted in Turner, "A Novelist Discovers a Novelist," p. 352.

[31] GWC to Scribner, Armstrong and Company, Jan. 18, 1875.

[32] GWC to Scribner, Armstrong and Company, Feb. 9, 1878.

[33] Turner, *Cable,* p. 84.

[34] H. H. Boyesen to GWC, Jan. 20, 1878, quoted in Turner, "A Novelist Discovers a Novelist," p. 354.

[35] H. H. Boyesen to GWC, Feb. 17, 1878, quoted in *ibid.,* pp. 356–358.

[36] GWC to H. H. Boyesen, March 6, 1878, quoted in *ibid.,* pp. 358–359.

[37] H. H. Boyesen to GWC, May 29, 1878, quoted in *ibid.,* p. 361.

[38] Turner, *Cable,* pp. 82–83.

[39] GWC to Charles Scribner III, Oct. 17, 1878.

[40] GWC to H. H. Boyesen, Nov. 5, 1878, quoted in Turner, "A Novelist Discovers a Novelist," pp. 361–364.

[41] Turner, *Cable,* p. 83.

[42] *Ibid.*

[43] GWC to Mary Louise Cable, Nov. 16, 1878.

[44] Turner, *Cable,* pp. 84–87; Ekström, *George Washington Cable,* p. 154.

[45] Turner, *Cable,* pp. 85–86.

[46] *Ibid.,* p. 89.

[47] GWC to Charles Scribner's Sons, Dec. 8, 1879.

[48] Turner, *Cable,* 115–116.

[49] *Ibid.,* p. 109.

[50] GWC to LBC, Sept. 16, 1880; see also GWC to LBC, Sept. 13, 1880, and Sept. 18, 1880.

VI: *The Grandissimes*

[1] Robert Underwood Johnson to GWC, Feb. 11, 1880, quoted in Turner, *Cable,* p. 95.

[2] As Turner notes, Russell's experience of race relations was that of plantation Mississippi, and his ignorance of the quadroon system sometimes made him misinterpret the particular nuances in Cable's fiction. Turner, *Cable,* p. 96.

[3] The rejected and amended chapters of *The Grandissimes* are in the collection of the Yale University Library.

[4] Robert Underwood Johnson to GWC, Jan. 20, 1880, quoted in Turner, *Cable,* pp. 98–99.

[5] Cable, "My Politics," in Turner (ed.), *The Negro Question,* p. 14.

[6] Cable revised *The Grandissimes* in 1883, simplifying the dialect throughout. All subsequent reprintings have been of the revised edition, and it is this edition that I have used *passim.*

[7] GWC to the editor of the *Literary World,* May 31, 1875.

[8] Turner, *Cable,* p. 93.

[9] Butcher, *George W. Cable,* p. 47.

[10] See for example Robert Underwood Johnson to GWC, Aug. 2, 1879.

[11] GWC to the editor of the *Literary World,* May 31, 1875.

[12] Butcher, *George W. Cable,* p. 48.

[13] As Turner says, the revisions Cable made in compliance with Johnson's objections were certainly gains for the artistry of the novel. Turner, *Cable,* p. 98.

[14] Robert Underwood Johnson to GWC, March 26, 1879.

VII: The Man of Letters

[1] Turner, *Cable,* p. 105.

[2] *Ibid.,* p. 100.

[3] *Ibid.,* p. 99.

[4] William Dean Howells to GWC, Oct. 2, 1881, in Mildred Howells (ed.), *Life in Letters of William Dean Howells,* Vol. I (New York, 1928), pp. 301–302.

[5] William Dean Howells to John Hay, March 18, 1882, in *ibid.,* Vol. I, p. 312.

[6] Quoted in Turner, *Cable,* p. 101.

[7] Turner, *Cable,* p. 101.

[8] Edward LaRocque Tinker, *Lafcadio Hearn's American Days* (New York, 1925), p. 122.

[9] *Ibid.,* p. 122–126.

[10] Turner, *Cable,* p. 102.

[11] Richard Watson Gilder to GWC, Jan. 13, 1881.

[12] Quoted in Julia Collier Harris (ed.), *Joel Chandler Harris: Editor and Essayist,* (Chapel Hill, N.C., 1931), pp. 46–47.

[13] Quoted in Turner, *Cable,* p. 105.

[14] GWC to William Dean Howells, Oct. 8, 1881.

[15] Quoted in Turner, *Cable,* p. 107.

[16] For once I must disagree with Turner, who declares that "with a touch of suggestion, a figure of speech, an ironic turn of thought, the reader is gently led through events that leave an effect as delicate as the odor of orange blossoms but also as haunting and unforgettable." Turner, *Cable,* p. 107.

[17] Philip Butcher praises the story for its power of social criticism. It has, he says, "the immediacy of a current newspaper." But that, it seems to me, is precisely what it lacks. The melodramatic love story and the lifelessness of the characters make the social criticism unconvincing. Butcher, *George W. Cable,* p. 59.

[18] Turner, *Cable,* pp. 108–109.

[19] *Ibid.,* p. 111.

[20] Smith, *The Editorial Influence of Richard Watson Gilder,* pp. 37–39.

[21] GWC to Charles Scribner III, Feb. 11, 1881.

[22] Turner, *Cable,* p. 112.

[23] GWC to Rebecca Boardman Cable, June 4, 1881.

[24] GWC to Louise Bartlett Cable, June 14, 1881, quoted in Biklé, *Cable: His Life and Letters,* pp. 69–70.

[25] *Ibid.*

[26] Turner, *Cable,* pp. 112–113.

[27] GWC to LBC, June 22, 1881.

[28] Turner, *Cable,* p. 113.

[29] GWC to LBC, July 2, 1881, quoted in Biklé, *Cable: His Life and Letters,* p. 71.

[30] Turner, *Cable,* pp. 113–114.

[31] GWC to LBC, July 16–17, 1881.

[32] GWC to LBC, Aug. 21, 1881.

[33] Turner, *Cable,* pp. 116–118.

[34] GWC to William Dean Howells, Oct. 8, 1881, quoted in Biklé, *Cable: His Life and Letters,* p. 73.

[35] Turner, *Cable,* pp. 118–119.

[36] Samuel L. Clemens, *Life on the Mississippi* (New York, 1917), pp. 354–355, 357.

[37] Paul M. Cousins, *Joel Chandler Harris* (Baton Rouge, La., 1968), p. 124.

[38] Clemens, *Life on the Mississippi,* pp. 379–380.

VIII: Reformer

[1] Turner, *Cable,* pp. 124–125.

[2] E. A. Burke to GWC, Dec. 16, 1881.

[3] Turner, *Cable,* pp. 124–127.

[4] Cable, "The Freedman's Case in Equity," in Turner (ed.), *The Negro Question,* pp. 67–68.

[5] Turner, *Cable,* p. 128.

[6] Ekström, *George Washington Cable,* p. 85.

[7] Turner, *Cable,* p. 128.

[8] GWC to Marion A. Baker, May 21, 1883.

[9] Turner, *Cable,* p. 130.

[10] Ekström, *George Washington Cable,* pp. 168–169.

[11] GWC to Charles Scribner's Sons, Feb. 11, 1881.

[12] Turner, *Cable,* p. 200.

[13] Ekström, *George Washington Cable,* p. 168.

[14] Grace King, *Memories of a Southern Woman of Letters* (New York, 1932), p. 45.

[15] Turner, *Cable,* p. 201.

[16] Cable limits his recognition of the historian to a single sentence, to the effect that "such pioneers as Peters, Burke, Touro, Martin, De Bow, and the Creoles Dimitry, Forstall, Gayarré, and others are gratefully remembered by a later generation for their labors in the cause of education." George W. Cable, *The Creoles of Louisiana* (New York, 1886), p. 258.

[17] Cable, "My Politics," in Turner (ed.), *The Negro Question,* p. 16.

[18] Turner, *Cable,* p. 129.

[19] *Ibid.*

[20] Ekström, *George Washington Cable,* pp. 151–152.

21 Cable, *The Creoles of Louisiana*, p. 40.

22 *Ibid.*, p. 139.

23 *Ibid.*, p. 275.

24 *Ibid.*, p. 320.

25 Turner, *Cable*, pp. 129–130.

26 For the text of the address, see Arlin Turner, "George W. Cable's Revolt Against Literary Sectionalism," *Tulane Studies in English*, V (1955), 5–26.

27 Years later, several persons who heard the lecture were interviewed by David H. Bishop, and it was then alleged that a minister had risen after the address to rebuke Cable for his anti-Southern views. Turner, however, doubts the authenticity of the claim, and declares that contemporary newspaper accounts would have indicated that such criticisms were made, if it were true. Quoted in Turner, *Cable*, pp. 134–135 and 135n.

28 Cable, "The Due Restraints and Liberties of Literature," in Turner (ed.), *The Negro Question*, pp. 47–48.

29 Turner, *Cable*, pp. 135–136.

30 Guy A. Cardwell, *Twins of Genius* (London, 1962), p. 5.

31 GWC to Samuel L. Clemens, June 29, 1882.

32 Turner, *Cable*, p. 136.

33 Samuel L. Clemens to William Dean Howells, Nov. 4, 1882, quoted in Turner, *Cable*, p. 137.

34 GWC to Louise Bartlett Cable, April 5–6, 1883.

35 Richard Watson Gilder to [GWC], Feb. 1, 1882, reprinted without Cable being identified as recipient in Rosamond Gilder (ed.), *Letters of Richard Watson Gilder* (Boston, 1916), pp. 389–391. See also Smith, *The Editorial Influence of Richard Watson Gilder*, pp. 96–97.

36 Turner, *Cable*, p. 132.

37 Richard Watson Gilder to [GWC], April 19, 1882, reprinted without Cable being identified as recipient in Gilder (ed.), *Letters of Richard Watson Gilder*, p. 391.

38 Turner, *Cable*, p. 132.

39 GWC to LBC, March 5, 1883.

40 GWC to LBC, March 7, 1883.

41 GWC to LBC, March 20, 1883.

42 Turner, *Cable*, p. 138.

43 GWC to LBC, April 5–6, 1883.

44 GWC to Rebecca Boardman Cable, April 7, 1883.

45 GWC to LBC, April 1, 1883.

46 Turner, *Cable*, p. 142.

47 GWC to LBC, April 13, 1883.

48 GWC to LBC, April 17, 1883.

49 GWC to LBC, Oct. 23, 1883.

50 GWC to LBC, Oct. 30, 1883.

51 Tinker, *Lafcadio Hearn's American Days*, p. 186.

52 GWC to LBC, Oct. 17, 1883.

[53] GWC to LBC, Oct. 1, 1883.

[54] GWC to LBC, Oct. 21, 1883.

[55] GWC to LBC, Oct. 27, 1883.

[56] GWC to LBC, Oct. 19, 1883.

[57] GWC to LBC, Nov. 21-22, 1883.

[58] GWC to LBC, Nov. 26, 1883.

[59] Quoted in Turner, *Cable*, pp. 147-148.

[60] Boston *Herald Supplement*, Nov. 28, 1883.

[61] *Ibid.*

[62] GWC to LBC, Nov. 24, 1883.

IX: Dr. Sevier

[1] Turner, *Cable*, p. 165.

[2] *Ibid.*, p. 168.

[3] Ekström, *George Washington Cable*, p. 159.

[4] Turner, *Cable*, p. 169.

[5] Ekström, *George Washington Cable*, p. 159.

[6] Turner, *Cable*, pp. 163-164.

[7] Richard Watson Gilder to GWC, Feb. 1, 1882.

[8] Baskervill, *Southern Writers: Biographical and Critical Studies*, Vol. I, p. 334.

[9] *Ibid.*, p. 335.

[10] George W. Cable, "New Orleans Before the Capture," *Century*, XXIX (April, 1885), 918-922.

[11] Butcher, *George W. Cable*, p. 72.

[12] Wilson, *Patriotic Gore*, p. 581.

[13] Richard Watson Gilder to GWC, Feb. 20, 1882.

[14] Richard Watson Gilder to GWC, June 18, 1883.

[15] Clarence C. Buel to GWC, July 16, 1885.

[16] Clarence C. Buel to GWC, July 25, 1885.

[17] Quoted in Ekström, *George Washington Cable*, p. 160.

X: Departure

[1] GWC to Louise Bartlett Cable, Jan. 19, 1884.

[2] GWC to LBC, Jan. 23, 1884.

[3] GWC to LBC, Jan. 28, 1884.

[4] Turner, *Cable*, p. 150.

[5] *Ibid.*, p. 151.

[6] GWC to Samuel L. Clemens, Feb. 21, 1884.

[7] Samuel L. Clemens to William Dean Howells, March 5, 1884, quoted in Cardwell, *Twins of Genius*, p. 97.

8 Samuel L. Clemens to William Dean Howells, Oct. 17, 1884, quoted in Cardwell, *Twins of Genius,* p. 97.

9 GWC to LBC, April 2, 1884.

10 GWC to LBC, Feb. 21, 1884.

11 GWC to LBC, Feb. 29, 1884.

12 GWC to LBC, March 24, 1884.

13 GWC to LBC, Feb. 24, 1884.

14 Biklé, *Cable: His Life and Letters,* p. 121.

15 Turner, *Cable,* p. 154.

16 *Ibid.*

17 *Ibid.,* pp. 154–155.

18 *Ibid.,* p. 155.

19 Cable, "The Freedman's Case in Equity," in Turner (ed.), *The Negro Question,* p. 20.

20 Turner, *Cable,* p. 159.

21 Cable, "The Due Restraints and Liberties of Literature," in Turner (ed.), *The Negro Question,* p. 48.

22 Quoted in C. Vann Woodward, *Origins of the New South, 1877–1913* (Baton Rouge, La., 1951), p. 216.

23 Editorial, *Century,* XXIII (1883), 945–946, quoted in Buck, *The Road to Reunion,* p. 295.

24 For a defense of Gilder's attitudes see Smith, *The Editorial Influence of Richard Watson Gilder,* pp. 99–103.

25 Butcher, *George W. Cable,* p. 83.

26 Turner, *Cable,* p. 156.

27 Woodward, *Origins of the New South,* p. 164.

XI: "Twins of Genius"

1 Cardwell, *Twins of Genius,* p. 8.

2 James B. Pond to GWC, June 18, 1884.

3 Cardwell, *Twins of Genius,* p. 8.

4 GWC to Samuel L. Clemens, July 11, 1884.

5 GWC to Mary Louise Cable, Aug. 2, 1884.

6 GWC to Mrs. James T. Fields, Aug. 2, 1884.

7 GWC to Anna L. Dawes, Oct. 21, 1884.

8 GWC to Samuel L. Clemens, Oct. 25, 1884, quoted in Cardwell, *Twins of Genius,* pp. 105–106.

9 Samuel L. Clemens to James B. Pond, Sept. 26, 1884, quoted in Arlin Turner, *Mark Twain and George Washington Cable* (East Lansing, Mich., 1960), pp. 47–48.

10 *Ibid.*

11 GWC to Louise Bartlett Cable, Nov. 6, 1884.

12 Cardwell, *Twins of Genius,* p. 16.

13 Quoted in *ibid.,* pp. 19–20.

[14] Quoted in *ibid.,* pp. 20–21.

[15] Paul Fatout, *Mark Twain on the Lecture Circuit* (Bloomington, Ind., 1960), pp. 205–206.

[16] Turner, *Cable,* p. 192.

[17] GWC to LBC, Dec. 16, 1884.

[18] GWC to LBC, Jan. 6, 1885.

[19] GWC to LBC, Jan. 30, 1885.

[20] Quoted in Cardwell, *Twins of Genius,* p. 64.

[21] GWC to LBC, Dec. 7, 1884.

[22] GWC to LBC, Feb. 8, 1885.

[23] Cardwell, *Twins of Genius,* pp. 33–34, 55–57.

[24] Quoted in Cardwell, *Ibid.,* pp. 65–66.

[25] Samuel L. Clemens, *Mark Twain in Eruption,* Bernard DeVoto (ed.) (New York, 1968), p. 216.

[26] Quoted in Cardwell, *Twins of Genius,* pp. 58–59.

[27] Cardwell, *Ibid.,* p. 71.

[28] *Ibid.*

[29] Turner, *Mark Twain and George W. Cable,* p. 135.

[30] GWC to Samuel L. Clemens, May 15, 1885 (telegram).

[31] GWC to Samuel L. Clemens, May 16, 1885.

[32] Samuel L. Clemens to GWC, May 18, 1885.

[33] GWC to the editor, Boston *Herald,* May 14, 1885.

[34] Quoted in Samuel Charles Webster, *Mark Twain, Business Man* (Boston, 1946), p. 322.

[35] Samuel L. Clemens to GWC, June 25, 1895, quoted in Cardwell, *Twins of Genius,* p. 111.

[36] The episode involved in the aftermath of the lecture tour is discussed at length in Turner, *Cable,* pp. 209–214; in Cardwell, *Twins of Genius,* pp. 107–109; and in Fatout, *Mark Twain on the Lecture Circuit,* pp. 228–231. Turner, in *Mark Twain and George W. Cable,* includes the text of Cable's two speeches on Clemens, pp. 124–136.

[37] Quoted in Cardwell, *Twins of Genius,* p. 25.

[38] GWC to Louise Bartlett Cable, March 2, 1885.

[39] Turner, *Cable,* p. 188.

[40] Fatout, *Mark Twain on the Lecture Circuit,* p. 231.

[41] Cable, "The Freedman's Case in Equity," in Turner (ed.), *The Negro Question,* p. 61.

[42] *Ibid.,* pp. 71–72.

[43] *Ibid.,* p. 72.

[44] *Ibid.*

[45] *Ibid.,* p. 74.

[46] Turner, *Cable,* pp. 197–198.

[47] Marion A. Baker to GWC, Feb. 5, 1885.

[48] Turner, *Cable,* p. 202.

[49] Quoted in Turner, *Cable,* p. 203.

50 Turner, *Cable,* p. 203.

51 Charles Gayarré to GWC, Aug. 6, 1882.

52 Charles Gayarré to GWC, April 23, 18[79?].

53 Turner, *Cable,* p. 208.

54 Marion A. Baker to GWC, March 9, 1885.

55 Quoted in Turner, *Cable,* p. 203.

56 Marion A. Baker to GWC, May 25, 1885.

57 Henry W. Grady, "In Plain Black and White: A Reply to Mr. Cable," *Century,* XXIX (April, 1885), 909–917.

58 Cable, "The Silent South," in Turner (ed.), *The Negro Question,* pp. 77–118.

59 Marion A. Baker to GWC, Aug. 31, 1885.

60 Quoted in Turner, *Cable,* p. 222.

61 King, *Memories of a Southern Woman of Letters,* pp. 60–61.

62 Butcher, *George W. Cable,* p. 86.

63 Turner, *Cable,* p. 223.

64 *Ibid.,* pp. 222–223.

XII: Northampton

1 Butcher, *George W. Cable,* pp. 88–89.

2 Turner, *Cable,* p. 280.

3 See Butcher, *George W. Cable,* pp. 85–90, and *passim.*

4 Louise Bartlett Cable to GWC, Nov. 26, 1889, quoted in Turner, *Cable,* p. 285.

5 Turner, *Cable,* pp. 274–279.

6 Cable, "Mark Twain's Seventieth Birthday," in Turner, *Mark Twain and George W. Cable,* pp. 124–129.

7 Philip Butcher, *George W. Cable: The Northampton Years* (New York, 1959), pp. 65–70.

8 *Ibid.,* pp. 83–84.

9 Turner, *Cable,* pp. 280–284.

10 *Ibid.,* pp. 288–289.

11 *Ibid.,* pp. 286–287.

12 *Ibid.,* pp. 227–232.

13 Richard Watson Gilder to GWC, Aug. 18, 1886.

14 Turner, *Cable,* p. 237.

15 *Ibid.,* pp. 238–239.

16 *Ibid.,* p. 240.

17 *Ibid.,* p. 241.

18 *Ibid.,* p. 242.

19 *Ibid.,* p. 248.

20 *Ibid.,* pp. 249–251.

21 King, *Memories of a Southern Woman of Letters,* p. 377.

[22] GWC to LBC, May 25, 1887.

[23] Thomas Nelson Page to Richard Watson Gilder, May 25, 1887, quoted in Smith, *The Editorial Influence of Richard Watson Gilder*, p. 72.

[24] GWC to LBC, May 25, 1887.

[25] Turner, *Cable*, p. 251.

[26] Cable, "The Negro Question," in Turner (ed.), *The Negro Question*, pp. 120–152.

[27] Quoted in Turner, *Cable*, pp. 251–252.

[28] *Ibid.*, pp. 264–265.

[29] *Ibid.*, pp. 265–266.

[30] Quoted in *ibid.*, p. 268.

[31] GWC to a Miss Ford, Dec. 27, 1889. The letter Cable sent to the Nashville *American* is apparently almost a word-by-word copy of this letter.

[32] William Malone Baskervill to GWC, Jan. 8, 1889, quoted in Butcher, *Cable: The Northampton Years*, pp. 102–103.

[33] GWC to William Malone Baskervill, Jan. 14, 1889.

[34] Baskervill, *Southern Writers: Biographical and Critical Sketches*, Vol. I, pp. 318–319.

[35] Cable, "A Simpler Southern Question," in Turner (ed.), *The Negro Question*, pp. 166–178.

[36] Cable, "What Makes the Color Line?," in Turner (ed.), *The Negro Question*, pp. 187–190.

[37] Woodward, *Origins of the New South*, pp. 63–64.

[38] Cable, "National Aid to Southern Schools," in Turner (ed.), *The Negro Question*, pp. 191–195.

[39] Turner, *Cable*, p. 255.

[40] Cable, "The Southern Struggle for Pure Government," in Turner (ed.), *The Negro Question*, pp. 213–244.

[41] See Buck, *The Road to Reunion*, pp. 279–281.

[42] Cable, "What Shall the Negro Do?," in Turner (ed.), *The Negro Question*, p. 163.

XIII: *John March, Southerner*

[1] GWC to Louise Bartlett Cable, May 3, 1889.

[2] GWC to LBC, May 5, 1889.

[3] GWC to LBC, Nov. 29, 1889.

[4] GWC to LBC, April 1, 1889.

[5] GWC to LBC, April 6, 1890.

[6] GWC to LBC, May 17, 1890.

[7] GWC to LBC, May 18, 1890.

[8] GWC to LBC, May 20, 1890. The Feltons were Georgia Independents known for their heresy not only on the Negro issue but on other issues central to Georgia politics of the day. Many years later, when the Populist and by that time Negrophobic Thomas H. Watson died, Mrs. Felton was appointed senator pro tem in his place, and by serving one day in the United States Senate became the first woman ever to sit in that body.

[9] GWC to Richard Watson Gilder, July 17, 1890.

[10] GWC to Richard Watson Gilder, Aug. 16, 1890.

[11] Richard Watson Gilder, to GWC, Aug. 29, 1890.

[12] Richard Watson Gilder to GWC, Oct. 20, 1890.

[13] Marion A. Baker to GWC, Sept. 6, 1890.

[14] Marion A. Baker to GWC, Jan. 4, 1891.

[15] Turner, *Cable*, p. 292.

[16] Richard Watson Gilder to GWC, June 23, 1893.

[17] Richard Watson Gilder to GWC, June 26, 1893.

[18] GWC to Richard Watson Gilder, June 26, 1893.

[19] GWC to Richard Watson Gilder, June 28, 1893.

[20] Richard Watson Gilder to GWC, July 5, 1893.

[21] Turner, *Cable*, pp. 292–293. Possibly the idea for the title came to Cable from a novel by T. C. DeLeon, published in 1893, entitled *John Holden, Unionist*. DeLeon's novel, a mediocre work, is also set in the Etowah country of north Georgia and Alabama, and toward the end involves mineral development and land speculation. The books are otherwise dissimilar in content.

[22] Wilson, *Patriotic Gore*, p. 579.

[23] Richard Watson Gilder to GWC, June 23, 1893.

[24] Turner, *Cable*, p. 294.

[25] Baskervill, *Southern Writers: Biographical and Critical Sketches*, Vol. I, p. 352.

[26] Butcher, *George W. Cable*, p. 122.

[27] *Ibid.*, p. 123.

[28] Wilson, *Patriotic Gore*, p. 583.

[29] Randolph Bourne, "From an Older Time," *Dial*, LXV (Nov. 2, 1918), 346.

XIV: Historical Romancer

[1] Butcher, *George W. Cable*, p. 137.

[2] Butcher, *Cable: The Northampton Years*, pp. 157–158.

[3] Butcher, *George W. Cable*, p. 119.

[4] *Ibid.*, p. 125.

[5] GWC to Louise Bartlett Cable, Aug. 4, 1897.

[6] Butcher, *George W. Cable*, p. 131.

[7] Turner, *Cable*, pp. 305–306.

[8] Entry for June 6, 1898, in diary kept in England and Scotland, 1898.

[9] Quoted in Turner, *Cable*, p. 309.

[10] Butcher, *Cable: The Northampton Years*, pp. 160–174.

[11] Turner, *Cable*, p. 316.

[12] GWC to LBC, Feb. 25, 1900.

[13] Turner, *Cable*, p. 316.

[14] Quoted in Turner, *Cable*, p. 318.

[15] GWC to Charles Scribner III, Oct. 8, 1901.

[16] Quoted in Turner, *Cable*, p. 325.

[17] Turner, *Cable,* pp. 319–320.

[18] GWC to Henry Van Dyke, March 5, 1904.

[19] GWC to Andrew Carnegie, Oct. 31, 1906.

[20] Butcher, *Cable: The Northampton Years,* pp. 212–225.

[21] *Ibid.,* pp. 223–240.

[22] GWC to Herbert Brewster, April 16, 1907; Herbert Brewster to GWC, April 19, 1907.

[23] Henry Taplin to GWC, April 20, 1907.

[24] Butcher, *Cable: The Northampton Years,* pp. 243–244.

[25] GWC to Andrew Carnegie, n.d. [1907].

[26] Turner, *Cable,* p. 340.

[27] *Ibid.*

[28] *Ibid.,* p. 335.

[29] GWC to Charles Scribner III, July 7, 1908.

[30] Quoted in Turner, *Cable,* pp. 337–338.

[31] Quoted in Turner, *Mark Twain and George W. Cable,* pp. 129–136.

XV: Engagement Renewed

[1] GWC to Mary Louise Cable, Jan. 4, 1909.

[2] Turner, *Cable,* p. 341.

[3] GWC to Charles Scribner III, Jan. 9, 1909.

[4] Woodward, *Origins of the New South,* p. 351.

[5] *Ibid.,* p. 361.

[6] Turner, *Cable,* pp. 332–341.

[7] *Ibid.,* p. 345.

[8] GWC to Andrew Carnegie, Jan. 9, 1913.

[9] Turner, *Cable,* p. 342.

[10] GWC to Margaret Cable Brewster, March 12, 1915.

[11] GWC to Charles Scribner III, March 23, 1915, quoted in Turner, *Cable,* p. 349.

[12] Boston *Evening Transcript,* Sept. 29, 1923, quoted in Turner, *Cable,* p. 350.

[13] King, *Memories of a Southern Woman of Letters,* p. 60.

[14] Joseph Pennell to GWC, Dec. 8, 1921, quoted in Turner, *Cable,* p. 351.

[15] Turner, *Cable,* p. 321.

[16] Charles Scribner III to GWC, Nov. 20, 1917, quoted in Turner, *Cable,* p. 352.

[17] Butcher, *George W. Cable,* pp. 158–159.

XVI: The Final Days

[1] Turner, *Cable,* p. 335.

[2] *Ibid.,* p. 355.

[3] See GWC to Benjamin B. Hampton, 3 letters, n.d. [1920–1921].

[4] GWC to Louise Cable Chard, Sept. 4, 1919.

[5] Turner, *Cable,* p. 356.

[6] Biklé, *Cable: His Life and Letters,* p. 298.

[7] *Ibid.,* p. 298.

[8] GWC to Charles Scribner III, Dec. 26, 1923.

[9] Biklé, *Cable: His Life and Letters,* p. 299.

[10] *The Bookman,* LXI (April, 1925), 249.

[11] The *Nation,* CXX (Feb. 11, 1925), 333.

[12] *The Outlook,* CXXXIX (Feb. 11, 1925), 213–214.

[13] Edmund Wilson, "Citizen of the Union," *New Republic,* LVII (Feb. 13, 1929), 352–353.

Selective Bibliography

Some 20,000 items of Cable material, including correspondence, manuscripts, and other items, are housed at the Howard-Tilton Memorial Library of Tulane University. There are also extensive Cable holdings at the Columbia University Library, and Cable's letters to his publishers are in the archives of Charles Scribner's Sons. The Berg Collection of the New York Public Library also has Cable material. Other repositories of Cable items include: American Academy of Arts and Letters, People's Institute of Northampton, Mass., Berea College, Duke University, Fisk University, Harvard University, Huntington Library, Joint University Libraries of Nashville, Tenn., Library of Congress, University of Virginia, Louisiana Historical Association, Louisiana State Museum, Louisiana State University, Xavier University, Yale University.

ANDERSON, CHARLES R., "Charles Gayarré and Paul Hayne: The Last Literary Cavaliers," in David K. Jackson (ed.), *American Studies in Honor of William K. Boyd,* Durham, N.C., 1940, pp. 221–281. [Includes some strong castigation of Cable by two patriotic Southrons]

ARVIN, NEWTON (ed.), Introduction to George W. Cable, *The Grandissimes.* New York, 1957.

BASKERVILL, WILLIAM MALONE, *Southern Writers: Biographical and Critical Studies,* Vol. I, Nashville, Tenn., 1897, pp. 229–356. [Contemporary estimate, often perceptive, by onetime associate who had come to disagree strongly with Cable's racial views]

BERTHOFF, WARNER, *The Ferment of Realism: American Literature, 1884–1919.* New York, 1965, pp. 83–88.

BIKLÉ, LUCY LEFFINGWELL CABLE, *George W. Cable: His Life and Letters.* New York, 1928. [Biography by Cable's daughter, containing numerous letters from Cable to Louise Bartlett Cable]

BLANCK, JACOB (comp.), *Bibliography of American Literature,* Vol. II. New Haven, Conn., 1957, pp. 1–12. [Bibliographical data]

BREWSTER, MARY, "George W. Cable," *Congregationalist,* CX (Dec. 10, 1925), 816–817.

BROOKS, VAN WYCK, *The Times of Melville and Whitman.* New York, 1947, pp. 396–404. [Cable as local colorist—with some inaccuracies]

BUCK, PAUL S., *The Road to Reunion, 1865–1900.* Boston, 1937. [Valuable discussion of local color as sectional conciliator, including role of magazines. See esp. Ch. V, pp. 115–143, Ch. VIII, pp. 196–219, and Ch. VII, pp. 220–235]

BUTCHER, PHILIP, *George W. Cable: The Northampton Years.* New York, 1959 [Detailed treatment of Home Culture Clubs; Butcher draws extensively on material furnished him by Adelene Moffat]

————, *George W. Cable.* New York, 1962. Vol. 24 in Twayne United States Authors Series. [Critical survey; emphasis on Cable's role as civil rights spokesman]

————, "George Washington Cable (1844–1925)," *American Literary Realism,* I (Fall, 1967), 20–25. [Excellent critical checklist]

————, "Cable to Boyesen on *The Grandissimes,*" *American Literature,* XL (November, 1968), 391–394. [Additional letter; see Turner below]

CARDWELL, GUY, A., "The First Public Address of George W. Cable, Southern Liberal," in *Studies in Memory of Frank Martindale Webster,* Washington University Studies, St. Louis, 1951, pp. 67–76. [Analyzes rumors of hostile reception of Cable when giving University of Mississippi address in 1883]

————, "George W. Cable Becomes a Professional Reader," *American Literature,* XXIII (January, 1952), 467–470.

————, *Twins of Genius.* East Lansing, Mich., 1953; London, 1962. [Detailed account of the Cable-Twain lecture tour, with correspondence]

CHASE, RICHARD, "*Cable's Grandissimes,*" *The American Novel and Its Tradition.* Garden City, N.Y., 1957, pp. 167–176. Originally published as "Cable and His Grandissimes," *Kenyon Review,* XVIII (Summer, 1956), 373–383. [*Grandissimes* seen as blend of novel and romance forms]

CLEMENS, SAMUEL L., *Life on the Mississippi.* New York, 1917. Chs. XLI–LI. [Description of visit to New Orleans, meeting with Cable and Joel Chandler Harris]

————, *Love Letters of Mark Twain,* ed. Dixon Wecter. New York, 1949. [What Clemens was writing to Livy during the lecture tour]

————, *Mark Twain in Eruption,* ed. Bernard DeVoto. New York, 1968, pp. 215–216. [Twain on his own and Cable's platform manner]

DENNIS, MARY CABLE, *The Tail of the Comet.* New York, 1937. [Memoir by daughter]

EIDSON, JOHN OLIN, "George W. Cable's Philosophy of Progress," *Southwest Review,* XXI (January, 1936), 211–216. [Emphasizes Cable's rejection of Southern tradition]

EKSTRÖM, KJELL, *George Washington Cable: A Study of His Early Life and Work.* Uppsala and Cambridge, Mass., 1950. [Valuable examination of Cable's early fiction in terms of its treatment of Creoles, and of reaction of Creoles to Cable]

EVANS, OLIVER, *New Orleans.* New York, 1959. [Fine study of the city]

GAYARRÉ, CHARLES, "Mr. Cable's 'Freedman's Case in Equity,'" in Thomas McCaleb (ed.), *The Louisiana Book: Selections from the Literature of the State.* New Orleans, 1898, pp. 198–202. [A vicious attack]

GILDER, ROSAMOND (ed.), *Letters of Richard Watson Gilder.* Boston, 1916.

GRADY, HENRY W., "In Plain Black and White," *Century,* XXIX (April, 1885), 909–917. [Grady's response to "The Freedman's Case in Equity"]

GRAU, SHIRLEY ANN (ed.), Foreword to George W. Cable, *Old Creole Days.* New York, 1961.

HARRIS, JULIA COLLIER, *The Life and Letters of Joel Chandler Harris.* Boston, 1918.

HEARN, LAFCADIO, *Creole Sketches,* ed. Charles Woodward Hutson. Boston, 1924. [Includes review of *The Grandissimes,* pp. 117-123]

——, "The Scenes of Cable's Romances," *Century,* XXVII (November, 1883), 40-47. Reprinted in *An American Miscellany,* ed. Alfred Mordell, Vol. II. New York, 1924, pp. 168-184.

——, *Essays on American Literature,* ed. Sanki Ichiwawa, introduction by Alfred Mordell. Tokyo, 1929.

HOWELLS, MILDRED (ed.), *Life in Letters of William Dean Howells.* Garden City, N.Y., 1928, 2 vols.

HUBBELL, JAY B., *The South in American Literature, 1607-1900.* Durham, N.C., 1954, pp. 804-822.

KING, GRACE, *Memories of a Southern Woman of Letters.* New York, 1932, pp. 49-50, 58-61, 377-378, and *passim.* [Memoirs of Creole local colorist who knew Gayarré well and resented Cable]

KING, KIMBALL, "George Washington Cable and Thomas Nelson Page: Two Literary Approaches to the New South," University of Wisconsin, Madison, Wis., 1964. [Doctoral dissertation contrasting Page's eulogy of Old South and defense of segregation with Cable's treatment of South and race]

KOWALEDSKY, WALDEMIR, "My Acquaintance with Cable," trans. Charlotte Adams from the *Viestnik Evropii* (May, 1883), in *The Critic,* III (July 28, 1883), 316-317. [Contains Cable's alleged criticism of Boyesen]

LORCH, FRED W., "Cable and His Reading Tour with Mark Twain in 1884-1885," *American Literature,* XXIII (January, 1952), 471-486.

MARTIN, JAY, *Harvests of Change: American Literature, 1865-1914.* Englewood Cliffs, N.J., 1967, pp. 100-105. [*Grandissimes* as attempt to reveal the myth of the false past]

PATTEE, FREDERICK LEWIS, *A History of American Literature Since 1870.* New York, 1915, pp. 246-253. [Includes Cable's remarks on beginnings of local color movement in South]

POND, JAMES B., *Eccentricities of Genius.* New York, 1900. [Impresario's view of Cable and Twain, along with trivia about various other celebrities]

PUGH, GRIFFITH THOMPSON, *George Washington Cable: A Biographical and Critical Study,* A Summary of a Thesis Presented to the Faculty of the Graduate School of Vanderbilt University. Nashville, Tenn., 1947.

[ROUQUETTE, ADRIEN,] *Critical Dialogue between Aboo and Caboo on a New Book; or, A Grandissime Ascension, by "E. Junius."* [New Orleans,] 1880. [Scurrilous pamphlet]

RUBIN, LOUIS D., JR., "The Road to Yoknapatapha: George W. Cable and *John March, Southerner," The Faraway Country: Writers of the Modern South.* Seattle, Wash., 1963, pp. 21-42. Originally published in *Virginia Quarterly Review,* XXXV (Winter, 1959), 119-132.

SIMPSON, CLAUDE, M. (ed.), Introduction to *The Local Colorists: American Short Stories, 1857-1900.* New York, 1960. [Excellent discussion of the local color movement]

SMITH, HERBERT FRANKLIN, *The Editorial Influence of Richard Watson Gilder, 1870-1909.* Ann Arbor, Mich., 1967 (University Microfilms), pp. 88-108, and *infra* [1961 Rutgers University dissertation]

STONE, EDWARD, "Usher, Poquelin, and Miss Emily: The Progress of Southern Gothic," *Georgia Review,* XIV (Winter, 1960), 433-443.

TALLANT, ROBERT, *The Romantic New Orleanians.* New York, 1950. [Excellent social history of city]

TINKER, EDWARD LAROCQUE, "Cable and the Creoles," *American Literature,* V (January, 1934), 313-326. [Though containing some serious factual errors, this essay is a discerning study of Cable's relationship with his native city]

TURNER, ARLIN, "George W. Cable's Literary Apprenticeship," *Louisiana Historical Quarterly,* XXIV (January, 1941), 168–186. [The "Drop Shot" columns]

———, "George W. Cable, Novelist and Reformer," *South Atlantic Quarterly,* XLVIII (October, 1949), 539–545.

———, "George W. Cable's Beginnings as a Reformer," *Journal of Southern History,* XVII (May, 1951), 135–161. [Cable's activities as opponent of Louisiana Lottery and advocate of prison reform]

———, "A Novelist Discovers a Novelist: The Correspondence of H. H. Boyesen and George W. Cable," *Western Humanities Review,* V (Autumn, 1951), 343–372. [The extensive Cable-Boyesen correspondence of the late 1870's]

———, "George W. Cable's Revolt Against Literary Sectionalism," *Tulane Studies in English,* V (1955), 5–27. [Text of University of Mississippi speech]

———, *George W. Cable, A Biography.* Durham, N.C., 1956. [The definitive work on Cable]

——— (ed.), *Creoles and Cajuns: Stories of Old Louisiana by George W. Cable.* Garden City, N.Y., 1959.

———, *Mark Twain and George W. Cable.* East Lansing, Mich., 1960. [Extensive description of their relationship, with much correspondence]

TWAIN, MARK—see Clemens, Samuel L.

VEDDER, HENRY C., *American Writers of To-Day.* New York, 1895, pp. 261–274.

WEAVER, RICHARD M., *The Southern Tradition at Bay,* ed. George Core and M. E. Bradford. New Rochelle, N.Y., 1968, pp. 308–315. [Discussion of Cable as critic of Southern attitudes; includes excellent analysis of *John March, Southerner*]

WEBSTER, SAMUEL CHARLES, *Mark Twain, Business Man.* Boston, 1946.

WILSON, EDMUND, "Citizen of the Union," *New Republic,* LVII (Feb. 13, 1929), 352–353. Reprinted in Wilson, *The Shores of Light: A Literary Chronicle of the Twenties and Thirties.* New York, 1952, pp. 415–420. [Review of Biklé biography in which Wilson sets forth the importance of Cable's work]

———, *Patriotic Gore: Studies in the Literature of the American Civil War.* New York, 1962, pp. 548–587, 593–604. Originally published as "The Ordeal of George Washington Cable," *The New Yorker,* XXXIII (Nov. 9, 1957), 172–216. [Highly influential essay, using Turner biography as point of departure]

WOODWARD, C. VANN, *Origins of the New South 1877–1913.* Baton Rouge, La., 1951. (Authoritative study of South during years of Cable's career, detailing the social and political conditions described in Cable's writings]

INDEX